ENGLISH TRAGEDY BEFORE SHAKESPEARE

by the same author

THE DEVELOPMENT OF SHAKESPEARE'S IMAGERY

English Tragedy Before Shakespeare

The Development of Dramatic Speech

BY WOLFGANG CLEMEN

Translated by

T. S. DORSCH

LONDON

METHUEN & CO LTD

36 ESSEX STREET W.C.2

First published in 1955 by Quelle and Meyer, Heidelberg, as
Die Tragödie vor Shakespeare: ihre Entwicklung im Spiegel der dramatischen Rede
This edition first published in Great Britain in 1961

Printed in Great Britain by
Richard Clay & Co Ltd, Bungay, Suffolk
Catalogue No. 2/6373/10

CONTENTS

PART ONE

PART TWO

PART THREE

TRANSLATOR'S NOTE

I should like to express my appreciation of the patience and understanding of Professor Clemen, who at all stages of the work of translating this book has made helpful suggestions, especially with regard to the treatment of technical terms. I also owe a debt of gratitude to my colleague Miss Mary Beare, of Westfield College, for the great kindness she has so often shown in helping me with knotty problems of translation.

ABBREVIATIONS

Alcazar	*The Battle of Alcazar*
Arraignment	*The Arraignment of Paris*
David	*David and Bethsabe*
Friar Bacon	*Friar Bacon and Friar Bungay*
Gismond	*Gismond of Salerne*
Gorb.	*Gorboduc*
Looking Glass	*A Looking-Glass for London and England*
Massacre	*The Massacre at Paris*
Misfortunes	*The Misfortunes of Arthur*
Oldcastle	*Sir John Oldcastle*
Orlando	*Orlando Furioso*
Span. Trag.	*The Spanish Tragedy*
Wars	*The Wars of Cyrus*
Wounds	*The Wounds of Civil War*

Anglia	*Anglia: Zeitschrift für englische Philologie*
Archiv	*Archiv für das Studium der neueren Sprachen und Literaturen*
JEGP	*Journal of English and Germanic Philology*
MLN	*Modern Language Notes*
MLR	*Modern Language Review*
MP	*Modern Philology*
NQ	*Notes and Queries*
PMLA	*Publications of the Modern Language Association of America*
RES	*Review of English Studies*
SP	*Studies in Philology*
TLS	*The Times Literary Supplement*

PART ONE

I

Introduction

In this volume an attempt is made to trace the history of serious drama before Shakespeare – by which is to be understood especially the tragedy written between *Gorboduc* and Marlowe's *Edward II* – by studying it in relation to the development of the dramatic set speech. This means that an element of special importance in the structure of Elizabethan tragedy will have to be detached from its setting in the plays and analysed in some detail. It will be found, however, that what may at first sight have seemed a restricted and one-sided critical procedure necessarily leads us to examine the plays more carefully as complete works, and thus gives us a fresh and clearer insight into their character.

It is hoped that a study of this kind, embracing not only the relationship of the set speech to the other formal elements of drama, but also its structure and its forms of expression, will provide a new approach to the history of pre-Shakespearian drama, and to developments within this period of which it has so far been difficult to give a clear account. Useful as are some of the existing studies which aim at describing the nature of this body of drama as a whole, they deal with it at best in general terms, and they are not of much value when we turn to them for exact information about the structure, the forms of expression, or the style of presentation of a particular play – in other words, about the various individual points that determine both its shape and the character of its dramatic art. It has therefore been thought best to limit this inquiry and confine our attention in the first instance to one of the more tangible components of these plays, to something which is of their very stuff and substance, which is, so to speak, the flesh and blood of drama, that is to say, the words which the characters speak in their longer unbroken speeches.

The term 'set speech' will be used for any continuous spoken passage that stands out noticeably from the general run of the dialogue by reason of its length and structure, its theme, or its significance. No attempt will be made to give an exact definition of the set speech as such, for by simplifying the forms that it may take and reducing them to an ordered scheme, any such definition would fail to do justice to their diversity. Clearly, too, we shall fall into difficulties if we try to lay down a dividing-line between the set speech and dialogue that will cover every case, for it is not always possible to differentiate them in this way. In the earliest stages of the course of development that is to be outlined in later chapters the difference between the two is obvious and unmistakable; but later the one merges into the other, and there will be occasions when it will be hard to decide whether a particular example should or should not have been included for analysis. With occasional passages, moreover, some readers will perhaps regret that what is said about the style of the set speeches could not have been supplemented by some discussion of the dialogue-technique, for in many plays the style cannot be adequately grasped if we take the set speech alone as our point of departure. But this would have demanded a fundamental widening in the scope of our study, no doubt involving some blurring of its main outlines, since the consideration of dialogue requires us to go back to different origins and different basic assumptions.

However, these distinctions are of less concern than the much more important question whether the set speeches in pre-Shakespearian drama stand out clearly enough and are an important enough phenomenon to warrant close study in connexion with the whole process of dramatic development at this time, and as a key to that process. This question can certainly be answered in the affirmative. For set speeches are an absolutely fundamental ingredient of pre-Shakespearian tragedy; they are the main pillars, indeed the very foundations of the play, and upon these foundations the whole building is designed. With the lapse of time they gradually occupy a less and less commanding position; nevertheless, the tradition of the dramatic set speech persists, and it has not yet entirely lost its force even in Shakespearian tragedy, where it occasionally makes its presence felt in the use of certain types of speech which, as will be suggested in Chapter 3, are among the characteristic set-speech types of pre-Shakespearian drama.[1]

There seems therefore to be every good reason for making a systematic study of the set speech in early Elizabethan tragedy. For this tragedy takes its very life from the exalted language in which the set speeches are couched. These speeches are extremely important for other reasons as well. In the first place, they are the sole medium by which the characters are presented and their states of mind and motives for action revealed; by their means, moreover, the dramatic import of the play is made clear, and the course of its action is unfolded. In these speeches is incorporated everything that later – in the realistic drama, and to some extent already in Shakespeare – is expressed by a whole variety of other methods: by means of gesture and movement about the stage, by means of eloquent silences, of misunderstanding, and of inarticulate utterance, by means of a significant reaction on the part of one of the characters in a particular situation, and by means of directly presented action and counter-action. In the rhetorical drama – and pre-Shakespearian drama is to a very large extent rhetorical drama – all these things are translated into words, into high-sounding speech. The characters in these plays must represent with their tongues alone everything that later on is conveyed to the audience in the various other ways already mentioned – though of course it has at all times been one of the paradoxical laws of drama that its characters should be allowed to say much more than they would in real life. However, the one-sidedness of this early rhetorical verse-drama is not without its positive aspects, in so far as the idea of 'eloquence', which played so great a part in the whole period under review, now acquires a new and deeper import. Instead of merely fulfilling its outward function as a polished, highly adorned and effective technique of oratory, eloquence comes to mean the ability to communicate by the medium of words alone a wide variety of man's deepest emotions. This ability we find in Shakespeare, but we should not find it had not the playwrights

[1] Cf. Milton Boone Kennedy, *The Oration in Shakespeare*, Chapel Hill, 1942.

who preceded him already contributed to dramatic verse that wealth of expression and of effect the potentialities of which were to be completely realized only after their time. Marlowe already must have been fully alive to these possibilities. It is reasonable to say, therefore, that the realistic drama, showing as it does an awareness that words are only a partial means of self-expression, was in a certain sense responsible for the impoverishment of the language of drama as a vehicle for expression, and for the decay of the art that had allowed, and indeed demanded, the complete expression of thought and emotion.

If then the set speech is of such central importance as an instrument of dramatic expression, it must be possible to learn a good deal from it about the style of the play as a whole, and about anything that is distinctive in the way in which its theme is presented and developed. This study will therefore deal not only with the structure, the style, and the movement of thought of the set speeches, but also with their function in the larger context of the whole play, with the way in which they are fitted into the framework of act and scene. An attempt will also be made to show what light these speeches shed on the total dramatic content, how far they serve the dramatist as a means of instructing his audience, and what part they play in the revelation of character. However, our first concern must be with the relationship of the speech to its immediate context, and to the other party in the exchange of which it forms a part. Other important matters to be discussed are the relationship between set speech and dialogue, the frequency with which the speeches occur, and the space they occupy in the play – in other words, the way in which they are used in building up its fabric. Consideration of these points in any particular play will bring us a step nearer to an understanding of its inner form, its thematic texture.

In these questions our attention is directed to the inner mechanism of the play and the relations that its various components bear to one another. Now this mechanism is itself part of a constant process of evolution. This is manifested in various ways. Thus developments of fundamental importance to drama come about when, for example, a stilted and disconnected dialogue between speakers who stand side by side and address one another without any real inner contact is replaced by a direct and closely interwoven means of communication between them; or again, when genuinely *dramatic* speech replaces a mere set speech – itself no more than rhetorical 'insertion' that lacks close connexion with the situation as a whole – and is integrated in a variety of ways with the action, the characterization, and the thematic structure of the play. In watching these things happen we can participate in that internal process of growth which is constantly modifying dramatic forms and carrying them to higher stages of development. In this sense the history of dramatic form is not a matter of externals, but rather the crystallization of the active processes of change that are taking place, not only within individual plays, but in the whole historical sequence of plays of the same type – in what is usually called the history of drama.

In the course of this book there will be some discussion not only of the development of dramatic forms, but also of the 'mode of expression' in pre-Shakespearian drama. This term has been chosen to suggest something more than a mere formal analysis of style, something that includes also the meaning that is brought out by means of the various stylistic devices. By style is generally understood only the 'how' of presentation, the technique of language by which a particular content of thought is clothed in words. Moreover, the 'devices' of style, especially those that turn up again and again as established stylistic artifices and 'figures', are very often removed from their context and considered as something existing in their own right. The extraordinary wealth of rhetorical figures still employed by Shakespeare,[1] and the influence of the academic exercises in rhetoric upon style as a whole, an influence that resulted from the dominant position of rhetoric throughout the period, do seem to suggest, indeed, that our first step should be to diagnose and classify the rhetorical figures that are so constant a phenomenon in the plays. But this kind of stylistic analysis, which can so easily degenerate into a more or less mechanical process of assembling and cataloguing, ought to be only one of several approaches to the texts, and we should never forget that the various figures that are used derive both their function and their effect from their relationship with the mean-

[1] See, e.g., Sister Miriam Joseph, *Shakespeare's Use of the Arts of Language*, New York, 1947.

ing that is expressed in any particular passage. The reader's attention will only occasionally therefore be drawn to the rhetorical figures which as a matter of course occur more frequently in the set speeches than anywhere else. For our first concern must be with the train of thought or the theme that underlies each of the various speeches under review, and the manner in which this content of thought is expressed.

It will be seen that the subject-matter and the themes that make up the content of these speeches are very often of a highly conventional nature. This is especially true of the 'type' speeches, the basic forms of which are enumerated in Chapter 3. These are speeches that are bound up with recurrent themes and recurrent emotional situations: laments for the dead, challenges, speeches of triumph over enemies, warnings against an imprudent action, and the like. As is shown in the final chapters of this book, where the lament is used for illustration, there is a stock of conventional formulas associated with the 'type' speech, an assortment of recurring ideas and themes and characteristic turns of phrase which are constantly met with, and which are always available for use when such a 'typical' situation presents itself.

However, these constant factors are blended with the variations in style which are due to gradually changing purposes, and with the individual impulse that lies behind the work of the various playwrights. For though pre-Shakespearian drama may at first sight appear to be dominated by convention, though innumerable passages give a stiff and stereotyped effect, thickly studded as they are with clichés, yet even here we find the clash between what merely conforms to type and what is due to the individual playwright's urge for expression. The 'typical' form of language with which an utterance was invested had at one time been the expression of a distinctive way of thought, of a distinctive attitude. With the lapse of years this association ceased to exist, and a particular form of utterance could be passed on from hand to hand, and taken into service again when the underlying way of thought that had once stamped this form as something individual had long since passed into oblivion, and was certainly not present in the consciousness of the writer.

It is of course the lesser playwrights, the mere craftsmen and the imitators, who write without any further concern for the forms which they have been able to take over from others and which have won the favour and acceptance of the audience. This is to a certain extent true even of the major playwrights. For what we have in Elizabethan drama is always a product of the reciprocal influence of the audience and the playwright on each other. The author's own individual urge for expression can develop only when he makes use of forms and conventions that have already been accepted by the audience and that have in a sense come to be looked for in every new play. This is certainly the case with the set speeches. Yet again and again, even in the pre-Shakespearian drama, we find places where the accepted patterns of speech are superseded, where the existing vehicles of language and style obviously no longer suffice for the expression of the author's intention. When this occurs we shall of course have to decide how far such departures are to be attributed to the playwright's own creative powers, and how far they may be due to other causes, such as, for example, the influence of other types of drama.

However, no convention of speech will have an enduring life once the ideas which originally lay behind it have to any considerable extent been modified. While recognizing the long currency and the force of certain effects that are due to conformity with type and convention, we have also, when dealing with pre-Shakespearian drama, to reckon with that other literary law, operating below the surface, according to which form and content strive towards a final harmony. In a negative sense, the exaggerated use of conventional devices of language and form may also be taken as an indication that this process of integration is at work. In this case we may be reasonably certain that the conventional formulas were taken over as mere empty shells, and were used solely for their power to raise the pitch of an utterance by their associations. However, in the course of time any form of overstatement and exaggeration becomes wearisome, even in a period so enthusiastically attached to every form of exuberance, of heightened effect and extravagance, as the Elizabethan age.

Another purpose of this book, then, is to contribute something to our knowledge of type-qualities in pre-Shakespearian drama; in this respect it aims at supplementing the important work of M. C. Bradbrook, L. L. Schücking,[1] and others, who have written full-length studies of the type-qualities that occur in Elizabethan drama as a whole. It is particularly necessary that the pre-Shakespearian period of this drama should be studied in this way, not only for our better understanding of the forms and techniques that are characteristic of the plays then being produced, but also because it is in these forms and techniques that Shakespeare's plays have their roots. Shakespeare's work is everywhere pervaded by conventional and stereotyped elements inherited from the past, always associated, however, with the new elements that are the product of his own remarkable creative urge. In the clash between convention and originality lies much of the secret of his art. At every stage of his work we can watch new forms growing out of old, and from the mixture of types and conventions that he took over from his predecessors and their reciprocal influence on one another he fashions something entirely new and entirely different. This is tantamount to saying, of course, that in Shakespeare the basic forms are no longer to be found in their purity, even where the subject of this book, the set speech, is concerned.

To get to know these forms and conventions as pure and unmixed types, we must look for them in pre-Shakespearian drama. Here we shall find them as they were before in Shakespeare they were outgrown by better things, or changed into something different and adapted to new settings. Any attention we can give to the material that lay behind Shakespeare – and often enough we shall be dealing with somewhat primitive material – will make us more fully alive to the uniqueness of Shakespeare's own achievement; we shall appreciate more thoroughly his ability to employ even primitive conventions in the composition of his plays without prejudice to their total artistic effect, and the brilliance with which he extended and reshaped and gave new life to the dramatic art-forms of his predecessors and his contemporaries.[2]

[1] M. C. Bradbrook, *Themes and Conventions of Elizabethan Tragedy*, Cambridge, 1935; L. L. Schücking, *Shakespeare und der Tragödienstil seiner Zeit*, Berne, 1947.

[2] Cf., among others, L. L. Schücking, *Character Problems in Shakespeare's Plays*, London, 1922; E. E. Stoll, *Art and Artifice in Shakespeare*, New York,

The conventional devices of style and expression which give pre-Shakespearian drama a character so essentially its own stand out most obviously in plays by the dramatists of the second and third ranks, the mere craftsmen who, having no marked talents of their own, have nevertheless applied themselves to authorship as to a technique that can be learnt. This is probably true, however, of the art and literature of every age; we can learn more about the styles and tastes of an age from the work of the mediocre performers, the lesser spirits of the time, than from the few great masterpieces created by the men of genius. In approaching subjects like those dealt with in this book, the literary historian must therefore give some of his time to works that do not amount to much by purely artistic standards. For the importance of these minor productions lies not only in what they tell us about the transmission of dramatic conventions and their hardening into standardized commonplaces, or about the continuity of dramatic styles; there are also times when they do more than the polished and successful masterpieces to explain the special technical problems with which the playwrights of the age had to contend.

Our study of the plays opens with *Gorboduc* and carries through to Shakespeare's immediate predecessors and early contemporaries, Marlowe, Peele, and Greene. Thus it deals at first with the set speech in English classical plays of the Senecan tradition; then, keeping pace with subsequent developments in pre-Shakespearian drama, it gradually extends its scope to cover finally the so-called romantic plays that verge on tragi-comedy, and it also includes the chronicle plays. Comedy has been deliberately excluded, as have any plays written earlier than *Gorboduc*, in order to concentrate attention on a limited number of developments which follow a more or less consistent course and which can be grasped as a whole. The plays singled out for special analysis have been chosen from the many dramatic works of this period because they seem to illustrate most clearly the developments under consideration.

1933; S. L. Bethell, *Shakespeare and the Popular Dramatic Tradition*, London, 1944; Henri Fluchère, *Shakespeare, Dramaturge élisabéthain*, Paris, 1948 (trans. Guy Hamilton, *Shakespeare and the Elizabethans*, London, 1953); Hardin Craig, *An Interpretation of Shakespeare*, New York, 1948.

In the second section of the book the functions and techniques of the set speech are examined within the bounds of single plays and with reference to the work of individual playwrights. In the third section the stress falls on the comparative analysis of passages exemplifying one and the same type of speech; in this way an attempt is made to cut a cross-section through the development of style and modes of expression as it applies to a single motif, that of lament.

It is hoped, finally, that the book may bring out the possibilities that lie in the detailed study of a single component of drama. It will at the same time reveal the limitations of such a method. A complete account of the development of pre-Shakespearian drama will require several further studies representing other lines of approach, culminating perhaps in a single comprehensive treatment of the subject.

2

The Set Speech in Renaissance Drama and Contemporary Theory

The over-riding importance attached to the set speech in the serious drama of England before Shakespeare's time is a characteristic of European drama as a whole in the Renaissance period. Some recapitulation of general developments in the literature of the fifteenth and sixteenth centuries will enable us to see this phenomenon in a clearer perspective. Many of the relevant facts can of course be only lightly touched on here.

A number of informative books have already been written about the significance of rhetoric in its bearings on all the literary kinds, and the important place allotted to rhetorical studies in school and university education, in poetic theory, and indeed in the common culture of the western world.[1] There is therefore no need in the present work to enter on the question of the relationship between the rhetorical theory of the Renaissance and of the ancients, or to show how a kind of amalgam was made of the literary theory of Aristotle, Cicero, Horace, and Quintilian, or to consider how far the rhetorical tradition of the middle ages continued to be operative at the Renaissance, or what was associated with the idea of rhetoric by the scholars of medieval and Renaissance times.[2] We should bear in mind, however, that during the middle ages it was normal 'to con-

[1] E.g., Charles Sears Baldwin, in *Renaissance Literary Theory and Practice*, ed. D. L. Clark, New York, 1939; Donald Leman Clark, *Rhetoric and Poetry in the Renaissance*, New York, 1922; Sister Miriam Joseph, *Shakespeare's Use of the Arts of Language*, New York, 1947; W. G. Crane, *Wit and Rhetoric in the Renaissance*, New York, 1937; J. H. W. Atkins, *English Literary Criticism: The Renascence*, London, 1947.

[2] See esp. E. R. Curtius, *European Literature and the Latin Middle Ages*, trans. Willard R. Trask, London, 1953, Chap. 4, 'Rhetoric', and Chap. 8, 'Poetry and Rhetoric'.

ceive of poetry as a species of eloquence', and to speak of 'the dominion of rhetoric over poetry'; these generalizations are still applicable to a major part of Renaissance poetry, just as the influence of the ancient conception that poetry and prose both come under the wider heading of 'discourse'[1] also makes itself felt in Renaissance literature in general. Although Aristotle's *Poetics* were being freshly and critically examined, most of the literary theorists of the sixteenth century continued to identify poetic theory with rhetorical theory, or thought of them as interchangeable, and this is only one of many indications of the supremacy enjoyed by rhetoric during the Renaissance. The recovery of Cicero's *De Oratore*, the classic exposition of the high claims of eloquence as an art based on an all-round cultivation of the spirit, and infinitely superior to any merely manual skill,[2] may have been one of the reasons for the extraordinary esteem in which rhetoric was held right down to the English Renaissance. And although in England some voices were raised against the authority of Cicero and in disparagement of the arts of rhetoric,[3] this was an exceptional attitude; the majority would have subscribed to Cicero's proposition, 'Est enim finitimus oratori poeta'.[4] In the narrower sense rhetoric is the art of applying to oratory a system of instruction in the use of decorative figures of speech, of structural devices, and of various types of style; in its actual operation it goes beyond its true province, and it became an all-important factor in the conception of poetry. The point was reached where all the poetic kinds were included under the general head of the art of eloquence; poetry was felt, by its skilful handling of the resources of language, to have exactly the same effect on the reader or hearer as highly-wrought oratory. An exaggerated value came to be placed on style for its own sake, and this in its turn led to the neglect of the claims of composition in the wider sense of the term.[5]

As far as the development of tragedy in England is concerned,

[1] Curtius, op. cit., pp. 145, 148, 147.

[2] Cf. Fr. Klingner, 'Cicero', in *Römische Geisteswelt*, Wiesbaden, 1952, Vol. I.

[3] E.g., John Jewel, Praelector of Humanity or Rhetoric at Oxford. Cf. Atkins, op. cit., p. 71.

[4] *De Oratore*, I. 70.

[5] On the influence of rhetoric on Elizabethan drama see Madeleine Doran, *Endeavors of Art: A Study of Form in Elizabethan Drama*, Madison, 1954, Chap. 2.

all this is of the highest significance. When Seneca's plays began to exert their influence, the ground was already very thoroughly prepared for the reception of this exceptionally powerful germinating agent, the strength of which can no longer be fully grasped today. For in these plays English playwrights were confronted with a form of drama which more than any other depends for its effects on the use of the set speech, developed at great length and embellished with all the resources of art. In these plays rhetoric was to be seen functioning within its own proper sphere, the formal speech; in these plays, too, were to be found all three 'kinds' of eloquence, the *genus iudiciale*, the *genus deliberativum*, and the *genus demonstrativum* [1] – terms which are explained in Chapter 3. Thus in serious drama the set speech came to be one of the most important places for the exercise of the arts of speech as they are comprehended in the arts of rhetoric. The 'occasional' speech, in particular the panegyric and the encomium, was revived in the Renaissance as a literary *genre* in its own right, but though it flourished in other literatures, it is not often found in England. However, in the English prose romances of the sixteenth century every opportunity is seized for the introduction of a set speech of one type or another. The episodic, discursive structure of these romances corresponds in many respects to the structure of early Elizabethan drama, and it was therefore quite natural that similar tendencies should manifest themselves in the plays of the period.[2] Thus the practical exploitation of the arts of language which it was the object of the favourite handbook of rhetoric of the time, Sir Thomas Wilson's *The Arte of Rhetorique* (1553), to inculcate, and which was given a fresh impulse after 1570 by the appearance of the English translation of the speeches of Demosthenes, became a matter of some importance in the domain of the drama. The theatre could therefore with some justification be described as the 'Academy of Speech', and with equal justification references could be made to the close connexion between the rostrum and the

[1] The three divisions of rhetoric, or kinds of speech, laid down by Quintilian, following Aristotle. See Chap. 3, p. 49.

[2] Cf. Kennedy, *The Oration in Shakespeare*, Chap. VII, 'Elizabethan Oratory'. Kennedy gives examples of set speeches in Elizabethan prose romances on p. 166.

stage.[1] In view of the heightened rhetorical consciousness of the period and the rhetorical education that every writer had been put through in his schooldays, it is not at all surprising that it is possible to trace step by step the influence of formal rhetoric on the design, the structure, and the embellishment of the set speeches in the contemporary drama. Every playwright, when he wished to introduce a set speech into his play, must have had in mind several prescribed patterns which he could follow.

However, as will be shown by illustration and analysis in later chapters, the dominating role of the set speech and counter-speech in the early days of English tragedy is only one side of a more comprehensive picture in which the conception of drama and the technique of drama are seen to be interrelated. For hand in hand with it went a specific form of dramatic representation in which events were explained or described in retrospect instead of being directly exhibited on the stage. Retrospective reports and soliloquies, deliberations on things to be done in the future, emotional speeches reflecting a character's state of mind in response to a situation, detailed discussions of the pros and cons of a course of action, these are the normal methods employed; it is not the immediate event, not life lived in the present moment, that are put before us, but what has gone before and what is still to come, while anything truly dramatic, anything that gives a sense of immediacy and actuality, seems almost to be outlawed from the drama. The result of all this is an indirect and oblique dramatic style, one which is to a large degree regulated by the narrative methods of the epic.[2] Action is pondered over, action is spoken about, but of itself it is not represented, or at most in snippets. It is a far cry from the inertia of this procession of massive, sluggishly-moving monologues and dialogues to the liveliness and variety of Shakespeare's history plays and tragedies. It is difficult to think of any dramatic style that could be further removed from true drama than that of the English classical tragedies written on the pattern of Seneca. And it might seem at first sight that there

[1] Cf. H. Gauger, *Die Kunst der politischen Rede in England*, Tübingen, 1952, p. 5.

[2] For some essential differences between the dramatic and the epic styles, cf. Emil Staiger, *Grundbegriffe der Poetik*, Zürich, 1951.

was nothing here that could lead to what we understand by true drama. Yet the transition was brought about, and in the process more was handed on than may at first be apparent.

The transition from the rhetorical tragedy of the early period to the Shakespearian type of drama is bound up with the most striking and impressive developments in form that English drama has undergone in the whole of its history. It is the purpose of the chapters that follow to trace this development primarily in terms of the set speech. As the story unfolds, we shall see how the formal set speech gradually becomes possessed of dramatic life; and it will emerge no less clearly that the weight and the splendour and the verbal artistry of the rhetorical set speech were handed on as a priceless legacy to Shakespearian tragedy. For what in a very special sense puts Shakespearian tragedy in a class of its own in the drama of the world is the fact that it derives its power no less from its rhetorical and poetic artistry and its sublime eloquence than from its representation of dramatic action reflecting real life in all its variety and complexity. Seneca was not merely someone who hindered the free development of English tragedy into a genuinely dramatic *genre*. By his example he also endorsed and reinforced the already existing tendency to express whatever has emotional potentialities in speeches of a heightened poetic quality. He was one of the generating forces that led not only to the rolling splendour of the verse of *Tamburlaine*, but also to the sublime apostrophes of Lear. It was Shakespeare's own special achievement that he brought about the fusion of the fast-moving, closely-packed drama of action with the tradition of the rhetorical tragedy which was dependent for its effects on the power of the spoken word, of eloquence. This he could not have done had it not been that for several decades the heroes of the Elizabethan stage had been in the habit of expressing their deeply-felt desires, emotions, and imaginings in the rhetorical language of the formal set speech.

A glance at the development of serious drama in France and Italy in the sixteenth century will be enough to show us that this coalition of two dramatic techniques originally diametrically opposed to each other was one of those happy conjunctions that are peculiar to the history of English drama. In these countries the transition from the rigid formality of the classical conventions to the liveliness of a drama of action did not come about until a very late period, and then was only partially carried through. For in France this evolutionary process leads, not to a Shakespeare, but to Racine, who represents the set-speech form of tragedy at its very highest. No such peaks were scaled in Italy; on the contrary, the development of Italian drama, from Trissino to Tasso, shows how extremely difficult it was to get out of the rut of a dramatic technique which was firmly based on exposition, retrospective narration, and the analysis of emotion. There are so many parallels and similarities between this sixteenth-century Italian tragedy and the contemporary English tragedy that they can surely not be put down entirely to a common influence proceeding from Seneca; some kind of influence of the Italian upon the English must also be assumed.[1] This relationship, which has so far been little explored, would be nothing out of the ordinary at a time when England was receiving so many different types of stimulus from Italy, and not only in the way of themes and subject-matter.

The characteristic handling of the set speech by the Italian dramatists throws some light on its development in England. Already in Trissino, who quite deliberately took Euripides and not Seneca as his model,[2] a great deal more space is given to retrospective narration, description, and introspection, all in the form of set speeches, than was ever the case in Euripides. In the famous *Sofonisba*, the first 'regular' tragedy, four-fifths of the play is narrated in soliloquies, duologues, and choral lyrics.[3] The choric mourning-song of Euripidean tragedy, the *Kommos*, is continually expanded by the Italian playwrights, in whose hands it assumes proportions far beyond those of its Greek models.[4] Thus the tendency towards the

[1] In his article, 'The Influence of Italian on Early Elizabethan Drama', *Mod. Phil.* IV, 1906, J. W. Cunliffe comes to the conclusion that in the earlier periods of Elizabethan drama the influence was very slight.

[2] On Italian imitations of Seneca in the fourteenth and fifteenth centuries see Wilhelm Cloetta, *Die Anfänge der Renaissancetragödie*, Halle, 1892, esp. pp. 51 ff., 85 ff., 190 ff.

[3] Cf. here, and later, Emilio Bertana, *La Tragedia* (*Storia dei Generi Letterari Italiani*), Milan, n.d., Chaps. II and III.

[4] E.g., in the *Scilla* of De Cesari.

expansion of the set speech and the amplification of its emotional content is quite apparent in the Italian dramatists even when they are consciously and deliberately following the Euripidean pattern. It is also characteristic of these Italian Euripideans that what they most signally failed to learn from their master should have been the simple naturalness of his diction and his pregnant phraseology.[1] In his famous *Treatise on the Composition of Comedies and Tragedies* (1554)[2] Giraldi Cinthio had expressly condemned simple diction as being inappropriate to the dignity of drama, and he had also on these grounds classed Seneca as superior to Euripides. Even earlier than this, however, dramatic style may be seen to have been developing in the direction of artificiality, affectation, and diffuseness, even when, as is the case with Trissino, there are very few instances of specifically rhetorical adornment. It is true that in his *Rosmunda* Trissino's successor Rucellai in several passages places sequences of rapid dialogue side by side with the more elaborate speeches; but even here what he is giving us is not dialogue in the true sense, but a clumsy imitation of stichomythia which in fact is merely a continuation of the sophisticated and formalized diction of the speech proper. Rucellai's *Oreste* is a free adaptation of Euripides' *Iphigenia in Tauris*, and it is therefore possible to trace with some particularity the twist towards the rhetorical and the sententious that has been given to Euripides' language and to observe the greatly increased length and prolixity of the speeches.

In Giraldi Cinthio the set speech is consciously 'dignified' and adorned with rhetorical figures; it is made into a kind of show-piece, and at the same time becomes the predominating medium of the drama. Indeed, all too many opportunities are taken of introducing set speeches and soliloquies. Without any regard to dramatic requirements or dramatic propriety, the characters are brought on the stage in little groups, usually in twos and threes (in so far as it is not a matter of 'one-man episodes'), and spout diffuse and endless

[1] Cf. G. Toffanin, *Il Cinquecento* (*Storia Letteraria d'Italia*), Milan, 1941, p. 515. In this connexion Toffanin differentiates two dramatic movements, one influenced more strongly by Seneca, the other by Euripides.

[2] *Discorsi intorno al comporre dei Romanzi, delle Comedie e delle Tragedie*, Venice, 1554.

set speeches filled with hollow-sounding emotional commonplaces. At the same time Cinthio, like his successors, makes increasing use of a well-tried expedient; even when his characters are not actually soliloquizing, he makes them on every possible occasion report their feelings and thoughts in some detail. He supplies them with confidants to whom they may open their hearts or confide their histories.[1] Thus there is a profusion of nurses, servants, waiting-women, and the like, usually nameless minor characters whose chief function is to be the recipients of confidences; nor must we forget the counsellors, who in the same way are made to assume the role of confidants and who respond with sage and moral counsels – which of course provides further opportunities for long set speeches. Characters of this type are far more extensively used in sixteenth-century Italian tragedy than was ever the way with Seneca; indeed, though they are no more than the merest ciphers, they are the figures it could least well dispense with.

However, while all these narrations and deliberations and counsellings and self-revelations are proceeding, the action is left completely at a standstill. An illustration of this is seen in Cinthio's *Altile*, where almost two whole acts go by before the so-called plot shows any signs of beginning. The second act of his *Arrenopia* opens with three soliloquies in a row, each of them marked as a separate scene, and it is only in the fourth scene that we are given a duologue, followed in the fifth scene, however, by yet another soliloquy. Cinthio differs from Seneca, of course, in that he makes more happen on the stage. The gruesome deeds and the horrors are no longer solely reported, as in Seneca; they are actually performed. But the set-speech technique is little affected by this innovation. Dramatic incidents are not yet at this stage conceived of as an amalgam of speech and action; it is something indeed that they should actually be represented, but they are hemmed in on either side by formal speeches of commentary and description, and

[1] In this way it was possible to avoid the excessive use of monologues, which were explicitly discouraged by the literary theorists. 'Dialogue' with confidants was a substitute for the 'forbidden' monologue in the classical plays of the period. Cf. Max J. Wolff, 'Die Theorie der italienischen Tragödie im 16. Jahrhundert', *Archiv*, LXVI, 1912, p. 351.

the two things, the incident that is displayed and the accompanying set speech, are kept apart as isolated units.

The number of lengthy set speeches in Seneca has often been remarked on; in Cinthio, however, they have become longer still. Cinthio's most famous tragedy, the *Orbecche*, contains about 2700 lines, whereas its model, the *Thyestes* of Seneca, has a mere 1113 lines. This expansion results almost entirely from the greater length both of individual speeches and of exchanges of set speeches.

Thus an examination of Cinthio's plays reveals a good many points of similarity between his practice and what we find in the classical tragedy of sixteenth-century England, not only in the outward structure of the plays and the dramatic technique generally, but even in details of style and speech-architecture. In his *Discorsi* Cinthio had laid down the various points in which Seneca was superior to the Greeks: 'Nella prudenza, nella gravità, nel decoro, nella maestà, nelle sentenze, tutti Greci che scrissero mai, quantunque nella eloquenza potesse essere più casto e più colto.' The first English tragedy, *Gorboduc*, is an imitation of precisely these qualities in Seneca; it is an attempt to acclimatize not so much his impassioned manner of speech as his stately dignity, his *gravitas*, and his moral tone. Neither in Italian nor in English tragedy does violent and passionate utterance make its appearance until rather later in the century. A further characteristic shared by the English and the Italian dramatists is the markedly moral and didactic undertone in the set speeches, their tendency to think of the play as a vehicle for instruction, as if indeed it was a morality play; in this respect the English went even further than the Italians.

It is true that a few of the later playwrights, Aretino in particular, manage to lighten the style; some of the ponderousness goes by the board, and at the same time there are rather fewer long set speeches. Furthermore, in Aretino, as also in Dolce, at least some attempt is made to individualize the characters and to approach them from a psychological point of view. But on the whole credible flesh-and-blood characters are seldom to be met with in sixteenth-century Italian tragedy. In England the playwrights did eventually manage to portray human beings; they managed to replace types by individuals. This the Italian tragic dramatists of the sixteenth century never achieved; they did not get beyond shadowy and easily interchangeable figures who either have a purely functional role in the plot or exist merely as personified abstractions. These personages – for one cannot dignify them with the name of 'characters' – have no clear outlines, and no humanity; they are soulless puppets [1] who are made to express well-worn and constantly reiterated sentiments and reflections. This again is most clearly apparent in the formal set speeches. If it is a question of offering counsel, or planning a course of action, or weighing the pros and cons of some matter, then it is this matter and not the personality of the speaker that is at the heart of the speech. But if it is love or despair, hatred or revenge, affliction or sorrow that is to be presented, we can be pretty sure of a set speech of the appropriate kind the emotional content of which is conveyed in conventional and very often purely stereotyped terms. In these circumstances it is usually immaterial who the speaker is, as long as the occasion for the speech brings it into one or other of these categories.

The tendency of the speeches to fall into types without any individuality of their own is accentuated by another characteristic that is common to Italian and Elizabethan tragedy. This is the practice of pitching all the emotions too high. The stereotyped emotions of hatred, revenge, grief, and the like are drastically overdrawn; they are depicted in the most glaring colours, exaggerated far beyond anything that could by modern standards be regarded as normal or probable. And in this an essential part is played by rhetoric. However, where everything is expressed *fortissimo*, there can be little room for differentiation. We shall see in later chapters that this standardizing of set speeches is a characteristic that persists for a long time; indeed we can trace it right through to the time of Shakespeare. Then at last, it is true, it begins to be overlaid with something new and entirely different which it is the specific purpose of this study to reveal. However, though it largely goes underground, its influence still continues to be felt for a long time as a subconscious basis for the terms in which the playwright will express himself. Again and again there are occasions when it can be

[1] Cf. Bertana, op. cit., p. 107.

detected even in the later stages of the developments we are discussing.

In sixteenth-century France the evolution of tragedy runs parallel to that of Italy in many ways. Seneca again provides the pattern, and we find a similar preponderance of rhetorical tragedy, matched by a similar handling of the set speech. The plays of Robert Garnier, whose influence on Elizabethan drama has been the subject of a valuable monograph,[1] are probably the best illustrations of what we may expect to find in set-speech tragedy at this time. It is not to act that the characters are brought on to the stage, but to make speeches; and indeed Garnier does not call them actors, but *interlocuteurs* and *entreparleurs*.[2] There is a minimum of action, and the narrative method, by which the substance of the play is embodied in a series of reports, retrospective narrations, and deliberative or persuasive speeches, seems on the surface to be identical with that of Seneca. However, Seneca in his speeches constantly gives the events and the elements of action in his plot some importance by his manner of relating them, whereas Garnier completely ignores the concrete particulars and the life-giving details of his stories. He is almost exclusively concerned with states of mind and with the spiritual reactions of his characters to the circumstances, usually the result of past events, with which they are faced. The speeches in his plays are the reflection of these inward states; they portray the relevant emotions and give expression to reflections of a highly lyrical quality, and they do so very much more extensively than Seneca's speeches.[3] Thus in Garnier the dramatic set speech has taken a further step away from the sphere of action; it has lost its connexion with real happenings and the events of life as it goes on around us. Through its emphasis on anything that was susceptible of emotional and lyrical treatment, and through the disciplined artistry of the style in which the emotion was embodied, it exercised some influence in the later phase of English classical tragedy for

[1] A. M. Witherspoon, *The Influence of Robert Garnier on Elizabethan Drama*, New Haven, 1924.

[2] Similarly Minturno calls the actors *recitanti*. Cf. Baldwin, *Renaissance Literary Theory and Practice*, p. 168.

[3] The differences between Seneca and Garnier are well brought out by Witherspoon, op. cit., pp. 40 ff.

which the attempts at reform of the Countess of Pembroke's circle were responsible. However, already before Garnier's influence has become apparent the style of the set speech in English drama has been running an almost parallel course and exhibiting similar tendencies. The style of expression for extremes of emotion and suffering has become sophisticated, formal, and pedantic; the emotional content of the speech is rationalized and anatomized down to the last detail in a sort of formalized ritual. Virtually therefore the emotional set speech is a subtle appeal to the intellect. In this connexion, then, the inferences drawn from a study of Garnier's plays are equally applicable to early English tragedy.[1]

Garnier represents the culminating point of rhetorical tragedy in France in the sixteenth century. Three decades after his death Alexandre Hardy gave a fresh impulse to French tragedy and turned it into new channels; he introduced a great deal of action, with an admixture of the romantic dramatic elements which had in the meantime been developing side by side with the regular form of tragedy, and he also abandoned 'regularity'. But he was not a dramatic genius like Shakespeare, in whose work a perfect fusion of the different styles was achieved, and at an altogether higher level.

Finally something must be said about the Latin tragedy of the sixteenth century, for it too is dominated by the set speech, similarly used as the chief medium of representation. Of those who carried on the Senecan tradition the Scottish playwright Robert Buchanan deserves special mention; his plays (*Baptistes*, 1541; *Jephthes*, 1554) enjoyed a certain renown even on the Continent. It is symptomatic of the strength of Seneca's influence that, although Buchanan had himself translated two of Euripides' plays into Latin, his own Latin plays are not in any way reminiscent of Euripides; they are very close imitations of Seneca, especially in their handling of the set speech.[2]

This short account of the dramatic methods of the Italian and French tragic playwrights has shown the importance they attached to the set speech, and their practice is fully sanctioned by the

[1] Cf. Witherspoon, op. cit., p. 31.

[2] Cf. Frederick S. Boas, *University Drama in the Tudor Age*, Oxford, 1914, p. 60; Baldwin, *Renaissance Literary Theory and Practice*, p. 138.

dramatic and poetic theory of the sixteenth century. For this too we are of course largely dependent on Italian and French sources, since there exists no systematic treatment of tragedy in England at this time, and there are only a few, though valuable, references to it in Sidney's *Defence* and other contemporary writings.[1] In the domain of tragedy the interdependence of theory and practice was closer in this century than at any other time, for tragedy was regarded as a 'learned art', and its practitioners deliberately set themselves to imitate ancient models, and were at pains to observe the 'rules' as well as was in their power.[2] It is true that not everyone would have concurred with Bernardo Tasso's view, to which his son Torquato also subscribed, that one could become a poet only by following the dictates of Aristotle;[3] yet the majority of writers evidently believed, with Giraldi, that the more closely a play kept to the rules laid down by the theorists, the better and more effective it would be.[4]

We can concern ourselves with these rules and theoretical systems only in so far as they have any significant bearings on the shaping of the set speech. Aristotle's requirement that the action of tragedy must be noble (carrying with it the assumption that it involves noble characters) was superficially interpreted and superseded by the demand that only persons of high standing should be represented in a tragedy. The rank of the characters was thus made a fundamental mark of distinction between tragedy and comedy.[5] Moreover, their

[1] Cf. Atkins, *English Literary Criticism: The Renascence*, p. 216: 'Except for Sidney's comments of 1582–3, and the conventional statements of Webbe and Puttenham, we look almost in vain for remarks on the plays produced or for theorizing on the dramatic art itself.' It is possible that the great freedom and lack of constraint with which Peele, say, or Greene, or Marlowe set about their dramatic experiments is bound up with the fact that England had no dramatic theory of its own, but only what operated at second hand.

[2] For what follows cf. Wolff, op. cit. On the influence of earlier theorists on the Renaissance conception of drama see Madeleine Doran, *Endeavors of Art*, pp. 105 ff.

[3] Bernardo Tasso, *Lettere*, II, p. 525; Torquato Tasso, *Dialogue of Pellegrino*. Cf. Wolff, op. cit., p. 174.

[4] *Discorsi*, p. 118.

[5] Already with the French theorists of the fifteenth century (cf. H. W. Lawton, *Handbook of French Renaissance Dramatic Theory*, Manchester, 1949), and similarly with the Italians (cf. Wolff, op. cit., p. 178).

speech had to be appropriate to their station in life. The question of what is appropriate, indeed the whole matter of linguistic decorum, is the subject of lively discussion on the part of almost all the theorists, and there emerged the further requirement that the style of tragedy should be grave and majestic. 'An ideal conception was formed of *gravità*, *maestà*, and *dignità* (Castelvetro); these qualities were to prevail through every part of the tragedy, and by those following the Senecan model they were considered necessary as properties of the grave Roman genius in contrast to the frivolity of the Greeks.'[1] As at the same time there was a desire to maintain a constant level of *gravità* in the style, the result was the unrelieved monotony and the stilted expression of emotion, so ill accommodated to the spontaneous overflow of powerful feelings,[2] which are characteristic of the early classical tragedy of England. Most of the literary theorists draw a clear distinction between the language of tragedy and of comedy, and consequently the style, together with the rank of the characters and some other purely external properties, comes to be regarded as the most important distinguishing feature of the two *genres*.[3] Thus for example Giraldi declares in his *Discorsi* 'Quel parlare della tragedia vuole esser grande, reale, e magnifico e figurato: quello della comedia, semplice, puro, famigliare, e convenevole alle persone del popolo.' Hence the style of tragedy could

[1] Wolff, op. cit., p. 179.

[2] Several of the theorists circumscribe the language of tragedy more narrowly; cf. Wolff, op. cit., p. 182, and J. E. Spingarn, *A History of Literary Criticism in the Renaissance*, New York, 1912, pp. 60 ff. Castelvetro speaks of the *favella magnifica* which must correspond to the *azione magnifica*, and as adornment for it he requires *figure nove* which will occur only to the learned (*Poetica d'Aristotile vulgarizzata e sporta*, Bâle, 1576, p. 973). On Castelvetro see also H. B. Charlton, *Castelvetro's Theory of Poetry*, Manchester, 1913. The same parallel between the *gravitas* of tragedy and *oratio gravis* is found in Scaliger, who describes this diction more accurately as '*oratio culta et a vulgi dictione aversa*' (*Poetices Libri Septem*, Rome, 1561, Chap. I. 4). The esteem in which detailed and dignified deliberation in the form of dialogue was held is shown by the *Giudicio sopra la Canace* (probably by Bartolomeo Cavalcanti), in which we read, 'Ragionamenti gravi sono il grandissimo ornamento alla tragedia'. (*Giudicio* printed in *Opere di Speroni*, Venice, 1740, Vol. IV, p. 90.)

[3] Cf. Spingarn, *A History of Literary Criticism in the Renaissance*, p. 66. There are many further illustrative quotations in Lawton, *Handbook of French Renaissance Dramatic Theory*.

never be appropriate in a comedy: 'Quelle pompe di parlare, que' superbi modi di dire, quelle similitudini, quelle comperazioni, quelle figure, que' contraposti, che i Greci chiamano Antiteti, e quegli altri ornamenti che convengono alla tragedia.'[1] It is true that some voices were raised in warning against too great a profusion of *ornamenti* in the diction and against diffuseness and circumlocution, but they remained in the minority and were not listened to.[2] Even in dramatic theory Euripides had lost the field to Seneca.

All these judgements – and others like them might have been cited [3] – are revealing as far as the subject of the present study is concerned. They indicate pretty accurately the stylistic traits that we shall meet with not only in the early English classical tragedies but also in those of a later period. In his definition of tragedy Aristotle laid down that it should be composed 'in an artistic style (ἡδυσμένῳ λόγῳ) which is appropriate to the nature of the various parts'.[4] Aristotle's conception of an 'enriched language' thus provided some sanction for the rhetorical adornment of the tragic style, and it was this aspect of tragedy that was especially cultivated. But Aristotle had also demanded suitability of style to subject-matter and corresponding variations in the diction employed, and this requirement being disregarded, the language took on a monotony beyond even that of Seneca. Apparently only one type of diction was ever considered, and that was the diction of the set speech. There was no discussion of the language appropriate to dialogue. This is true even of Minturno's claim [5] that the style of tragedy should be 'vividly descriptive', by which is meant only the language of the reports and narrative speeches, not the dramatic diction of the

[1] Both passages from the *Discorsi*, p. 96. There are similar remarks in the French theorists, e.g., Jodocus Badius Ascensius (Lawton, op. cit., pp. 30 ff.).

[2] Cf. Wolff, op. cit., p. 183. Under Seneca's influence the faults censured by Cavalcanti became commonplace in the classical tragedy as a whole: '*inutili abbellimenti, copia di parole di gran suono, e aggiramenti di sentenze e di voci gonfiate*' (*Giudicio*, p. 121).

[3] Several of the texts mentioned are published in English translations by Barrett H. Clark, *European Theories of the Drama*, New York, 1947.

[4] *Poetics*, VI. ii.

[5] *De Poeta Libri Sex*, Venice, 1559.

dialogue. Thus tragedy was regarded as something which was primarily spoken and listened to; it relied for its effect above all on the power of the spoken word. Apart from Castelvetro,[1] whose views are in many respects original and in advance of his times, no one seems to have realized that the words and the action are interdependent and work together to produce a single overall impression. Even Minturno draws a clear distinction between the pleasure that the tragic poet provides by 'the sweetness of his verse and the elegance of his speech' and that which he provides 'by the use of song and dance'.[2] But in that last phrase he is thinking rather of masque interludes than of the drama proper.

Again from the theoretical angle, a good deal of light is thrown on the use of the set speech in dramatic composition by the scenario of a tragedy which Scaliger offers as a pattern for works of this nature. It is the ground-plan for a tragedy having for its plot the story of Ceyx and Alcyone as Ovid relates it (*Metam.*, XI). What is so significant is the closeness with which this 'ideal' pattern corresponds to the structure of sixteenth-century classical tragedy, allowing a great deal of space to set descriptions, reports, formal laments, and reflections by the Chorus.[3]

Scaliger gives a closer account elsewhere in the *Poetics* (VII. 3) of his conception of the nature and purpose of drama as it is illustrated in this scenario. According to him the chief aims of tragedy are to represent the passions and to teach – that is, to influence – the audience. The plot is merely a means to these ends: 'Quare erit quasi exemplar aut instrumentum in fabula; affectus vero finis.' Here Scaliger was laying down a very important principle, one which applies Renaissance psychological theory to the composition of drama. In doing this he was also meeting the interest of the whole age in new techniques for the representation of emotion and the

[1] Cf. Charlton, *Castelvetro's Theory of Poetry*; Baldwin, *Renaissance Literary Theory and Practice*.

[2] *De Poeta Libri Sex*.

[3] *Poetices Libri Septem*, III. 97: '*Primus Actus* est conquestio, hinc Chorus detestans navigationes. *Secundus Actus:* Sacerdos cum votis, colloquens cum Halcyone et nutrice: arae ignis, piae sententiae, hinc Chorus vota approbans. *Tertius actus*: Nuncius de orta tempestate cum rumoribus, hinc Chorus exempla adducens naufragiorum, multa apostrophe ad Neptunum. . . .'

analysis of character.[1] It is obvious that there is a connexion between the importance of the set speech as a medium for representing the passions in drama and this universal preoccupation with 'the passions of the human heart'. Needless to say, the 'representation of the passions' then meant something quite different from what it does today. In the same way as clear-cut distinctions were drawn between the various 'temperaments', and fixed conventions existed as to the speech and conduct and appearance appropriate to a particular temperament, so also with regard to the passions (the *passioni*) there appears to have been a fixed system of classification, a theory of types which involved the recurrent use of certain stereotyped forms of utterance and certain conventional stylistic usages.[2] And when in the course of the play a particular emotion was represented in a set speech, the person actually concerned was left in the background, for it was merely the type of the emotion that had to be expressed; interest was centred on the general, not the individual. The particular character and the specific circumstances which lay at the back of the emotion and which were responsible for its expression in the set speech were of much less importance than that the typical forms of utterance always associated with this emotion should be employed in the speech. And since it was the function of tragedy to exemplify *pathos*, even as in comedy the emphasis was laid on *ethos*, there grew up with regard to the set speech a clearly defined typology, as will be more fully illustrated in later chapters. In this way the ancient conceptions of the nature of *pathos* and *ethos*, those of Aristotle and Quintilian among others, were during the Renaissance as drastically simplified and schematized as Aristotle's teachings on the nature of tragedy and Cicero's reference to the 'attributes' according to which a person is to be characterized.[3]

This dependence on conventional methods, including the stereo-

[1] Cf. Otto Regenbogen, 'Schmerz und Tod in den Tragödien Senecas', in *Vorträge der Bibliothek Warburg 1927–1928*, Leipzig, 1930. Regenbogen stresses the significance of the researches of W. Dilthey, 'Zur Weltanschauung und Analyse des Menschen seit der Renaissance und Reformation' (*Gesammelte Schriften*, II), where these ideas are more fully discussed.

[2] Here and for what follows cf. Madeleine Doran, *Endeavors of Art*, pp. 237 ff., and Chap. 9.

[3] *De Inventione*, I. xxiv ff.

typed representation of the characters,[1] is a very strongly marked feature of the set speech in pre-Shakespearian drama. In this connexion the idea of 'decorum' plays a significant part. Decorum was the most important standard by which the choice, not only of the most appropriate language, but of all the other components of a play as well, was regulated; it meant, not that the writer must try to give the impression of something transferred immediately from life to the pages of a book, but that he should aim at representing what was considered appropriate to particular types of character, states of mind, and situations. Decorum was therefore no mere abstraction; on the contrary, it presupposed that the richness of real life, with its constant mixing of types, its inconsistencies, and its infinite and ever-shifting variety, could be broken up into a carefully organized system of phenomena which could be separately identified and authoritatively defined.

However, some distinction must be drawn here between theory and practice, just as there are differences in the way in which these conventions are observed in Italian, French, and English drama. English plays, especially the comedies, quite soon begin to approximate more closely to life and to give their characters more individuality, whereas on the Continent the drama takes a very much longer time to break away from conventional usages and schematic patterns. Of course a highly gifted playwright will on his own initiative begin discarding the accepted forms with all their rigid limitations, and will handle the existing conventions in such a way as to gain the most vivid dramatic effects. To show this happening in Elizabethan drama is one of the objects of this book.

In view of the emphasis laid on the set speech as a dramatic medium and on the representation of the passions by means of the spoken word alone, it is not surprising that almost all the theorists

[1] Cf. Ruth L. Anderson, *Elizabethan Psychology and Shakespeare's Plays*, Univ. of Iowa Humanistic Studies, Vol. III, No. 4, 1927; Hardin Craig, *The Enchanted Glass*, New York, 1936. Doubts over the application of Elizabethan psychological theory to literary interpretation are expressed by Louise Turner Forest, 'A Caveat for the Critics against Invoking Elizabethan Psychology', *PMLA*, LXI, 1946. Critical comment on relevant literature is provided by Francis R. Johnson, 'The Elizabethan Science of Psychology', in *English Studies Today*, ed. C. L. Wrenn and G. Bullough, Oxford, 1951.

gave short shrift to such matters as the structure of a play and the conduct of its action. Here again Aristotle's views were interpreted in a misleading manner. Thus it could be said of Minturno, 'Tragedy is discussed as a poem with parts like those of a speech and with descriptive amplification.' [1] Apart from Castelvetro, who, with a probable debt to Aristotle, stresses the primacy of plot over character, no one seems to have concerned himself, even theoretically, with the structural laws of drama. This corresponds with what we can learn for ourselves by studying the part the set speech plays in the total structure of the plays throughout the early period.

Attention must also be drawn to the heavy emphasis that the theorists laid on the moral and didactic purpose of tragedy. One went to comedy to be amused, to tragedy to be instructed, the accompanying boredom being openly admitted.[2] Sir Philip Sidney, indeed, in the few observations he has left us on the subject of drama, wishes to extend this notion of moral profit also to comedy; however, it is as the special merit of *Gorboduc* that he stresses it, otherwise, characteristically, finding nothing in the play worthy of special praise except the style and the set speeches: '*Gorboduc* . . . as it is full of stately speeches and well sounding Phrases, clyming to the height of Seneca his stile, and as full of notable moralitie which it doth most delightfully teach, and so obtayne the very end of Poesie . . . .'[3]

If we are to consider not only the style and structure of dramatic set speeches, but also their subject-matter and their relationship to the characters of those who deliver them, we shall do well to remind ourselves of the misleading conception of the tragic which to a large degree determines the nature of early English tragedy. Aristotle's famous doctrine of catharsis was construed as meaning that tragedy purges the onlooker of the emotions of pity and terror in that it gets him used to the sight of suffering by piling on the horror, and thus teaching him to accept it with composure.[4]

Aristotle had declared, though presumably this represents only a part of his belief, that the *pathos* of tragedy 'is a destructive or

[1] Quoted from C. S. Baldwin, *Renaissance Literary Theory and Practice*, p. 166.

[2] Cf. Wolff, op. cit., p. 341.

[3] Cf. Sidney, *An Apologie for Poetrie*, Cambridge, 1948, p. 51.

[4] Wolff, op. cit., pp. 340 ff.

painful occurrence, such as a death on the open stage, acute suffering and wounding, and the like'.[1] These words were accepted in so literal a sense that a tragedy without bloodshed was regarded as quite out of the question.[2] The suffering was seen primarily, and even exclusively, as physical suffering, dispossession, wounding, mutilation, and other things of this nature.

Once more Shakespeare was the first to attach a deeper meaning to the idea of suffering. This is true also of his new conception of the tragic, which had so far been dominated by the medieval view of tragedy as the fall of a great man from high estate into great misfortune, it being unthinkable that such a fall should not be accompanied by outward manifestations of violence, by bloodshed, deprivation of rights, defeats in battle, rape, and the like. What we understand nowadays by 'inward' tragedy was unknown. Shakespeare was the first to see its potentialities and give them shape, though there is some approach to it in Marlowe. But even Shakespeare used the materials of 'outward' tragedy as a groundwork on which to build his inward tragedy; he started from the kinds of happening which were regarded during the Renaissance as the essential prerequisites of tragedy, and which are perhaps described in the most characteristic terms by Scaliger: 'The materials of tragedy are on the grand scale and fearful, such things as royal decrees, slaughter, desperation, suicide, banishment, rapine, incest, destruction by fire, bloody battles, the plucking out of eyes, weeping and wailing and lamentation, burials, dirges, and funeral hymns.'[3] As will be shown later, these 'catch-words' describe themes and motifs that lend themselves to type-speeches which are not the expression of individual feelings, but a string of the commonplaces that are associated with particular recurrent motifs.

Accepting the fact that serious drama before Shakespeare was pre-eminently speech-drama, gaining its effects more from the power of the spoken word than from any liveliness in the stage-action, some reference must now be made to recent studies of the arts of

[1] *Poetics*, XI. 10. [2] Cf. Wolff, op. cit., p. 352.

[3] Scaliger (VI): 'Res tragicae grandes, atroces, iussa regum, caedes, desperationes, suspendia, exilia, orbitates, parricidia, conquaestiones, funera, epitaphia, epicedia.'

acting on the Elizabethan stage.[1] Research has made it seem probable that in the Elizabethan theatre we must think in terms of a somewhat restricted and formalized histrionic art which, in its heavily stylized character, its strict observance of decorum, and its scanty and apparently rather stilted use of movement and gesture, corresponded closely to the declamatory style of the contemporary drama. The authors of these studies, whose findings, however, cannot yet be regarded as certainly established, have come to the conclusion that the players probably merely declaimed their parts and did not allow themselves to act freely and naturally, and that on the Elizabethan stage much more concern was shown for the arts of speech than for skill in movement. Even if we are not prepared to go as far as this, and keep some reservations as to the supremacy of declamation, we must accept the fact that these arts of declamation assumed a large and important role in the Elizabethan theatre, and that in the majority of plays ensemble-acting was continually interrupted by long set speeches and soliloquies which the more distinguished actors treated as 'object-lessons in their declamatory art, their irresistible stage-rhetoric'.[2] Attempts have been made to see even in the design of the Elizabethan stage a desire to give further countenance and prominence to this art of declamation; indeed this stage has been conceived of as being more a 'speech-stage' than an acting-stage. Finally, analysis of production methods and of contemporary principles of dramatic composition has shown how far these must have been governed by the dominance of declaimed speech.[3] Yet it would be dangerous to come down exclusively either on the one side or the other in such matters as these. There are plenty of intermediate steps between a speech-stage and an acting-

[1] Cf. B. L. Joseph, *Elizabethan Acting*, London, 1951; Alfred Harbage, 'Elizabethan Actors', *PMLA*, LIV, 1939; M. C. Bradbrook, *Elizabethan Stage Conditions*, Cambridge, 1932, and *Themes and Conventions of Elizabethan Tragedy*, Part I. Attention should be drawn, however, to Marvin Rosenberg's strictures on these views in 'Elizabethan Actors: Men or Marionettes?', *PMLA*, LXIX, 1954. There is also some more recent literature on the subject

[2] Rudolf Stamm, *Geschichte des englischen Theaters*, Berne, 1951, p. 115. Stamm also discusses the relationship between declamation and acting.

[3] Cf. Fluchère, *Shakespeare, Dramaturge élisabéthain* (English title, *Shakespeare and the Elizabethans*).

stage, and it is among these that the true character of the Elizabethan theatre is to be sought. It is the object of later chapters of this book to bring out the changing relationships between the arts of declamation and events acted on the stage, and to show how speech and action became interdependent. Shakespeare himself maintains a balance between the two extremes. In his tragedies he gives as much importance to vigorous action on the stage as to the language of emotion in the long speech.

And now finally a few words must be said about this matter of emotional language in tragedy. Nowadays we exert ourselves (as in the present chapter) to discover what lay behind the growth of an ornate and elevated, an 'emotionalized', form of language in Renaissance tragedy; at the same time we must admit that we have lost any sense such as former times possessed of direct contact with this particular way of expressing emotion. An Elizabethan theatregoer would not have found it either unnatural or improbable that the tragic hero should express himself in an elaborate verse-speech, full of rhetorical figures, overdrawn images, and far-fetched allusions, that he should move in a world of highly exaggerated forms of language such as he would never use in real life. It is only the realistic attitude of much later times that has made it all seem so disproportionate, and has caused us to think inadmissible in tragedy, or all but inadmissible, much that to earlier periods must have seemed entirely proper and matter of course.[1] However, a different attitude has perhaps been growing up of late years with the revival of poetic drama in England[2] and the beginnings of a more critical view of naturalism.[3]

The Elizabethans had a decided taste for inflated sentiments, for

[1] Cf. Staiger, *Grundbegriffe der Poetik*. Even Dryden describes the use of the heroic couplet in tragedy as natural. As we are concerned in tragedy with 'nature wrought up to a higher pitch', and as it sets 'noble persons' before us, it would follow that 'heroic rhyme is nearest nature' (*Essay of Dramatic Poesy*).

[2] Cf. T. S. Eliot's various essays on the problems of verse-drama, e.g., *A Dialogue on Dramatic Poetry*, 1928, and *Poetry and Drama*, 1951.

[3] Cf. Rudolf Stamm, 'Christopher Fry and the Revolt against Realism in Modern English Drama', *Anglia* 72, 1954; see also the literature on poetic drama there cited. On the idea of 'naturalness' and 'the language of tragedy' cf. also Cleanth Brooks and Robert Heilmann, *Understanding Drama*, New York, 1945, p. 32.

the proud bearing and arrogant, high-sounding self-revelations of the man who had grown conscious of his own worth. Although to us such sentiments – and they appeared in many guises on the Elizabethan stage – seem theatrical, extravagant, or eccentric, the contemporary spectator would have felt and accepted them as an enlarged reflection of the kind of feelings that he himself experienced. In the emotional set speech of the Elizabethan drama there vibrates some of the dynamic thrust of the Renaissance man, and we today can still catch some of the notes.

But ultimately such a vigorous, high-flown form of expression had its own special *raison d'être* on a stage which, in comparison with later times, was poorly equipped with properties, scenery, and decorative effects, and had at the same time to suggest frequent changes of scene. For on this stage the spoken word alone, working on the imagination of the audience, had to give shape to everything that would be visibly present on the stage of later days. Language could be, and indeed had to be, used more boldly and vigorously because it had to create not only scene and atmosphere, but often too the illusion necessary to a particular role. Its potentialities for conjuring up many different kinds of picture before the eye of the imagination were not yet restricted by the realism of the picture actually presented on the stage.

Thus the form and style of the Elizabethan dramatic set speech are governed by a great many conditions and assumptions, and these will all have to be taken into consideration when we begin analysing examples. The main object of the present short survey has been to describe in outline certain of the usages and conventions according to which the developments to be traced in the following chapters were to take place. It will perhaps prevent us from judging by the wrong standards.

3

The Basic Types of Dramatic Set Speech

In the last chapter reference was made to the way in which dramatic set speeches fall into distinctive types. This is to be seen especially clearly in the frequent recurrence of particular types of speech which are always associated with particular varieties of type-situation. The Elizabethan playwrights, even those who came after Shakespeare,[1] thought much more in terms of the individual situation than of the whole play conceived as a single entity, and in their plays certain well-established basic situations constantly reappear; the playwrights have recourse to them again and again, as often, indeed, as the nature of their plots allows. Thus in the pre-Shakespearian drama it is possible to differentiate as *typical* dramatic episodes the judgement-scene, the triumph-scene, the siege-scene, the council-scene, the deathbed-scene, the farewell-scene, the conversion- or 'talking-over'-scene, and the wooing-scene, and there are a few other kinds of situation that regularly conform to type in the same way. These have only very recently been analysed and defined. Of course we must distinguish between different categories represented in this list. For example, the 'talking-over'-scene represents a situation that is fundamental to drama; it is a 'primeval' situation that occurs in the drama of all ages. On the other hand, the triumph-scene and the siege-scene are limited to the historical themes of the Renaissance. It will be seen that for each of these type-situations a particular and distinctive pattern evolves which each playwright varies and develops in his own way. However, right up to the time of Shakespeare certain features of these patterns remain constant.

If we analyse these recurrent type-scenes and situations closely and compare them with one another, we discover one important

[1] Cf. the observations of F. L. Lucas in the Introduction to his edition of Webster's plays, London, 1927.

reason for the stereotyped character of pre-Shakespearian drama, and the same might be said of the set speeches that conform to one or other of the accepted types. In Elizabethan drama, and especially in the pre-Shakespearian drama, there were obviously more set speeches of this kind than in the drama of any other period. That is to say, not only were certain recurrent sets of circumstances in the serious drama that preceded Shakespeare treated as suitable occasions for the delivery of long set speeches, but such a speech was entirely dominated by the type-theme that lay behind it; this was treated as what might be called a 'set-speech theme', and it was usually elaborated far beyond what was appropriate to the dramatic occasion. In most cases, indeed, these speeches protract a single moment in the course of the action a very great deal further than is dramatically necessary or desirable, and in structure and manner of proceeding they always display certain special characteristics which are peculiar to the type of speech demanded by the circumstances.

This must not be confused with what we find in the drama of the ancients when particular kinds of recurrent situation give rise to the interchange of set speeches. In classical drama, indeed, it would be much nearer the mark to speak of basic set-speech attitudes than of the set speech proper. Moreover, we can always see how the composition of these speeches has been influenced by the original situations to which they owe their form. For example, the large-scale speech advising for or against a course of action, the speech of accusation, the messenger-speech, the speech of instigation or provocation, the reprimand, the judgement-speech – all these may be identified in various phases of their development throughout the drama of antiquity. In many cases it is also possible to specify whether these speeches should be classified under the basic headings of *epideictic*, *symbouleutic*, or *dicastic*. However, even with Euripides, the influence on whom of the rhetorical system of the sophists is taken for granted, the classification of speeches by *genera* that has been attempted by some scholars proves both inadequate and unfruitful. That he owed much to this system, which had been developing outside the drama, and that the speech-types laid down by the rhetoricians have had some influence on the dramatic set speech, certainly does not mean that Euripides could draw on a ready-made system of rhetoric in the composition of his speeches. Thus in the latest study of the set speech in Euripides (that of Franz Tietze, 1933) the conclusion is drawn that 'the dramatist cannot be adequately judged if only standards based on rhetorical theory are applied to his work'.

While therefore the great majority of set speeches in pre-Shakespearian drama can be classified according to certain clear-cut types, no valid distinctions of this kind can readily be drawn for ancient drama. Yet such a classification of speech-types has been devised for the ancient epic. In the epic, and this not in Homer alone, set-speech types appear to stand out much more clearly and are much more sharply defined than in the drama. And it is interesting to find that most of the types of set speech which, as later chapters will show, can be distinguished in pre-Shakespearian drama are to be found also in the Homeric epics.[1] This does not mean, however, that Homer is following anything like a rigid system when his speeches fall into types. On the contrary, for all their generic qualities, his speeches carry an individual stamp and are coloured by specific situations and speakers. Thus, too, in ancient drama the *genus*, the type of the speech, is not the really decisive factor; certainly it is apparent below the surface, and it may be the starting-point for the speech, or provide its broad framework, but more important in each case are the individual style, the relevance of the speech to the play as a whole, to the character of the speaker, and to the particular situation involved, and all the other various factors that might bring about modifications of the type. In Euripides the type-qualities one would expect from any classification according to rhetorical *genera* seem to be outweighed by qualities of an entirely different kind, in that the nature of the speech is determined by the type to which the speaker belongs; thus it is quite often possible to say that such and such a speech is typical of a barbarian, or of a woman, or an egoist. However, Euripides does not always detract from the individuality of his characters by nar-

[1] The following Homeric set-speech types have parallels in pre-Shakespearian drama: summons to battle, speeches of triumph, laments, petitions or supplications, invective and threatening speeches, panegyrics, speeches of greeting and farewell, and messenger-speeches.

rowing them down to types in this way, for in some of his plays there seems to be a movement away from this devitalizing process of adapting characters to types; they remain individuals, preoccupied with their own personal problems, and endowed with a rich humanity that goes far beyond the types they represent. Thus the speeches do not lend themselves at all readily to general statements as to their nature.

It might be thought that the plays of Seneca, who is incomparably more important to the history of pre-Shakespearian drama than the Attic playwrights, would show a much stronger tendency to employ speeches that conform to specific types. For Seneca makes a great deal more use of conventional methods, and indeed of accepted patterns, and, as has been widely recognized, he is a writer who tends to seize upon and emphasize the typical. However, this tendency is revealed rather in a certain uniformity of style, in which the same commonplace expressions are used in passages of very different kinds, than in any differentiation of speeches according to a complex system of clear-cut types. There is one situation occurring in several of Seneca's plays in which a particular pair of stereotyped set speeches appropriate to this particular situation is habitually employed. 'In a frenzy of love or hatred the mistress makes a passionate speech in which she works herself up towards some frightful deed; the nurse foresees the mischief that must result from it and tries to restrain the mistress.' This '*domina-nutrix* scene', as it has come to be known, is found in one form or another in five of Seneca's plays, and it is therefore possible to isolate what runs according to type in the themes and the structure of the emotional speeches delivered in such very similar circumstances. Together with the messenger-speech, the emotional set speech is the most characteristic speech-type of Senecan drama, and Seneca quite deliberately increased both its scope and its importance. Embodied in it, and treated rhetorically but at the same time with real psychological insight, are all those passions and those states of mind the effective and constantly varied presentation of which was Seneca's special preoccupation: despair, uncertainty and vacillation, execration, threat, lamentation, and frenzy.[1] Seneca introduces the widest possible variety of these

[1] Cf. Otto Regenbogen, 'Schmerz und Tod in den Tragödien Senecas'.

prepossessions into an emotional set speech and mixes them all together; in the pre-Shakespearian drama, however, single motifs are detached and worked up into types of set speech that exist in their own right, so that we can differentiate between laments, speeches of execration, death-bed-speeches, and the like. Apart from messenger-speeches, used also for purposes of exposition, the only types that Seneca developed at all extensively were speeches of advice and dissuasion; on the other hand, he made much less use than Euripides of the dispute, that is, the battle of words presented as a series of consecutive set speeches of some length.[1]

However, we need hardly be surprised that there are so comparatively few set-speech types in Seneca's plays.[2] For in a species of drama that concerns itself almost entirely with the narration of past events and with reflection and introspection, there is no room for episodes centring upon concrete happenings, or for outward events providing occasion for long set speeches of types other than those that have already been mentioned. So that, although Seneca did in fact exercise a very strong influence on their handling of the set speech, it was not from him that the English playwrights acquired their great variety of set-speech types. What they did was to adapt to their own purposes his technique of making the long set speech the principal medium for the presentation of the play and giving it a much greater prominence than was warranted by the events that occasioned it, so that it was puffed up into something of a show-piece, a kind of 'insertion' almost independent of its context. The result of this, of course, was that the plot, which in any case was presented largely by report and other indirect means, was much interrupted, and often diverted from its course. Thus the 'disintegration of the play'[3] which is characteristic of Seneca is a mark also of many of his imitators in the pre-Shakespearian period.

The growth of a multiplicity of set-speech types is something

[1] Cf. C. W. Mendell, *Our Seneca*, New Haven, 1941, p. 111.

[2] Mendell (op. cit.) has examined the longer speeches in one of Seneca's plays, the *Hercules Furens*. He comes to the conclusion that the only set-speech types represented in this play are 'the messenger speech, the extended dialogue speech, the argument scene, and the monologue' (Chap. V, 'Long Speeches', p. 107).

[3] Regenbogen, op. cit.

that appears to be a special characteristic of English Renaissance drama. Several things helped to bring it about. Apart from the rhetorical tradition derived from Seneca, there were traditional strains of other kinds. There was the influence, for example, of the Morality Plays and other types of allegorical representation, of the tableaux, and of everything that was associated with the ceremonial of medieval and Renaissance life, so that we have various sources for what has been described as 'pageantry on the stage'.[1] Thus in connexion with the half-romantic, half-historical dramatic plots of the period there came into existence a whole range of recurrent 'set scenes' the effect of which could be enhanced by splendid occasional speeches or rhetorical show-pieces: the ceremonial welcome, the coronation-scene, the triumph-scene, in fact all the ritual of court and political life, embellished with appropriate speeches of greeting and homage as well as with panegyrics of a king or a queen or of England. The meeting of hostile armies – a very common event in historical plays, and one of which Shakespeare himself remains fond – offered opportunities for the exchange of arrogant challenges. This short and incomplete list will suffice to show how much richer English drama was in 'set-speech occasions' of various kinds than the more subjective plays of Seneca, so entirely lacking as they were in events actually pictured on the stage.

The question now arises how far the set-speech types of pre-Shakespearian drama can be classified according to the three *genres* of set speech that the poetic theorists of the Renaissance took over from the rhetorical systems of the ancients; these were the *genus demonstrativum*, the *genus deliberativum*, and the *genus iudiciale*. The *genus demonstrativum* (ἐπιδεικτικόν) has to do with *laus et vituperatio*, or in Elizabethan parlance *praise and dispraise*.[2] Into this class therefore would fall panegyrics and funeral orations, as well as speeches of disapprobation. The *genus deliberativum* (συμβουλευτικόν) embraces *suasio et dissuasio*, and thus includes speeches for or against a course of action, among which must be counted all speeches designed to change a point of view, the speech imparting good counsel (*paraenesis*), and the reprimand. Finally the *genus*

[1] Alice S. Venezky, *Pageantry on the Shakespearean Stage*, New York, 1951.
[2] Wilson's *Arte of Rhetorique*, ed. G. H. Mair, Oxford, 1909.

iudiciale (δικανικόν) covers speeches of indictment and defence (*accusatio* and *defensio*). This method of classification was of course familiar to all Renaissance authors, and there can be no doubt that it had some influence on the technique of dramatic set speeches. However, it is not comprehensive enough to embrace and clarify all the types of set speech; indeed there are several to which it does not apply at all, and anyone who tries to make it do so will soon find himself in difficulties. For example, the formal reproach, which is a common type of speech, is often indistinguishable from the formal indictment; is it to be placed in the *genus demonstrativum* (as *vituperatio*), or the *genus iudiciale*? Overlapping of this kind occurs elsewhere too, and involves us in fruitless argument about the most appropriate classification. An attempt has actually been made to allocate all the 'orations' in Shakespeare's plays to one or other of the three rhetorical *genera;* it is an interesting attempt, but it is not wholly convincing. To give it validity, the *genus demonstrativum* in particular would have to be extended to include much more than properly belongs to it.[1] The relevance of rhetorical conceptions and rhetorical categories to Renaissance drama should not be exaggerated, and facts should not be drastically simplified for the sake of a system of classification which contributes only in a very limited sense to our understanding. We shall find it more helpful to

[1] Kennedy, *The Oration in Shakespeare*. Among the 'demonstrative orations' Kennedy includes: the messenger-speech about the engagement in France in *1 Henry VI*, I. i. (but he ignores many messenger-speeches of the same kind), and such expository speeches and speeches announcing plans and projects as Claudius's speech from the throne in *Hamlet*, I. ii, Iachimo's self-revelatory speech in *Cymbeline*, V. v, Prospero's farewell in *The Tempest*, V. i, Montjoy's ambassadorial speech on behalf of the French King in *Henry V*, III. vi, etc. But dozens of similar speeches would have to be included under this heading. Kennedy's classifications are rendered even more dubious by the fact that he makes the idea of the 'oration' dependent on the presence of several hearers, of an 'audience', whereas he uses 'declamation' to describe the set speech delivered to only one or two hearers. But the distinction is not as clear-cut as this. Kennedy describes as a 'deliberative oration' Katherine's speech to King Henry in *Henry VIII*, I. ii, yet here there is only one listener. Kennedy goes on, 'The ideal use, however, directs the oration to a group' (p. 32). In this case the set speeches in the English classical drama, surely in the formal sense typical examples of orations, would almost all have to be rejected, since most of them are addressed only to one or two hearers.

begin by setting out the types of set speech in pre-Shakespearian drama, and then we can go on to draw our inferences.[1]

The undeveloped dramatic technique of the earlier phases of the English Renaissance is shown up at its clumsiest in its methods of exposition, for in many plays this function is assumed by the set speeches. Seneca's expository soliloquies and the prologues of the Morality and Mystery Plays provided models of different kinds for set speeches in which a character introduces himself in some detail [2] while at the same time preparing us for future events. This convention remains the basis of Gloucester's opening soliloquy in Shakespeare's *Richard III*, where Gloucester's introduction of himself is combined with a partial revelation of his own designs and some account of the present state of affairs. However, even in the course of a play the set speech is continually used for exposition, partly in the guise of formal *Report-speeches*,[3] which are especially common in plays of the Senecan tradition, and partly as speeches which discuss plans of action. These *Planning-speeches*[4] were to become a characteristic feature of the Elizabethan drama as a whole; their object is to make a situation clearer by bringing the audience into the picture, letting them know in good time what is afoot, and preparing them in advance for what is in store for them. This tendency to explain everything, to make it obvious and clear, is widespread in pre-Shakespearian drama. At a higher level the planning-speech – which sometimes takes the shape of a soliloquy or of a monologue delivered in the presence of other persons – can show decisions being formed and maturing, can represent the mental processes that lead to a decision or judgement, and then it may turn into a *Resolution-speech*. But in the earlier periods it is devoted merely to the announcement of plans that are already fixed. Even within the

[1] The lists of passages cited hereafter are not exhaustive; in each case only a few examples are given.

[2] *Gismond*, I. i; *Selimus*, I. i. 7; ii. 231; *Wounds*, II. i; *Wars of Cyrus*, I. ii. 188.

[3] *Gorb.*, IV. ii. 247; *Gismond*, IV. ii; V.; *Misfortunes*, II. i; *Wars*, 225, 1008, 1098, 1514, 1623; *Span. Trag.*, I. ii. 22; *Selimus*, 1922.

[4] *Selimus*, 530, 725, 1075, 1539, 1671; *Locrine*, II. i. 78; *Span. Trag.*, III. ii. 100; *Edward I*, VII. 66; *Orlando*, 249; *James IV*, 197; *1 Tamburlaine*, III. iii. 30; *Massacre*, II. 34.

compass of Shakespeare's work we can trace the development of the planning-speech and the resolution-speech from this primitive state to more complex and mature forms. The greater the amount of the material the plot has to deal with, the more necessary the playwright finds it to remind the audience what has already happened and what still has to happen. This he does in yet another of the set-speech types of Elizabethan drama that are designed to enlighten the onlookers, the *Review of the Situation*,[1] which is often combined with the planning-speech.

Although important as exposition, speeches in which characters introduce themselves or merely give information are essentially static in nature; they are not part of an interchange of speeches by means of which events are set in motion, a situation changed, or a dramatic tension created which advances the action. This is true also of the planning-speech, at any rate at the lower, more rudimentary level. A type of speech that is dramatic and 'kinetic' in the true sense is the *Conversion-speech*,[2] although in the earliest phases of the period under review, as examples will show, it too is used undramatically. Among variants of the conversion-speech – which may be used either for persuasion or for dissuasion – mention should be made of the *Appeasement-speech*,[3] its opposites the *Incitement-speech* and the *Exhortation*,[4] and the *Wooing-speech*[5] and the *Petition*,[6] for all of these aim at influencing another person in some way, whether by getting something out of him or by changing his mind. When it is not the paramount object of the speech actually to exert an influence in this way, but merely to give good advice, the result is the *Counsel-speech*;[7] this is a speech type that is common in Italian tragedy, where the stock figure of the *consigliere* appears

[1] More fully treated in Chap. 6.

[2] *Gorb.*, II. i; *Gismond*, II. ii; *Misfortunes*, I. ii; III. i; *Wounds*, 537, 1814; *1 Promos and Cassandra*, III. iv; *Alcazar*, 722; *Arraignment*, II. i; *James IV*, II. ii. 328; *1 Tamburlaine*, I. ii. 164; *David*, 892.

[3] *Gorb.*, III. i. 44; *Gismond*, I. iii.

[4] *Gorb.*, V. ii; *Misfortunes*, III. iii; *Wounds*, V. i; *Wars*, IV. iii; *Locrine*, II. iii; *Edward I*, I. xiv.

[5] *Orlando*, I. i; *1 Tamburlaine*, I. ii. 82.

[6] *1 Tamburlaine*, V. i. 1.

[7] *Gorb.*, I. ii; *Wounds*, I. i; *Selimus*, 1031; *James IV*, I. i. 39; II. iii,

beside that of the confidant. The *consigliere* often makes speeches, in the main undramatic, in which his advice takes the form of sententious commonplaces, elaborated in some detail and with more than a touch of pedantry. This character, the 'Good Counsellor', also makes his appearance in English drama; Shakespeare's Gaunt in *Richard II* and Kent in *King Lear* may be recognized as later derivatives of the original stock figure. At all periods, of course, conversion-speeches have constituted one of the basic forms of the genuinely dramatic speech in drama. They receive their peculiar stamp in the plays of the English Renaissance from the rhetoric with which they are impregnated; for in these plays the rhetoric assumes its original function as a means of *persuasio*. The conversion-speech belongs to the 'conversion-scene', the ancestry of which stretches back to certain Morality episodes, especially those in which a man is torn between the counsels of the Good and the Evil Angel, and to Seneca (e.g. *Troades*, 203 ff.). It is not long before dialogue becomes associated with the conversion-speech, and either partially or entirely replaces it.

Reference has already been made to 'occasional' speeches designed to fit special sets of circumstances. The *Panegyric*[1] is a direct development of the stock expressions of praise which go back to the classical tradition earlier discussed under the heading of the *genus demonstrativum*; there are abundant examples of its use in medieval and Renaissance literature.[2] *Triumph-speeches*,[3] *Greeting-speeches*,[4] and *Challenges*,[5] the last a derivative of the classical speech of provocation, occur in the romantic history plays and the chronicle plays.

Finally there are various examples of '*Tribunal*'-*speeches*,[6] such as *Indictment-speeches* and *Justification-speeches*,[7] and those winding-

[1] *Wars*, 1455; *1 Tamburlaine*, II. i. 7; *Edward I*, I. 211; III. 73.

[2] Cf. Curtius, *European Literature and the Latin Middle Ages*, Chap. 8, sect. iv.

[3] *Selimus*, 2512; *Locrine*, III. iv; IV. i; *Wounds*, II. i (371); III. iii (1077); *2 Tamburlaine*, IV. iii.

[4] *Wars*, I. i; *Alcazar*, I. i (71); II. ii (422); *Edward I*, I. 66; *Arraignment*, I. i. 163; *Friar Bacon*, II. i (430).

[5] *Selimus*, 1202; *Edward I*, XXI. 1 ff.; *James IV*, V. iii.

[6] *Arraignment*, IV. i.

[7] *Selimus*, 604; 2272; *Gorb.*, IV. ii; *Gismond*, IV. iii.

up speeches in which judgement is delivered over the contending parties. Any reader of Shakespeare will at once call to mind Othello's apologia before the Duke of Venice (*Othello*, I. iii), the court-scene in *The Merchant of Venice* (IV. i), and similar occasions in the history plays and in *The Winter's Tale* and *Measure for Measure*.[1]

However, by far the largest group of set speeches in pre-Shakespearian drama must be classed as *emotional* set speeches, such as laments, speeches of execration or of threat, vows of vengeance, and deathbed-speeches.[2] The deaths of major characters are invariably accompanied by set speeches of some considerable length, as is still the case in the early plays of Shakespeare. It is true that in his later tragedies Shakespeare allows his heroes to die without such speeches, giving them only the briefest of utterances, or even a wordless death; but in doing this he is breaking with a convention observed by every playwright before him. In these emotional set speeches, of which there are several examples in almost every serious play before Shakespeare, the high passions of the Elizabethan age are given free vent. In some of the early classical plays the passions are torn to tatters, although in expression the speeches remain stiff and stereotyped; at the other end of the scale stands *Tamburlaine*, with its grandiloquence and intensity and its amalgamation of speech and impressive gesture. It is in the laments that the pre-occupation of the Elizabethan playwrights with high-wrought feeling and declamation is most clearly visible, and also the almost constant hyperbole which has with justice been described as being of the essence of Elizabethan drama.[3] And it is for this reason that the

[1] There are a few types of set speech that occur less frequently than those that have been listed: e.g., the speech of instruction (*2 Tamburlaine*, V. iii; *Friar Bacon*, III. ii), and the speech of disclosure (*James IV*, III. iii; *Span. Trag.*, IV. iv).

[2] Cf. Chap. 15. Other examples occur in *Gismond*, I. ii; III. ii; V. i; V. ii; V. iv; *Misfortunes*, I. iii; III. i; IV. iii; V. i; *Wounds*, I. i. 182; *Wars*, 1021, 1643; *Selimus*, 1278, 1303, 1316, 1472, 1503, 1750, 1774, 1841, 2008; *Locrine*, II. iv; III. vi; IV. ii; V. ii; V. iv; *Alcazar*, II. iii; V. i; *Cambises*, 444, 577; *Edward I*, XXIV; *James IV*, 1466; *Orlando*, 1409; *Oldcastle*, V. i; *Looking Glass*, II. ix; III. i; V. ii; *Clyomon and Clamydes*, 872, 1378, 1512, 1597.

[3] Cf. Schücking, *Shakespeare und der Tragödienstil seiner Zeit.*

dramatic laments of the period have been singled out for special treatment in the last section of this book.

The types of set speech we have been discussing do not always occur in their pure forms. They may be combined in various ways and appear as hybrids, as some of the examples in later chapters will show. As of course we should expect, the unmixed types occur very largely in the earlier stages; as time goes on they tend increasingly to merge with one another. The more self-contained speeches devoted to a single specific theme illlustrate that practice, so characteristic of the early period, of isolating topics for separate and individual treatment; instead of continuity and constant reference to a total effect, the speech proceeds step by step, stone piled upon stone, so to speak, and the various motifs are developed independently of one another.

The object of the short catalogue of speech-types set out in the last few pages has been to lay down the basic assumptions and principles by which our procedure in the following chapters is to be governed. Now it is time to turn to the real concern of this book, which is to study the handling of the set speech in individual plays, the various functions it assumes, and the various modifications it undergoes.

PART TWO

4

Gorboduc

The history of rhetorical tragedy in England opens with *Gorboduc*. In this play the *genre* Drama has assumed a very strange garb; it is so stiff in movement and so full of elaborate set speeches that it is difficult for us nowadays to appreciate it as drama at all. Yet *Gorboduc* exerted an unusually powerful influence on English drama. It must have been accepted as a model not only by the literary theorists, but even by the playwrights. We must not, therefore, in trying to set it into historical perspective, start from any preconceived notion of Drama *per se*, or judge it according to any later conception of what a play should be. In spite of all dramatic and poetic theory, there is no such thing as Drama, in the abstract, to be set up as a norm of value against which to measure the dramatic production of different ages. In the five decades alone between 1550 and 1600 we find half a dozen dramatic forms in England, each possessing its own laws and characteristics.[1]

Speech is the life-blood of *Gorboduc*, the almost exclusive medium by which it is given the character of a play. It is true that the several acts are prefaced by dumb shows,[2] in which, perhaps in imitation of Italian models, the didactic intention of the succeeding episodes is

[1] T. S. Eliot: 'The forms of drama are so various that few critics are able to hold more than one or two in mind in pronouncing judgment of "dramatic" and "undramatic"' ('Seneca in Elizabethan Translation', *Selected Essays*, London, 1948, p. 75).

[2] On the dumb shows in *Gorboduc* see George R. Kernodle, *From Art to Theatre*, 1944, p. 145. Kernodle makes a convincing case for the street tableaux as a major influence on the dumb shows.

allegorically and symbolically foreshadowed in mime. These dumb shows are not, however, to be taken as indicating any tendency to carry movement into the recited scenes and make them less stiff. They have a purely didactic purpose; their function is to bring out the moral presented in *Gorboduc*. No spark of animation passes from them into the spoken scenes. The sphere of vivid but mute action and the sphere of stiff declamation unaccompanied by action stand indeed in close juxtaposition, but they are entirely unrelated to each other. It may be, however, that subconsciously the authors felt the need to make some concession to the eyes of their audience in a work where such immoderate demands were being made on their ears.

It will be easier for us to understand the nature and role of the set speech in *Gorboduc* if we examine the way in which Sackville and Norton transformed their raw material into a play, with its mechanism of acts and scenes, its entrances and exits, its grouping of the characters, and its dialogues and soliloquies. For this business of dramatizing narrative sources can result in very different types of plays; the way in which it is done is far more important for the structure of the play, its own individual pattern, than the material itself. An outline of the plot of *Gorboduc*[1] might suggest that it is a fast-moving play, full of bustling scenes and animated dialogue. But it is the very reverse of this. From material that abounds in incident the authors have taken for their nine scenes only those portions that might be described as 'points of rest' between the actual incidents.[2] The incidents themselves have been left out of the play: we hear about them only by report, or alternatively they are reflected in the reaction that they produce in the characters. This reaction, however, is manifested only in speech.

This procedure of giving in a play only the antecedents and the consequences of actions, and not the actions themselves, and of presenting these antecedents and consequences very largely in long speeches and soliloquies, is the basis also of the tragedies ascribed to

[1] E.g., in Holzknecht's *Outlines of Tudor and Stuart Plays, 1497–1642*, New York, 1947.

[2] Cf. Rudolf Fischer, *Zur Kunstentwicklung der englischen Tragödie*, Strassburg, 1893.

Seneca. For in these plays the thoughts of the characters turn chiefly on happenings of the past and future; we are shown the states of mind and the reflections to which the happenings themselves give rise. The 'dramatic present' plays a negligible part. We very often get the feeling that the 'real play' is being performed elsewhere, on another stage, and that the speakers are gazing across at this stage from the enclosed space in which they are sitting quietly together like a play-reading society, merely telling us what is going on and giving expression to the appropriate reflections and feelings. The plays of Seneca were very probably designed for reading aloud,[1] and it was only under a misapprehension that the Elizabethans took them as plays intended for performance. When such an unbroken succession of long speeches, declaimed without any accompanying action, was given the actuality of theatrical performance, some curious antinomies were bound to arise. The elimination of these, necessary as it was, did not come about until much later. There are not yet any signs of it in *Gorboduc*; on the contrary, in comparison with Seneca, there is a further increase in the undramatic element.[2] The proportion of long speeches in any particular scene of *Gorboduc* is even higher than in the Senecan tragedies. In Seneca, moreover, the run of long speeches is often

[1] Disagreement with this view is expressed by Léon Herrmann, *Le Théâtre de Séneque*, Paris, 1924.

[2] The view is maintained here that the composition of *Gorboduc* in the larger sense was influenced by the practice of Seneca. However, this thesis has been strongly contested by Howard Baker in *Induction to Tragedy*, Louisiana State U.P., 1939. Many of the views put forward in this stimulating book can be accepted, but not that Senecan influence on *Gorboduc* is all but non-existent. This is no place to take up the large and often discussed problem of Seneca's influence on Elizabethan tregedy. Some relevant studies are J. W. Cunliffe, *The Influence of Seneca on Elizabethan Tragedy*, London, 1893; F. L. Lucas, *Seneca and Elizabethan Tragedy*, London, 1933; H. B. Charlton, *The Senecan Tradition in Renaissance Tragedy*, Manchester U.P., 1946 (earlier as the Introduction to the Dramatic Works of Sir William Alexander, Earl of Stirling 1921); Hardin Craig, 'Shakespeare and the History Play', in *Joseph Quincy Adams Memorial Studies*, Washington, 1948; Theodore Spencer, *Death and Elizabethan Tragedy*, Harvard U.P., 1936; Henry W. Wells, 'Senecan Influence on Elizabethan Tragedy', in *Shakespeare Assoc. Bull.* XIX, 1944; S. R. Watson, 'The Senecan Influence in *Gorboduc*', in *Studies in Speech and Drama in Honor of Alexander M. Drummond*, New York, 1944.

interrupted by dialogue-passages of shorter speeches; at times there is even stichomythia, or lines of verse broken up between several speakers. In *Gorboduc*, on the other hand, the shorter dialogue-passages occur much less frequently, and some scenes have none at all; nor is there any sustained stichomythia. Often immoderately long, the speeches follow one another in massive and ponderous array, and we can scarcely think of them as dialogue.

Apart from their narrative or descriptive function, the majority of the speeches in Seneca's plays are essentially a medium for the expression of rage or despair, or of intense emotion of some other kind. In *Gorboduc*, however, only a few scenes, indeed only a few speeches, have strong feelings as their basis.[1] And for this reason the play lacks one of the primary driving-forces of tragedy. For in most of the scenes we find nothing but cold deliberation and the endless debating of pros and cons. In Seneca most of the speeches are the outward manifestation of highly emotional states of mind; in *Gorboduc* they serve the ends of hair-splitting argument. The temperature, one might say, is many degrees lower than in Seneca; in place of the sultry heat of emotion we have the frigid atmosphere of a legal process. And in fact both authors of the play were Inns of Court men, so perhaps it is not surprising that a legal cast of thought should be constantly reflected in their style and language.

There are further differences. In many scenes in Seneca's plays something that could be called development takes place. One mood perhaps gives way to another, some resolution is formed, the relationship between two characters changes, and the situation at the end of the scene is different from what it was at the beginning. Speech is the dramatic instrument by means of which Seneca brings this change about and communicates it to the reader. Of disclosures and developments of this kind within the limits of a single scene there is hardly a sign in *Gorboduc*. Most of the spoken scenes are entirely static. We mark time, as it were, or go round in a circle, and it is nearly always obvious from the situation at the beginning of the scene what its ending will be.

Even with Seneca we can scarcely speak of characters in any true sense of the word. We get no impression of physical presence, of a

[1] In the main they are the scenes by Sackville.

flesh-and-blood personality behind the parade of emotion. The language of the plays seems remote from the concrete reality of human life of which it ought to be a reflection, seems indeed to be quite independent of it. However, with Seneca the main characters at least are presented as human types with continuous parts in the plot, and they are shown in a variety of situations. Their speeches serve the purpose of revealing their roles as types, and of setting them against the appropriate emotional backgrounds.

In *Gorboduc*, on the other hand, the speeches are almost entirely unrelated to the characters. Gorboduc himself appears in only three scenes, Ferrex and Porrex each in two, and most of the other characters only once. Furthermore, since the number of characters is greater than in Seneca's plays, new characters make their appearance in practically every scene, and then disappear. There is therefore no continuity in the appearance of the characters on the stage to serve as a constant factor on which to fasten; instead we have a succession of abruptly broken-off situations which have no connexion with one another. For this reason the individual speeches give an even more completely detached impression than they do in Seneca; often indeed there are single speeches by characters who make only single appearances. In addition, in some scenes more characters are present than are ever on the stage in Seneca, and some of these open their mouths only once or twice. When finally we compare the speeches of *Gorboduc* and Seneca with regard to their bearing on the action of the play, we find that the Senecan speeches have a much closer relevance to such incidents as, we learn, have preceded them in the intervals between the acts and scenes, and this in spite of the often long-drawn description, narrative and reflection that they contain.

Again the reason for this is the way in which the authors have turned their subject-matter into plays. Seneca invariably dramatizes only the closing phases of his story; he begins his action either just before or at the catastrophe, so that a comparatively brief lapse of time is covered by the rapid succession of scenes and speeches. *Gorboduc* deals with a much longer period; it covers the last part of Gorboduc's reign, and also takes in the events that follow his death. More therefore 'happens' in *Gorboduc* than in a play by Seneca, and thus the discrepancy between the underlying action and the speeches is increased, for the events are so numerous that the speeches cannot cover them satisfactorily, not even by means of outright report, a method naturally also used in *Gorboduc*. The course of these events remains to some extent obscure; a good deal escapes us altogether, and a good deal becomes clear only in retrospect, after we have been shown the reactions produced by the events. Some of the actions, too, appear to have been inadequately motivated and prepared for; examples are the slaughter of the King and the Queen, of which we are told only in passing in the fifth act (V. i. 7), and the motivation of Ferrex's assassination by Porrex. Then again, because Seneca's plays are more closely knit as a result of his more drastic curtailment of the material that he uses in his plots, his narrative background is less extensive, and is better integrated by his methods of report and description.

However, the ultimate reason for the lack of relationship in *Gorboduc* between speech and character, speech and action, is not to be found in the management of its characters or the particular way in which its story has been dramatized. The true reason is that in this play the characters are merely an expedient whereby a train of events, essentially impersonal in itself, and designed solely to impart a moral, may be split up and distributed among a number of different speakers. *Gorboduc* is not conceived in terms of a dramatic conflict between living people, but as an 'exemplum' for a moral discourse, the 'dramatic action' becoming a mere side-issue.

This is made clear by analysis of the speeches. Much space is given to reflections on the serious consequences of civil war and dissension, on the mischief that arises from an irregular succession to the throne, and on other political topics, and this shows what the authors were driving at. They were warning their audience against the insurrection and political disorder so easily stirred up by uncertainty about the succession.[1] This warning and this moral, constantly reinforced in one form or another, and combined with other political doctrines, provide the vital thread which runs through the play from beginning to end. The true centre of interest of the play

[1] Cf. S. A. Small, 'The Political Import of the Norton Half of *Gorboduc*', *PMLA*, XLVI, 1931; also Baker, op. cit.

lies in its didactic political import, and its 'hero' is something supra-personal, the welfare of the body politic. In contrast to Senecan practice, there is no 'protagonist'.[1] *Gorboduc* is a 'Mirror for Magistrates' in dramatic form.

This heavily stressed didacticism, this emphasis on the political and moral application of the play, constitutes the main divergence from Seneca. In *Gorboduc* the essential thing is not what happens, but the political and moral implications of what happens.[2] *Gorboduc* thus follows the didactic tradition of the Morality Plays;[3] the Senecan influence lies more in matters of technique than in anything else, and is less dominant than used to be thought. What a study of the distribution of the speeches and their function in the play reveals is reflected also in their structure. It will be seen that a method of composition taken over from another writer must be modified in several important respects when the later work is informed by a different spirit.

Let us begin with the council scene in the first act and see if we can discover just what it is that lies at the back of the style of speech in *Gorboduc*. In this scene (I. ii) Gorboduc gets the advice of three of his Lords about the proposed division of the realm. First we have a preamble[4] in which Gorboduc informs the Lords that he intends to

[1] Cf. H. E. Fansler, *The Evolution of Technic in Elizabethan Tragedy*, Chicago, 1914; and Baker, op. cit.

[2] On the didacticism of *Gorboduc* cf. C. F. Tucker Brooke, *The Tudor Drama*, London, 1912, pp. 192–3; E. M. W. Tillyard, *Shakespeare's History Plays*, London, 1948, pp. 93 ff.

[3] Cf. W. Farnham, *The Medieval Heritage of Elizabethan Tragedy*, Berkeley, 1936, pp. 352 ff. Important remarks on the influence of the Morality Plays on later English drama will be found in A. P. Rossiter, *English Drama from Early Times to the Elizabethans*, London, 1950.

[4] As a sample of the style, here are the first 26 lines, which together form a single sentence:

My lords, whose graue aduise & faithful aide,
Haue long vpheld my honour and my realme,
And brought me to this age from tender yeres,
Guyding so great estate with great renowme:
Nowe more importeth me, than erst, to vse
Your fayth and wisedome, whereby yet I reigne;
That when by death my life and rule shall cease,
The kingdome yet may with vnbroken course,

ask for their advice, speaking of the significance for the country at large of the question to be decided and pointing out that the 'common peace' is a matter of universal concern. Arostus in his reply expresses his readiness to give advice and his devotion to the interests of the King. This reply is a ritual form of address, so to speak, a studied and ceremonious act of courtesy before we come to the matter in hand. This matter, 'the case', is first broached by Gorboduc at line 46. The greater part of the scene consists of the three long speeches in which Arostus, Philander, and Eubulus turn over the plan put forward by the King, weigh it up from different points of view, and retail the grounds for their own opinions, which are partly favourable to the project, partly unfavourable. In their train of thought and their argumentative manner these speeches are like legal pleas; they can scarcely be described as 'persuasion-speeches' attempting to bring the King round to a different way of thinking. Although Gorboduc himself is several times addressed in person, the speeches are directed less at him than at some higher authority, just as in the courtroom it is not any particular individual that is addressed. They are the formal voicing of different attitudes to a matter that is still *sub judice*. In their organization, the way in which they break up into separate and distinct sections, these speeches are

---

Haue certayne prince, by whose vndoubted right,
Your wealth and peace may stand in quiet stay,
And eke that they whome nature hath preparde,
In time to take my place in princely seate,
While in their fathers tyme their pliant youth
Yeldes to the frame of skilfull gouernance,
Maye so be taught and trayned in noble artes,
As what their fathers which haue reigned before
Haue with great fame deriued downe to them,
With honour they may leaue vnto their seede;
And not be thought for their vnworthy life,
And for their lawlesse swaruynge out of kinde,
Worthy to lose what lawe and kind them gaue:
But that they may preserue the common peace,
The cause that first began and still mainteines
The lyneall course of kinges inheritance,
For me, for mine, for you, and for the state,
Whereof both I and you haue charge and care, . . .
(I. ii. 1–26)

examples of a clear rhetorical 'disposition',[1] according to which the points at issue are taken up and settled one by one, as in a legal plea. Eubulus's speech even follows fairly closely the scheme of speech-division that Sir Thomas Wilson laid down on the authority of Quintilian, though it does not correspond with it in all particulars.[2]

A more important point, however, is that these three speeches, for all their length and detail, do not in any way advance the action of the play. The 'case' is considered from various theoretical standpoints, yet Gorboduc's closing speech shows that he has not changed his own point of view: 'In one self purpose do I still abide,' he says (l. 342).

The syntax, style, and diction are all appropriate to this static quality of the speeches whereby a thesis is impersonally and dis-

[1] Quintilian (*Institutio Oratoria*) divides the juristic speech into five sections: *prooemium*, *narratio*, *probatio*, *refutatio*, *peroratio*. To these Wilson added the 'proposition' and the 'division', on which W. F. Schirmer remarks that they 'have no independent existence' ('Shakespeare und die Rhetorik', in *Kleine Schriften*, Tübingen, 1950 p. 90). In Eubulus's speech we may distinguish the following: Introduction, with the request for a favourable hearing ('the Entrance . . . whereby the will of the standers by of the Judge is sought for, and required to heare the matter'), the apodeictic formulation of his divergent standpoint ('narration is a plaine and manifest pointing of the matter . . .'), in which this particular standpoint is corroborated by a maxim of general application and further confirmed by examples drawn from human experience and history ('The proposition is a pithie sentence comprehended in a small roome, the somme of the whole matter.'). Then we are shown how the decision that is contemplated will affect Ferrex and Porrex. The King is exhorted not to take this course, but to keep his sons longer under his own supervision. (This section only approximately conforms to the Wilsonian scheme.) Finally the King is asked again to keep the government in his own hand (Conclusion). Howard Baker's contention (*Induction to Tragedy*, p. 39) that Eubulus's speech corresponds exactly to the Wilsonian disposition is true only of certain parts of it.

[2] Philander's 100-line speech exemplifies this preconceived disposition. Before he develops his theme in the body of his speech, Philander in the first part (217–29) introduces the two points of view to be discussed (agreement with the division of the realm, 219–24, and rejection of a premature abdication by the King, 225–9); then in the *divisio*, the development of the theme, he argues both sides in greater detail (230–303), on general grounds as well as from historical precedents, answers possible objections (*confutatio*), and puts forward his own counterproposals. In the *conclusio* he refers to the will of the gods in support of his advice.

passionately amplified. As a rule extremely long, carefully constructed sentences are used to convey with great prolixity a simple and often quite commonplace idea, and the impression is given of a stilted attempt at dignity and of a too obviously organized structure. This impression is reinforced by the continual parallelism of half-lines and of line-beginnings and line-endings. As far as metre is concerned, the authors systematically and consistently use the single line as their unit, and subordinate their sentence-structure to it. We scarcely ever find several lines overlapping metrically and building up into the kind of verse-paragraph that we are familiar with in Shakespearian blank verse. The result is a rigidity of pattern and a monotonous uniformity of style which are not only quite undramatic, but also impress the modern reader, through the inflexible regularity with which the iambic rhythm is used, as being wearisomely pedantic and long-winded.[1] Retaining their natural accentuation, the nouns and adjectives dutifully accommodate themselves to the exigencies of the iambic pentameter; there is none of that clash between natural stress and metrical stress, none even of those displacements and inversions of stress, that can be so effective.

A reflection of the objective and didactic treatment of the subject may be seen in the 'substantival' nature of the style in *Gorboduc*; it is a style in which verbs are heavily outnumbered by nouns and adjectives. The nouns are nearly all, by way of *amplificatio*, qualified by empty and colourless adjectives, which hang from them like clogs and still further slow down the movement of the speech. Many noun-adjective combinations of this kind, often cemented by alliteration, are paired off and arranged antithetically in symmetrically divided lines, or are made to balance each other at the ends of lines. The commonest pattern of all, the combination of a disyllabic adjective with a monosyllabic noun, lends itself especially well to this arrangement.[2] The frequent use of hendiadys leads to constant

[1] There are some general comments on the language of *Gorboduc* in Moody E. Prior, *The Language of Tragedy*, New York, 1947, p. 32.

[2] Thus the first and second or the second and third stresses of the line must fall on the first adjective and its noun, and the fourth and fifth stresses must always fall on the last adjective and noun. Cf. lines 12, 13, 21, and 25 in Gorboduc's lament reproduced in Chap. 15, p. 253.

tautology, and furthers the efforts of the authors to be weightily reflective, and at the same time explicit, in their speeches. A whole series of other rhetorical devices, anaphora, climax, parallelism, alliteration, and chiasmus, all serve the purpose of imparting order and clear organization to the speeches; their effect is much more to clarify the meaning than to enhance the effect of what is said.

The almost exclusively abstract vocabulary, lacking the force of concrete expression and devoid of figurative quality, also contributes to the uniformity and the dry objectivity that are so characteristic of the style. Whether we have a scene involving strong emotion or a conference scene, the diction remains fundamentally the same. Everything is stamped with the same die; the speech has become merely an impersonal, and homogeneous, means of communication, treating subjects of very different kinds in exactly the same way, and moreover treating them so generally that they are all reduced to the same level of cold, rational abstraction.

Everything conspires, then, to strip away from *Gorboduc* all the ebb and flow of mental excitement and changing humours, all the colour that goes with diversity of character-interest and fluctuations in style and tempo at different stages of the action. Everything works to this end: the monotonous regularity of the blank verse, the colourless and abstract diction, the systematized clarity of the syntax for all its involutions, the prolixity of the speeches and their lack of connexion with one another, the absence of movement and development in the scenes, and the stiff and lifeless grouping of the characters. All these features of the play are mutually interdependent. Corresponding to the singular lack of subtlety with which the rhetorical figures are used, we have the over-elaborate organization of the speeches and the explicit, minutely detailed exposition. This again has a close bearing on the static, uncomplex structure of the whole scene, which is connected with the preceding or following scene by nothing more than some simple contrast or parallel. Matched with this, finally, is the symmetrical and all too obvious grouping of the characters, which is a legacy from the Morality Plays.[1]

[1] Cf. J. W. Cunliffe, *Early English Classical Tragedies*, Oxford, 1912, pp. 301–2; and Baker, op. cit.

Thus in every way the style and language of *Gorboduc* are calculated to further the main endeavour of the two authors, that is, to make their 'matter' as easily intelligible as possible. And as far as they are concerned, intelligibility is synonymous with generalization. Nothing that cannot be adapted to the general formulas that swarm on every page of *Gorboduc* is capable of being expressed in the medium they devised. In such a style there could be no room for any differentiation or complication in the 'matter' such as might have been brought about by the clash of different temperaments and personalities, or by development and change in these personalities – assuming that Sackville and Norton had been capable of conceiving dramatic personalities, which on the face of it does not seem very likely. However, the real reason for the generalized and 'depersonalized' character of this style was not merely the lack of dramatic power in the authors; it was much more the didactic spirit in which they wrote their play.

Their purpose is not revealed gradually as the play proceeds; the gist of their argument emerges quite clearly at the very beginning. And once it has been stated, their moral is constantly recapitulated. It is repeated by the Chorus, by the dumb show, by the various characters, and, moreover, both at the beginning and at the end of scenes. A prose paraphrase of the whole play would be revealing; it would show, first, how few ideas it really contains, though they are paraded with the maximum of verbiage, and secondly, how often these few ideas are repeated in the course of the play. With other playwrights the paraphrasing of a speech always involves some loss, the loss of just that quality which gives the play its special character, but that is not true of *Gorboduc*. In *Gorboduc* very long speeches can be paraphrased quite briefly, and there would be no loss at all if odd lines here and there, or even whole periods, were left out.

The highly inflated language of *Gorboduc* reflects the ideal of 'copiousness' that was so dear to the hearts of Elizabethan writers.[1] But the great abundance of verbiage has not yet been assimilated in this play, and employed in such a way as to give intensity to the sentiments expressed or to produce striking poetic effects. On the

[1] Cf. Madeleine Doran, *Endeavors of Art*, pp. 46 ff.

contrary, the copiousness here is useless adornment, mere patchwork, involving a lavish expenditure of artistry for a limited end. Nor is it copiousness in the sense of exuberance, as it so often is in Marlowe and Shakespeare; it is sheer affectation, a pedantic fondness for reduplicating ideas, merely a means of amplifying a statement with a whole paraphernalia of parallels, antitheses, and other rhetorical devices.

As has already been shown, it is natural to this whole way of writing that the emphasis should fall on what is impersonal, general, and didactic. It is therefore no accident that the 'counsel-speech', the *paraenesis*, as we have seen it exemplified in Act I, Scene ii, should so often be used in *Gorboduc*. For this is the very type of speech, since it consists of admonition, instruction, advice or dissuasion, that gives the speaker the best opportunities to refer continually to the impersonal higher authority of general moral principles, and this means of course that his own personal feelings and opinions have to be suppressed. The more purely objective he can be, and the better he can succeed in keeping his own personal concerns out of it, the more persuasive the counsel-speech will be. The characters in *Gorboduc* are not therefore made to change their views, as are those of Marlowe and Shakespeare later, by the impact on them of a forceful personality which works on them rather by psychological means than by argument; they are won over by the objective logic of supra-personal facts, which is independent both of the speaker and of the character who is being worked on.

This is well illustrated in the two scenes that make up the second act. In both we have a situation involving persuasion and dissuasion. The first time it is Ferrex who is addressed by a good and an evil counsellor, the second time Porrex. The basic situation of the Morality Play, that of the man who is exposed to equal pressure from the Good and the Evil Angel, is here carried a stage further. In this particular exchange there is no dispute between the speakers; the speeches are an eloquent affirmation of the principles of good and evil, maintained on both sides on general political grounds. The person spoken to, whether it is Ferrex or Porrex, is virtually left out of account; to all intents and purposes the speeches are directed at the audience. There are, it is true, a few occasions when the interlocutor appears to be addressed personally (e.g., II i. 68, 168), but generally speaking the characters 'speak past' one another, as we have already observed in Act I, Scene ii.

It is interesting to see how the moral bearing of this debate between the principles of good and evil is immediately conveyed to the audience. The moment Hermon has finished his inflammatory speech, we are given Dordan's revealing comment:

> O heauen was there euer heard or knowen,
> So wicked counsell to a noble prince? (II. i. 162–3)

In every scene of *Gorboduc* remarks of this kind are addressed to the audience, and are clearly interposed for their benefit. The same type of revealing commentary is used also in later plays, where it runs side by side with the more strictly dramatic forms of representation, and provides pointers to the authors' intentions. It is a device which is common, indeed, to the whole of Elizabethan drama, and even Shakespeare makes frequent use of it,[1] though in him it is increasingly assimilated and in some subtle fashion made dramatic.

If we examine pre-Shakespearian drama in this light and go through the plays line by line, we shall be astonished to find how strong is this tendency to introduce explanatory comment. Nor is this necessarily true only of specifically didactic plays. The practice stems from the technique of the Morality Play, and the frequency with which these passages of comment crop up in *Gorboduc* shows better than anything else that in this play we are not dealing with mere slavish imitation of Seneca, but with a work that stands in the line of *English* tragedy. Certainly Sackville and Norton learned much from Seneca as far as style and structure are concerned, but in several very important respects they were carrying on the English dramatic tradition.[2]

For this particular device is not found in Seneca. Seneca can indeed be edifying, and his lavish use of epigram and sententious maxim might at first sight appear to be a means of elucidating his intentions. In the final analysis, however, the shrewd *dicta* scattered

[1] Cf. Schücking, *Character Problems in Shakespeare's Plays*, passim.
[2] Cf. A. P. Rossiter, op. cit., p. 134.

through his plays are a product of his preoccupation with rhetoric.[1] They are his way of adding rhetorical point and colour to his writing, and of giving his emotional outbursts a sophisticated and rational form of expression, which, with the admixture of Stoic doctrine, turns them into a species of hybrid creation, a compound of thought and feeling. But Seneca's *sententiae* are not meant as hints to the audience, pointing the way to his meaning, the role that such forms of expression so often assume in Elizabethan drama. Where different functions are involved, apparent similarities are not real similarities.

With Senecan usage in this matter we may compare the sententious maxims so freely introduced into the speeches of *Gorboduc*, where they are sometimes made to stand out of the surrounding text by means of quotation-marks:

> Within one land, one single rule is best:
> Diuided reignes do make diuided hartes.
> (I. ii. 259–60)

> O most vnhappy state of counsellers,
> That light on so vnhappy lordes and times,
> That neither can their good advise be heard,
> Yet must they beare the blames of ill successe.
> (II. ii. 69–72)

In the first of these maxims the moral underlying the whole play is propounded; the second passage, in which a proverbial saying is amplified into a general reflection, gives Philander the opportunity to explain in his own words his role as a counsellor.

Sometimes, however, whole speeches could be said to consist of elucidatory comment; such are, for example, the closing speeches of Dordan and Philander in II. i and II. ii, the final speech of Eubulus (V. ii. 180 ff.), and of course the speeches of the Chorus. A function which in ancient tragedy is reserved for the Chorus alone is taken over in Elizabethan drama by the acting characters as well, and, moreover, so very extensively that, when in the course

[1] Cf. Howard Vernon Canter, *Rhetorical Elements in the Tragedies of Seneca*, Univ. of Illinois Press, 1925.

of time the Chorus itself disappears, the 'choric utterance' remains and is almost universally employed by the dramatists.

The fourth act of *Gorboduc* is by Sackville. In contrast to Norton, whose scenes have a predominantly political and didactic stamp and in structure are a pretty close approximation to the Morality technique, Sackville tends to lay his greatest stress on powerful emotion and sensation.[1] This does not mean, however, that the different subject-matter in which he deals is presented in an essentially different style. The long lament spoken by Videna at the beginning of Act IV is his work,[2] but it can scarcely be said to differ in any considerable respect from the lament that Norton gives to Gorboduc in Act III, Scene i. As far as technique is concerned, however, it is characteristic that in this soliloquy by Videna a more intense relationship with another character is to be observed than in any of the speeches addressed to a person who is actually present. For paradoxically the interlocutor is missing in this case; it is in his absence that Porrex is 'addressed' in the soliloquy. Once more an opportunity for the really dramatic presentation of characters confronting one another face to face has been missed. It is true that in the maledictions hurled at Porrex and the sorrowful invocations of the dead Ferrex the style of this soliloquy at first glance appears to communicate a stronger pathos than is usual in *Gorboduc*; but this impression is at once counteracted by the systematic way in which the antitheses and parallels are grouped. Moreover, in the structure of the soliloquy as a whole, as in these smaller units within it, we find the same rationalizing tendency at work as in the counsel-speeches; there is the same insistence on subdivision and explanation. For like the counsel-speeches, Videna's soliloquy breaks up into distinct and independent sections, which again are capable of further subdivision. Each of the six or seven ideas it contains is sorted out into one such compartment, and usually these ideas are expressed in several alternative ways.[3] So that here, too, we

[1] Apart from the opening scene, the first three acts are by Norton, as is also the final scene of the play. Cf. Baker, *Induction to Tragedy*, p. 44.

[2] Analysed in Chap. 15, p. 257.

[3] Why have I not died before this time? (1–14, four times asked). Then should I not need to be suffering thus (15–22, in three different forms). Apostrophe to Ferrex (23–6). Apostrophe to Porrex (27–9). Declaration of

have that rigid organization of material according to which the various points are 'disposed of' one by one. There is still no overriding central idea, and none of that surge of feeling which, rising and falling in intensity, can go flooding through a whole speech. In this style emotions are rationalized, generalized, and subordinated to an impersonal pattern in just the same way as ideas and decisions.

Smacking as it does of academic theory, this same speech-style, in which a 'case' is weighed and debated as it were from the outside even when the speaker's own interests are at stake, is carried into the following scene. Here father and son confront each other, and in such a meeting might have lain the potentialities of a highly dramatic scene, for Porrex is to be called to account for the murder of his brother. It is turned into a 'tribunal-scene', however, with a speech for the prosecution from the father followed by two speeches for the defence, of which the first is a speech expressing remorse, and the second a 'report', in which Porrex gives an account of the events leading up to the murder. Not even in this situation, fundamentally dramatic as it is, do we find anything approaching a genuinely dramatic conflict, even though Gorboduc and Porrex speak with the express intention of influencing each other. The speeches and their speakers are juxtaposed, but there is no contact between them.

Even when later in the scene Marcella comes running in with cries of lamentation to announce the death of Porrex, there is no real departure from the normal pattern on which the speeches in this play are built. It is true that the other characters, Gorboduc, Eubulus, and Arostus, interrupt Marcella's report with exclamations and questions; but to all intents and purposes this report is a continuous speech, and one completely detached from its environment at that, for though it has auditors it has no counterpart to match it. Admittedly Marcella's speech, in which in striking contrast to the usual style of *Gorboduc* there is even for once a concrete situation

---

vengeance against Porrex (30–5, three times). Was there no one else you could have slain? (36–57, three times). Then Ferrex would still be with us (58–60). But why do I speak thus? Can I still think of you as my child? (61–4). No, I renounce my motherhood (65–76, four times). Do you think that you can escape vengeance? (77–81, four times).

pictured (l. 219), is more expressive than anything that precedes it, as Charles Lamb remarked. But even so no dialogue develops in this episode.

This is true also of the last act, although to the eye there is something here, in the succession of short speeches, that has the appearance of a dialogue-structure. However, the four utterances of the British leaders with which the scene opens are not related to one another in the manner of dialogue; they constitute a commentary which is divided between the four speakers. And in this undramatic sequel to the tragedy that has already been played out, the action for which the leaders have met together is less important than the expression of opinion. The core of the scene, however, lies in the excessively long speech by Eubulus. In its comprehensive statement of political principles, this is a key-speech for the whole play, although it stands outside the main drama of Gorboduc and his sons. Two further speeches by Eubulus, those which open and round off the final scene, serve the same purpose; they consist of admonition and instruction directed at the audience, and are intended to sum up the moral which has been offered in the 'exemplum' represented by the action of the foregoing acts. From the 'Expositor' or 'Doctor' of the Morality Play, who came on to the stage as Epilogue and spoke the final words, there has grown up the part of the 'Good Counsellor', to whom the author assigns this function of commentator.[1]

Gorboduc lends itself to disparagement as a pretty sorry piece of work, and it is easy enough to point to its artistic and dramatic deficiencies.[2] Yet the play represents a landmark in the history of English drama, and in it we find a significant starting-point for the development of dramatic speech. It was not for nothing that Sidney praised the 'stately speeches' and 'well sounding phrases clyming to the height of Seneca his stile'.[3] We must grasp the prob-

[1] It is no wonder that the final words correspond closely to a passage in a parliamentary speech delivered, probably by Norton himself, on 16 January 1552. Cf. L. H. Courtney, 'Ferrex and Porrex', *NQ*, ser. 2, pp. 261–3; cited by Baker, op. cit., p. 222.

[2] 'The play belongs rather to antiquarianism than literature' (F. L. Lucas, *Seneca and Elizabethan Tragedy*, p. 96).

[3] *An Apologie for Poetrie*, ed. E. S. Shuckburgh, Cambridge, 1948, pp. 51–2.

lems of form and style that manifest themselves in this play if we are to understand rightly the further development out of which eventually Shakespearian drama was to come into existence. The task which was laid down for the English drama of the future, as well as some of the conventions that were to persist in this later drama, may be very clearly seen in *Gorboduc*.

5

English Classical Plays

Gismond of Salerne. The Misfortunes of Arthur

In the early days of the regular English drama we encounter a curious dichotomy of dramatic method which was not properly resolved for several decades. At much the same time as *Gorboduc* appeared, with its clumsy juxtaposition of unrelated, formalized set speeches, the first comedies constructed on the Roman pattern began to be written, modelled on the plays of Plautus and Terence. But in these comedies we find a dialogue which is realistic and dexterously handled, and a dramatic movement which, even if it is not yet particularly subtle or artistic, is at least fluid and lively. One would have thought that the intermixture of these two extremes would soon produce good drama. But the two worlds were kept apart as though by a wall; they represented two entirely different conceptions of dramatic style for which the poetic theorists laid down quite distinct rules and requirements. It is true that in the popular drama attempts were made to bring tragedy and comedy together, but these attempts were quickly followed by reaction. It was in fact the genius of Shakespeare that first succeeded in bringing about an artistically perfect fusion of the different styles of comedy and tragedy.

The dramatic form of *Gorboduc*, in which the set speech is the dominating element, remained alive even after Kyd's *Spanish Tragedy* and Marlowe's plays had brought a new type of drama into existence. For Thomas Hughes's *Misfortunes of Arthur*, though it did not appear until 1588, shows the influence of Seneca much more obviously even than *Gorboduc*. Then there are plays like *Selimus*, *Locrine*, and *The Wounds of Civil War*, which were written at about the beginning of the 1590s, and for which we may presume that *Tamburlaine* was the chief model; it is clear from these plays too that, in the over-emphasis that they laid on the role of the set speech, individual playwrights continued to imitate the Senecan technique for some decades. The purely classical drama in the style of Seneca must of course be seen as a specialized product, designed solely for university, Inns of Court and royal audiences. We must not forget, however, that in the 1580s and 1590s there were different tastes to be catered for, corresponding with the particular sections of the public for which the plays were intended.[1] The influence of the early classical plays on the popular stage, and for that matter on the later development of English drama as a whole, was slight and indirect;[2] in contrast to what happened in France and Italy, it never got a proper foothold in England, in spite of Garnier's influence,[3] which was responsible for a second renaissance in the works of Daniel, Fulke Greville, and Sir William Alexander. Nevertheless, at a time when there was such a lively interchange of ideas between the playwrights and the representatives of the rival dramatic traditions, we must take some interplay of influences for granted, and the handling of the set speech in the early English classical plays therefore requires some consideration.

Gismond of Salerne (1567–8),[4] an Inns of Court play, shows how the Senecan method of composition might be applied even to a romantic story, a love-story taken from Boccaccio's *Decamerone*. But while the long set speech was not out of place in the political tragedy of *Gorboduc*, where so much counsel is to be imparted, its use in a romantic love-story was bound to produce a marked discrepancy between form and content. Yet *Gismond of Salerne* is completely dominated by set speeches. Two years earlier had appeared Gascoigne's *Jocasta*, a play which, through an Italian and a Latin intermediary, goes back to the *Phoenissae* of Euripides.[5]

[1] Cf. Alfred Harbage, *Shakespeare and the Rival Traditions*, New York, 1952.

[2] 'The influence of Seneca upon Elizabethan tragedy was immense, but it was transmitted to the drama of the people by poet-playwrights who had studied Seneca at school. Straight Senecan drama in English had but a brief temporary period.' – T. M. Parrott and R. H. Ball, *A Short View of Elizabethan Drama*, New York, 1943, p. 39.

[3] Cf. Witherspoon, *The Influence of Robert Garnier on Elizabethan Drama.*

[4] Reprinted in J. W. Cunliffe, *Early English Classical Tragedies*, Oxford, 1912.

[5] Cf. F. L. Lucas, *Euripides and his Influence*, Boston, 1923.

This English Euripidean work, whose place of origin, Gray's Inn, puts it into the dramatic tradition of the Inns of Court plays, makes some use of the stichomythia which Euripides introduces so freely among his longer speeches; the authors of *Gismond*, on the other hand, never use this device as a possible means of relieving the tedium of an unbroken succession of long speeches. Only in two scenes do we find dialogue-passages of short speeches; otherwise the play is made up entirely of long speeches and long soliloquies. To an even greater extent than in *Gorboduc*, the set speech is what makes the play. For although Boccaccio's story provides plenty of contrasts, plenty of dramatic event and situations, in the play based on it almost everything has been rejected which might possibly have produced dramatic scenes, as the term is normally understood.

Indeed it would be hard to think of a better example than *Gismond* of how material that was originally dramatic can be 'undramatized'. Never once are the two lovers brought face to face; moreover, a great many dramatic encounters, disclosures and conflicts described in the source-story are either removed from the action and made to take place 'between the acts',[1] or are explained in soliloquy to a character who is not on the stage. Thus everything possible has been done to strip the play of action, and even to prevent the characters from meeting face to face. The outstanding feature of the work is its indirectness of presentation; report-speeches, lyrical meditations and laments have taken the place of stirring scenes of action.

Thus the soliloquy now has to do the work of a scene of action. Sometimes there are what might be called 'one-man scenes'. For example, there is the scene (III. iii) in which Guishard enters carrying the walking-stick that Gismond has given him. He suspects that the stick hides a secret, breaks it in two, and finds Gismond's letter. This he reads out, and then breaks out into a rapturous declaration of his love. Here the soliloquy is not merely the expression of Guishard's inner thoughts; it is at the same time a kind of protracted stage-direction for the one-man scene that is being enacted – a device that Kyd was also to resort to. This tendency to make an entire scene consist of a single speech may lead to an increased use

[1] Cf. Fischer, *Zur Kunstentwicklung der englischen Tragödie*, p. 60.

of gesture and stage-business. Of this some better examples will be seen later.

Other scenes consist merely of two long speeches, a communication of some kind, and an answer to it; examples are the three scenes of Act II. If we examine these answers we shall see how quickly they lose touch with their counterparts and assume an independence of their own as monologues. Thus in Act II, Scene ii, Lucrece tells Gismond's father Tancred about Gismond's desire to marry again. But it is only in the opening sentences that Tancred's reply is directed to Lucrece; after this he gives himself up to a woeful contemplation of his own situation, and finally (l. 59) he 'addresses' Gismond herself, though she is not present.[1] Not until the very end of the speech does he give Lucrece the answer she is to take to Gismond.

This tendency for speeches to change into monologues, even when by their very nature they form part of a dialogue-sequence, is very common. It determines the structure of the speech in Elizabethan tragedy in several phases of its development. However, it is not quite the same thing as the soliloquizing tendency within dialogue which is found in Attic tragedy. There the soliloquizing is the result of an inner compulsion; some spiritual disharmony, some emotional upheaval, or some momentary internal conflict compels the speaker to go down below the superficial level of mere statement and answer, so that something of his inner life is revealed. At times, it is true, especially in their later development by Euripides, the soliloquies do not show this inner compulsion; but even then, when viewed in the context of the play as a whole, they possess some special significance. In the early English classical drama, on the other hand, the inner compulsion is never apparent.

How far the influence of Euripides' *Phoenissae*, transmitted through the adaptations of Dolce and Gascoigne, stimulated this tendency of the speeches to develop into monologues, until it became an accepted pattern, and how far the authority of Seneca contributed to the same end, it is not easy to determine. At all events, the early English tragic dramatists were at extraordinary

[1] Such addresses to absent characters are frequent. Cf. III. iii. 80; IV. ii. 17; and *Gorb.*, IV. i.

pains to incorporate pseudo-soliloquy of this kind into their speeches. Not all such passages can be accounted for in the same way, and we shall have to watch for the moment in the course of its development when the pseudo-soliloquy is giving place to the soliloquy proper.

From the very first, of course, there is a reason for many of the soliloquies which does not apply to their use in Attic tragedy. In English drama the soliloquy is a means of self-explanation devised for the benefit of the audience, a pointer to the speaker's innermost feelings, aims and motives;[1] it is also a means whereby the author may make clear the moral purpose of his work, as well as introduce any other relevant material for whose presentation he has not been able to find room elsewhere. It is, therefore, one of those forms of expression which are designed for the enlightenment of the audience, and some of which have already been discussed.

In *Gismond of Salerne* the commonest reason why speeches are made to drift into soliloquy is the authors' desire to introduce as many passages of melodramatic emotion as possible. No opportunity is let slip of bringing into the speeches either exaggerated and rhetorical expressions of grief or passages of moral reflection. The latter function is for the most part served by the Chorus. Here the important factor is once more the didactic intention, the wish to offer guidance or admonition, and this wish links *Gismond of Salerne*, in the same way as *Gorboduc*, with the Morality tradition.

However, both elements come to the fore in practically every speech. Violent passions and sophisticated, pseudo-philosophical moral reflection form the two poles round which the speeches are continually made to revolve. The authors of *Gismond* must have thought that both were particularly suitable for dramatic treatment. But the antithesis between restrained good sense and exaggerated passion – an antithesis which runs through the whole of Elizabethan tragedy[2] – is here set before us in a crude and as yet dramatically unintegrated form. For both the emotional passages and the moral reflections could often quite appropriately be interchanged among

[1] Cf. Schücking, *Character Problems in Shakespeare's Plays*, passim.

[2] Cf. e.g., Lily B. Campbell, *Shakespeare's Heroes Slaves of Passion*, Cambridge, 1930.

the characters. For example, Gismond's train of thought at the beginning of her soliloquy in Act I, Scene ii, might just as properly have been put in the mouth of the Chorus, and the two speeches in which Gismond and Tancred in turn contemplate suicide (V. ii, V. iv.) could with only trifling adjustments be interchanged. These two characters, moreover, Gismond as well as Tancred, both speak as much in terms of rationalistic moral deliberation as in the accents of raging, ungovernable passion or hopeless grief. These are, ultimately, the only styles that they have in their repertoire.

What then can be described, with these reservations, as 'speech deviating into monologue' may be exemplified from Tancred's long opening speech in Act IV, Scene ii.[1] Accompanied by Renuchio and Julio, Tancred comes out of Gismond's chamber, where all unobserved he has witnessed the meeting of Gismond and Guishard. He begins with an invocation to Jove, whom he calls upon, as the god of vengeance, to destroy him. He continues in the same vein with two parallel apostrophes to Earth and Hell, both opening in the same rhetorical fashion as the first invocation – 'O great almighty Jove', 'O Earth', 'O hell'; these give way to rhetorical questions, and accusations directed against Gismond. Then come six more rhetorical questions in which he asks whom he ought most to blame for his woe, followed by his deliberations as to who is first to be destroyed:

> . . the naughty traitor first, to fede my boyling ire,
> my cursed daughter next, and then the wretched sire.

[1] Of the 84-line speech the first 12 lines may be quoted as a sample:

> O great almighty Ioue, whome I haue heard to be
> the god, that guides the world as best it liketh thee,
> that doest with thõder throwe out of the flaming skies
> the blase of thy reuenge on whom thy wrath doeth rise;
> graunt me, as of thy grace, and as for my relefe,
> that which thou pourest out as plages, vnto the grefe
> of such, whoes siñes haue whet thy sharp and deadly ire.
> Send down, o Lord, frõ heuen thy whot cõsuming fire,
> to reue this rutheful soule, whome tormẽtes to and froe
> do tosse in cruel wise with raging waues of woe.
> O earth, that mother art to euerie liuing wight,
> receiue the woefull wretch, whom heuen hath in despight.

And then at last an abrupt transition carries us into the narration of what he has seen. The division of the speech into several clear-cut sections, distinct from one another though at times related to the same theme, is characteristic; there are the three apostrophes, the address to his daughter, the questions he puts to himself, his report of what took place in Gismond's chamber, and the further questions to himself.[1] These ended, there is an equally abrupt transition to dialogue with his companions, for he suddenly turns and addresses Renuchio.

In the long speech of Tancred which follows, we again find him digressing into monologue, a monologue which to some degree approximates to soliloquy. The state of mind to be brought out here, as well as in other passages,[2] is that of vacillation, of internal conflict. This is a new motif in English drama, for comparable speeches in *Gorboduc*, those of Ferrex and Porrex in Act II, though they contain self-questioning, do not bring out any sense of internal conflict.

Now this type of conflict is by its very nature highly dramatic, and it is worth examining the form in which it first makes its appearance in English tragedy. In the Moralities it is for the most part removed altogether from the consciousness of the person concerned, and is transformed into a dispute between the principles of good and evil. And if, as in *Everyman*, we do find some monologues which express vacillation, they very seldom go beyond the mere question of what ought to be done. In Seneca, on the other hand, the authors of *Gismond* could have found many examples of spiritual conflict expressed in soliloquies; but with his usual understanding of human psychology, Seneca depicts this vacillation as a mental agitation in which emotion and intellect are mutually active. In contrast, Tancred's speech, and all similar speeches expressing indecision, show all the characteristic marks of academic pedantry. The vacillation is brought out by means of question, protestation, argument and counter-argument, until at last a resolution is arrived at which is given an academic justification.[3] By his skill in psychological

[1] With this pattern cf. Marcella's speech in *Gorb.*, IV. ii.

[2] IV. iii; V. ii; V. iv.

[3] IV. ii. 86 ff. Shall I slay them both? (five times repeated). Alas, that one of the two, my daughter, is so dear to me! She cannot die and leave me still

analysis Seneca had managed in the soliloquies of his characters to give the impression that the spiritual conflicts were actually taking place in the minds of the speakers, and that they were giving expression to them as their own immediate experience. In the English classical drama, on the other hand, the monologues are seen entirely from the outside. The character approaches himself from the outside as a subject for contemplation, dramatizes himself, and describes what is happening to him, in physical as well as psychological terms, as something that is taking place wholly outside himself. Thus the same style of presentation is adopted for spiritual experiences as for political deliberations.

In view of the weakness of *Gismond of Salerne*, the analysis of these details in it could scarcely be justified were we not concerned with phenomena which, in varying degrees, were to determine the path of English tragedy for some decades. For this rationalized treatment of emotion, this argumentative manner even in speeches voicing passionate feeling, this self-contemplation and self-description from the outside – all these things are still to be found in the early Shakespeare, and indeed in his somewhat later contemporaries such as Chapman, Webster and Tourneur. The over-abundant use of rhetorical forms is only one of the ways in which this rationalistic spirit is manifested.

The tendency of the speeches in *Gismond* to become monologues is not, however, the only thing that prevents an exchange of set speeches from developing into dialogue. It is true that in speech and counter-speech attitudes are put forward which are fundamentally related to one another, and which might sometimes even suggest a

---

alive. Sooner could my hands tear the heart from my breast than take away her life, which would bring on me deadly suffering worse than death. But what if my mighty rage should bring me to the point of killing Gismond? Would that be the end, and put a close to my conflict? No, her ghost would haunt me for ever. Therefore will I . . . This kind of analysis of a conflict is even more strongly marked in the long speech that Tancred makes to his daughter in the next scene. Here is a conflict of duties that is presented to us by a sophisticated process of argument ('I fight within my self'). And Gismond's answer employs just the same style of utterance, arranged in careful clauses and limited by conditions; in her 27 lines there are no fewer than five *either-or* or *neither-nor* constructions.

'conversion-scene', as for example in the recurrent situation in which a desperate person, in the grip of powerful emotion, is to be consoled, calmed or inhibited from rash actions by someone who counsels prudence.[1] But even in these episodes the two parties concerned seem entirely to ignore each other's presence; they 'speak past' each other, as it were. The two standpoints, those of reason and passion, are sharply differentiated; as they are put forward here, they have no relation to each other, and the development of a dramatic conflict is therefore out of the question. (Act I, Scene iii, is a good example.) As a result the psychological situation at the end of such scenes is usually the same as at the beginning. It makes no difference if the duologue of speech and counter-speech is diversified with stichomythia, giving the appearance of a conflict in dialogue form which draws the speakers into a more intimate relationship with each other. The authors were obviously not interested in either the dramatic encounter or the dramatic conflict, and, in short, they were not aiming at realistic dialogue, but merely at a juxtaposition of representative motives and attitudes.

All the greater is their attempt to elevate their style and to trick it out with rhetorical flourishes which far outdo *Gorboduc* in their uninhibited straining after effect, and which have to serve as the medium both of spine-chilling despair and of hair-splitting argument. For an illustration we have only to glance at lines like

> The hye despite herof, that griped my grefefull brest,
> had wellnere forced my hart wth sorrow all distrest
> by sodein shreke to shew some parcell of my smart;
> (IV. ii. 67–9)

or

> Ah pleasant harborrow of my hartës thought.
> Ah swete delight, ioy, cõfort of my life.
> Ah cursed be his crueltie that wrought
> thee this despite, and unto me such grefe . . .
> (V. ii. 25–8)

The excessive use of alliteration, the qualification of almost every noun by an emphatic epithet that adds nothing to its

[1] Seneca's *domina-nutrix* scene was the model.

meaning,[1] the reiteration and reduplication, and above all the rhyme, which either links together alternate iambic pentameters or (as in IV. ii) pairs of alexandrines: all these devices, helped by frequent enjambement (in contrast to the practice in *Gorboduc*), give the lines a melodramatic urgency and an exaggeratedly sentimental tone far removed from the restraint of the deliberate and carefully balanced blank verse of *Gorboduc*.

In a letter to Robert Wilmot,[2] William Webbe speaks of the applause with which *Gismond of Salerne* was performed before Queen Elizabeth. He adds:

> Yea, and of all men generally desired, as a work, either in stateliness of show, depth of conceit, or true ornaments of poetical art, inferior to none of the best in that kind; no, were the Roman Seneca the censurer.

In 'true ornaments of poetical art' he is presumably referring to the emotional and reflective speeches, with all their rhetorical trimmings. The words 'stateliness of show', however, are an allusion to another characteristic which is not unimportant in the development of the rhetorical drama.[3] At the very beginning of Act I we read, as the stage-direction for Cupid's soliloquy, 'Cupide cometh downe from heaven'; and in Act IV Megaera's speech is prefaced by the words, 'Megaera ariseth out of hell'. The introduction of spectacular theatrical effects of this kind, made possible by the resources of the Court stage,[4] sprang from the desire to give animation to scenes in which speech in unaccompanied by action. The later history of rhetorical tragedy shows how often stage-effects are introduced into plays where the predominance of speech precludes movement and action.[5] Speech and action run parallel and in virtual isolation from one another. It was only after some time that the two were blended in a dramatic unity.

[1] It is full of clichés: gentle heart, cruel death, fond delight, tender breast, hideous sights, raging heat, joyful news, pining woe, cruel destiny, etc.

[2] Quoted in Cunliffe, *Early English Classical Tragedies*, p. lxxxviii. The letter is dated 8 Aug. 1591. Cf. E. K. Chambers, *The Elizabethan Stage*, Vol. III, p. 514.

[3] Cf. Cunliffe, op. cit., p. lxxxix.

[4] Cf. Chambers, op. cit., Vol. III, p. 30.

[5] Cf. Alice S. Venezky, *Pageantry on the Shakespearean Stage*,

In 1591, twenty-three years after its first appearance, *Gismond of Salerne* was revived by Wilmot in a modified version with the title *Tancred and Gismunda*.[1] The alterations are revealing, especially where the handling of the set speech is concerned. For we now have much more dialogue to counteract the effect of the long set speeches, more movement within the scenes, and fuller stage-directions at the beginning of the scenes. Situations which in the earlier version were represented by means of two long speeches are diversified in the new version with some lively dialogue—compare, for example, the third scene of Act II in *Gismond* with the second scene of Act II in *Tancred and Gismunda*. Megaera's long soliloquy at the beginning of Act IV does not now begin immediately; before it there is a new stage-direction: 'Megaera riseth out of hell, with the other furies, Alecto and Tysiphone, dancing an hellish round; which done, she saith:

> Sisters, begone, bequeath the rest to me,
> That yet belongs unto this tragedy.'

A great many additions of this kind might be mentioned; their purpose is to introduce more movement and action into the play.[2] The Chorus is no longer entirely dissociated from what is going on in the scenes proper, but takes part in the dialogue. Each act is preceded by a dumb show,[3] which, however, no longer demands an allegorical interpretation, as in *Gorboduc*, but shows the actual characters of the play giving a realistic representation of the events which are to follow. Deeds of horror are no longer merely reported, but are brought on to the stage, the poisoning of Gismunda, for example. The exuberance of the style is toned down, and the use of blank verse contributes to this end. Clearly the dramatic developments of the previous three decades had a not inconsiderable influence on the revision.

Thomas Hughes's *The Misfortunes of Arthur* (1588), although it

[1] Ed. W. W. Greg, Malone Society Reprints; also in Dodsley.

[2] The statement on the title-page, 'Newly revived and polished according to the decorum of these daies', makes it clear that we are concerned with a conscious adaptation to the 'new taste'. Cf. A. Klein, 'The Decorum of These Days', *PMLA*, XXXIII, 1918, p. 244.

[3] On the dumb shows cf. Kernodle, *From Art to Theatre*, pp. 144 ff.

is an extremely close imitation of Seneca, also shows a greater freedom in its dramatic structure in that stichomythia and rapid exchanges of dialogue are frequently used; indeed it is only in a few scenes that long set speeches are associated with them. The dumb shows which introduce the several acts contain much more movement than those of *Gorboduc* and *Tancred and Gismunda*, and suggest more splendid settings; they seem to have constituted the most important dramatic effects of the play, and in fact they once more stand as a substitute for the action which is wanting in the actual scenes.

The Misfortunes of Arthur shows to a unique degree how far a playwright could carry the process of taking phrases straight out of Seneca and fitting them together like a mosaic. As Cunliffe has demonstrated, it is possible to indicate step by step the material taken from the various plays of Seneca; in one speech of twenty-eight lines, for example, only one single line is Hughes's own work.[1] These borrowings bring out very clearly what it was in Seneca that was particularly valued, and what, in consequence, determines the style of the speeches. At one time it is the pithy moral maxims and *dicta*, at another the passionate outbursts in which the heroic figures of Seneca give expression to their inordinate desires, and with which they stifle the dictates of reason and voice their rebellious fury and their emotions of hate, rage and revenge.[2]

The object of scraping together exaggerated utterances of this kind from different plays by Seneca, and piling them on top of one another in a single speech, seems to be to produce an impression of frenzy and conflicting passions, and if possible to outdo Seneca himself in the accumulation of purple passages. This may be illustrated from the two longer speeches of Guenevora in Act I, Scene ii (ll. 1–16, 19–47); here eleven passages taken from three different plays of Seneca (*Thyestes*, *Agamemnon*, *Hercules Oetaeus*) have been run together to produce this cumulative effect.[3] The method

[1] Cf. Cunliffe, op. cit., p. xci, and pp. 326–342.

[2] On the exaggerated expression of will and emotion as characteristics of numerous characters in Elizabethan drama, cf. Schücking, *Shakespeare und der Tragödienstil seiner Zeit*, esp. Chap. IV.

[3] Cf. Cunliffe, op. cit., p. 328.

of translation itself further betrays this craving for exaggerated sentiment. A passage from *Thyestes*,

dira Furiarum cohors
discorsque Erinys veniat et geminas faces
Megaera quatiens; non satis magno meum
ardet furore pectus, impleri iuvat
maiore monstro; (250–54)

appears thus in the English play:

Come spitefull fiends, come heapes of furies fell,
Not one, by one, but all at once: my breast
Raues not inough: it likes me to be filde
With greater monsters yet. My hart doth throbbe:
My liuer boyles: some what my minde portendes,
Vncertayne what: but whatsoeuer, it's huge.
(I. ii. 39–44)

In her famous first soliloquy Lady Macbeth makes a similar appeal to the Furies (*Macbeth*, I. v. 39–44); but a comparison of the two passages will show how very different they are. It is not only the exaggerated style, for which there are parallels even in Shakespeare, that turns Guenevora's apostrophes to the Furies into a mere hollow outburst of passion which wastes itself on the empty air; it is also the entire lack of preparation for such an outburst and the fact that it bears no relationship to Guenevora's world of ideas – to which might be added the lack of structural coherence in the whole treatment of the situation.

Yet the theme of the scene in which these lines occur is one of the common type-themes of Elizabethan tragedy, that is, the conflict between reason and passion.[1] In this particular instance we can see how the representation of this theme was given a welcome sanction by the authority of Seneca, who laid down the pattern for it in one of his recurrent type-situations, the so-called '*domina-nutrix* scene'.[2] The equivalent here to the Senecan situation is the conflict between Guenevora's passionate raving and Fronia's appeal for

[1] As already in *Gismond*; cf. p. 79. [2] Cf. Chap. 3, p. 47.

restraint, which is paralleled in Seneca, if not in actual words, at any rate in sense:

> Good Madame, temper these outragious moodes,
> And let not will Vsurpe, where wit should rule.
> (I. ii. 17–18)

This is only one of many passages in *The Misfortunes of Arthur* where this conflict, expressed as an antithesis between 'will' and 'wit', is represented;[1] one too of the many appeals for calm which assume the conventional rhetorical form of the 'appeasement-speech'.[2]

The last lines of the passage quoted from Guenevora's speech ('some what my minde portendes . . .') require a note. Foreboding of the future is yet another common device of Senecan drama which was taken over by English playwrights. In the rhetorical tragedies it is used chiefly for its immediate theatrical effect, but later, in Shakespeare for instance, it is developed into a subtle device for tightening the structure of the play by drawing past and future closer together; in other words, it becomes genuine foreboding and anticipation.[3] It is used in several other passages in *The Misfortunes of Arthur*.[4]

The procedure of picking out passages from speeches in several different plays by Seneca and fitting them together to make a new speech is of course not likely to produce either unity in the structure or cohesion in the thought of the speech, even when the joining is done with some skill. It was possible to carry out such a strange procedure to this extent only because there existed as yet no conception of an organically developing dramatic speech, all its elements closely interwoven, and possessing both unity and continuity. The only method of structure observed at this time was that of dealing with a series of points one after another, and the seams are always only too obvious. *The Misfortunes of Arthur* illustrates therefore how little progress had been made towards any principle of composition which would embrace the whole speech and weld its several parts into unity, for the effect is exactly the same even when

[1] Cf., e.g., II. iv. 77. [2] An example already in *Gorb.*, III. i. 42.

[3] Cf. Clemen, 'Anticipation and Foreboding in Shakespeare's Early Histories', *Shakespeare Survey 6*, 1953.

[4] E.g., II. iv. 81.

the author is writing for himself and is borrowing comparatively little from Seneca.

This may be seen in two of Arthur's long set speeches in the third act (III. i. 1–21; III. iii. 1–65). These speeches break up into a series of clear-cut sections entirely unconnected with one another as far as subject-matter is concerned, and each of them developing a single thought or motif.[1] Even when the various motifs appear to be related to a common end, as in Arthur's long address to his comrades-in arms (III. iii), one never gets the impression that the thought is being expressed at all directly, much less concisely. On the contrary, such a speech may contain a good deal of irrelevant material, for the introduction of which the use of the rhetorical device of *amplificatio* offers plenty of opportunities. It is obvious that in the process of amplification the relation of the speech to the person spoken to will be pushed into the background.

In this play, as in *Gismond of Salerne*, the Chorus encroaches on the dialogue (V. i). What they say, however, does not amount to true dialogue; it is much more a mournful reflection, largely retrospective and recapitulatory in character, in which several members of the Chorus take up the theme in turn.[2] The lament does the rounds, so to speak; it is passed from the one to the other somewhat in the manner of antiphonal responses or chants.

[1] III. i. 1–21, Arthur's speech on the arrival in England: 1–4, five questions giving variations on the opening question, 'Is this the welcome that my Realme prepares?' 5–8, conjecture about Mordred's behaviour. 9–10, is it to be attributed to Mordred's youth? 11–14, lament over the badness of the world (taken from Seneca's *Hippolytus*). 15–21, so has Fortune dealt with me, and now misfortune has free rein (20–1 from Seneca's *Troades*). Turning now to the second speech, III. iii. 1–65, Arthur's *exhortatio* to his confederates and soldiers: 1–4, apostrophe to his comrades-in-arms. 5–7, has the blood we have shed merited such dishonour? 8–17, review of the situation, winding up with a question. 18–28, must we put up with this? No, let them only come on! 29–34, they will have to pay a heavy price, and you too, Mordred, shall realize this. 35–8, the traitor Gilla, too, is among the rebels. 39–42, five parallel questions: where may we find a little rest? 43–6, yet we must fight. 47–52, apostrophe to the earth and to the realm. 53–6, here stand I, the conqueror, and Arthur the King. 57–60, here I renounce all ties and resolve on war. Fortune, be thou my protector. 61–5, order to the herald to announce to Mordred that Arthur his father approaches to chastise him.

[2] Cf. Chap. 15.

In the previous act there is a scene (IV. iii) in which, in just the same way, the speeches are merely set side by side without any true interconnexion. This time it is the mournful farewell to the fallen British warriors and heroes, a commemorative speech shared by two speakers, Gildas and Conan, and their recital, with its figurative language, gives much the same impression as an obituary or an inscription on a war-memorial. Once more the speech takes the by now well-worn form of a didactic commentary. This is a device which is comparable to the outstretched forefinger of the 'commentator' in late medieval paintings who, himself a part of the picture, brings home to the beholder the significance of the representation as an *exemplum*, a warning or a lesson to be followed. Several other passages in *The Misfortunes of Arthur* are to be taken in the same way; in them the author imparts political counsel which was intended to be applied to the contemporary situation in the England of Queen Elizabeth.[1]

Here then is a further illustration of how, even in a classical play like this, crammed with quotations from Seneca, the native tradition retains its force. On the other hand, Seneca's influence on the style and diction of the play is strongly marked, which is not surprising when we consider the large number of Senecan phrases woven into its texture. Indeed, the neatness and conciseness of Seneca's Latin were at times able to communicate to the English style, for all its propensity to expand into prolix detail, a compactness and pregnancy which deserve to be noted as new elements in the stylistic development of English tragedy.[2]

[1] Cf. E. Waller, 'A Possible Interpretation of *The Misfortunes of Arthur*', *JEGP*, XXIV, 1925, p. 2. Even without going as far as Waller in identifying the various characters with political personalities, the reference of the play to political conditions under Queen Elizabeth cannot be denied.

[2] Some passages show beyond doubt that Seneca was the linguistic model. E.g.:

> Not death, nor life alone can giue a full
> Reuenge: joyne both in one. Die: and yet liue.
> (I. iii. 49–50)

or

> Death is decreed: what kinde of death, I doubt.
> (I. iii. 15)

If we review the speeches and their disposition in *The Misfortunes of Arthur*, and study the arguments which precede the acts, we can appreciate how exactly the various set-speech types are marked out. For instance, in the argument of Act I we read:

> In the third scene *Gueneuora* perplexedly mindeth her owne death, whence being diswaded by her sister she resolueth to enter into Religion;

and in that of Act III:

> In the first Scene *Cador* and *Howell* incite and exhort *Arthur* vnto warre: Who . . . notwithstanding their perswasions resolueth vpon peace.

Here the patterns are laid down for the 'dissuasion-speech' and the 'conversion-speech', just as in other scenes we find such type-speeches as the lament (IV. iii), the 'instigation-speech' (III. iii), the 'counsel-speech' (IV. i), and of course the report. These types stand out quite clearly. We are still dealing with a one-dimensional method of composition in which only one situation or line of thought at a time can be represented in speech or dialogue.

---

or

> I inwards feele my fall.
> My thoughts misgeue me much: downe terror: I
> Perceiue mine ende . . .
>
> (II. iv. 81–3)

6

Locrine

When *The Misfortunes of Arthur* appeared, other plays had already been written which combined two types of drama in that they mixed certain elements from the classical tragedy with others taken from the popular drama. Shakespeare's immediate predecessors, Kyd, Peele, Greene, and Marlowe, contributed to this development; their contributions will be discussed in later chapters. First, however, we must consider an anonymous play of decidedly mediocre quality in which this mixing process is very crudely carried out. *Locrine*, written probably in the late 80s or at the beginning of the 90s,[1] and almost certainly the work of one of the University Wits, mixes the tragic and the comic, the verse declamation of high tragedy and the prose clowning of low-life characters. Yet though they are allowed to appear side by side, the two stylistic levels are never brought any closer to each other. Indeed, there is scarcely any other play in which the emotional rhodomontade assumes so highly exaggerated a form, and this even when, as sometimes happens, it is found in the same scene immediately next to some realistic comic prose, which might be expected to exert a corrective influence. This play shows, therefore, that the rhetorical, declamatory style, the style that out-Senecas Seneca, is able to hold its own even when it is not artificially preserved, when it is not encouraged and fostered by the specialized taste of a particular type of audience.

Locrine is not a pure set-speech play. It contains some scenes of vigorous action, and there is a good deal of bustling movement on the stage and much coming and going of the characters; here and

[1] It is dated 1591 by Irving Ribner, *The English History Play in the Age of Shakespeare*, Princeton U.P., 1957. Other scholars give it an earlier date: cf. Thornton Graves, 'The Authorship of *Locrine*', *TLS*, 8 Jan. 1925; Kenneth Muir, '*Locrine* and *Selimus*', *TLS*, 12 Aug. 1944.

there, too, some lively dialogue, sometimes quite dexterously handled. We do not find, however, that the long set speeches, with all their pretentious rhetorical paraphernalia, have on this account been any more effectively integrated with the dramatic movement of the play, or with the dialogue of which they may form a part.[1] In *Locrine*, as in earlier plays, the set speech is merely a self-contained passage of declamation which, introduced at every opportunity, is expanded and elaborated like an operatic aria, little regard meanwhile being paid to its dramatic setting. Many scenes give the impression of having been written with the express object of creating situations in which these declamatory set-pieces can be made to seem in place.

If we analyse the emotional speeches that have been supplied in such profusion, once more we shall find that they fall in line with the types of set speech described in Chapter 3. For in *Locrine* there are no fewer than five long point-of-death speeches and eleven laments, so that the title *The Lamentable Tragedie of Locrine* seems peculiarly

[1] Well illustrated in, e.g., III. iv. 1–21, where Locrine, entering with his comrades-in-arms, first describes his triumph in three parallel statements ('Now . . . Now . . . Now . . .'), and then 'addresses' his absent enemy Humber and prophesies his downfall. Then, but only in the last two lines, he turns and speaks directly to Thrasimachus. It is interesting to see, too, how few of the characters on the stage in many of the scenes are allowed to speak at all. This mute standing by of characters who are not drawn into the dialogue also results from the dominance of the long set speech, even now that the number of characters in individual scenes has increased, in comparison with the classical tragedies. Thus there are some curious 'dialogue-episodes' such as that which occurs in III. ii; here, after Humber's opening speech, spoken in the presence of Estrild, Hubba, Trussier, and some soldiers, the Ghost of Albanact enters, unseen by the others, and comments on Humber's hopeful words as a presage of his own downfall; Humber's next speech, still in no sense dialogue with his friends, is a vision of a bloody battlefield on which the Ghost makes further prophetic comments. It is only in line 36 that another character, Hubba, speaks, and the 'resumption' of dialogue is unconvincing. There is another remarkable example of dialogue that is not dialogue at the meeting of Locrine and Estrild in IV. i. Estrild's lamenting monologue (46–75) is followed by an exchange of four speeches in five lines between Camber and Locrine, then by Locrine's long aside, which is also a lamenting contemplation of his own state, and then by a kind of antiphonal lament employing the technique of stichomythia in which Estrild and Locrine are the speakers, but neither is heard by the other.

appropriate. In the same way the other set speeches can be classified under such headings as the report or messenger-speech, the threat and the execration-speech, the proclamation, and the instigation-speech. Most of them have very little to do with the plot. They are moments which have been singled out from the course of events to serve as points of rest, and because they involve typical situations, the author has seized on them as occasions for declamatory set speeches. All association with any of the other characters present goes by the board, or at best is brought to our attention in the last few lines of the speech, as, for example, at III. iv. 20.

Lament and accusation provide the material for the most frequently exploited situations.[1] When we examine the other types of speech and the attitudes inherent in them and the corresponding situations, we find that they turn upon certain recurrent themes common also to the chronicle plays; they suggest the probability that Marlowe's *Tamburlaine* had already appeared. There are, for instance, the boastful claims and the supremely arrogant proclamations in which a character speaks of his own deeds and plans. Thus in the very first scene Thrasimachus declares:

> I, in the name of all, protest to you,
> That we will boldly enterprise the same,
> Were it to enter to black *Tartarus*,
> Where triple *Cerberus* with his venomous throte,
> Scarreth the ghoasts with high resounding noyse.
> Wele either rent the bowels of the earth,
> Searching the entrailes of the brutish earth,
> Or, with his *Ixions* ouerdaring sonne,
> Be bound in chaines of euerduring steele.
>
> (I. i. 73–81)

[1] In the opening scene it is first the dying Brutus who bewails his approaching death and reflects mournfully on his succession. At the end of the scene it is Locrine that grieves, clothing his lament in an indictment of the stars and the gods. In II. v the wounded Albanact bewails his fate and accuses 'injurious fortune'. In III. i Locrine, Guendoline and Camber mourn Albanact's death. In III. vi there is the grotesquely bombastic speech of cursing and lamentation in which the conquered Humber undertakes 'to bewaile mine ouerthrow'. In IV. i Estrild laments her fate, and a few moments later Locrine laments his: '*Locrine* may well bewaile his proper griefe.'

Other passages employ much the same hyperbolic terms of protestation or malediction or provocation, arrogantly challenging the heavens or summoning up the direst torments of hell.[1] In this declaration of the speaker's purposes and the threats with which they shake the very foundations of heaven and earth, they are strongly reminiscent of Marlowe's Tamburlaine:[2]

> Ile passe the Alpes to watry *Meroe*,
> Where fierie *Phoebus* in his charriot,
> The wheels whereof are dect with Emeraldes,
> Casts such a heate, yea such a scorching heate,
> And spoileth *Flora* of her checquered grasse;
> Ile ouerrun the mountaine *Caucasus*,
> Where fell *Chimæra* in her triple shape
> Rolleth hot flames from out her monstrous panch,
> Scaring the beasts with issue of her gorge;
> Ile passe the frozen Zone where ysie flakes,
> Stopping the passage of the fleeting shippes,
> Do lie like mountaines in the congeald sea.
> (II. v. 48–59)

In contrast to the usual style of the classical plays so far dealt with, the language of the emotional speeches in *Locrine* is metaphorical and highly coloured. The fondness for exaggerated sentiments finds its expression in a corresponding type of imagery, which continually takes the form, now of a comparison with something grand and lofty, now of a merely imagined reality; and this is

[1] I. i. 157 ff.; III. ii. 46; III. iv. 29; IV. i. 29.

[2] Cf. also V. iv. 4–7:

> The fire casteth forth sharpe dartes of flames,
> The great foundation of the triple world
> Trembleth and quaketh with a mightie noise,
> Presaging bloodie massacres at hand.

Or there are III. ii. 46 ff.; III. iv. 30 ff.; III. vi. 6 ff., 28 ff. Also reminiscent of Marlowe is III. iv. 6–9:

> Now sit I like the mightie god of warre,
> When, armed with his coat of Adament,
> Mounted his charriot drawne with mighty bulls,
> He droue the Argiues ouer *Xanthus* streames.

so even in passages which do not occur in speeches expressly designed to appeal to our emotions, as when Humber says in the closing lines of the second act:

> Now let vs martch to *Abis* siluer streames,
> That clearly glide along the *Champane* fields,
> And moist the grassie meades with humid drops.
> (II. vi. 25–7)

Thus a new style has come to the fore in dramatic speech, a style which was very rarely employed by earlier playwrights, and then largely for didactic purposes. How far this considerable enrichment of Elizabethan dramatic diction is to be put down to the influence of Peele [1] and Marlowe, and how far the author of *Locrine* was himself responsible for it, are questions which still require investigation. In any case it brings a new element into dramatic speech, a lyrical beauty which counterbalances the abstract and rational character of the language employed in the purely classical tragedies. In *Locrine*, it must be confessed, these means of expression are used without any discrimination. The infinity of mythological and classical allusions, the repetition of words and phrases,[2] the unfailing supply of rhetorical questions and figures of speech, the excessive use of apostrophe: all these devices the author assiduously presses into his service in the building up of his purple passages. And in his endeavour to gain the most striking effects possible, he crowds them all together without any regard for their appropriateness to their context or their mutual harmony.

[1] Reminiscent of Peele are such passages as the following:

> The aierie hills enclosed with shadie groues,
> The groues replenisht with sweet chirping birds,
> The birds resounding heauenly melodie,
> Are equall to the groues of *Thessaly*,
> Where *Phoebus* with the learned Ladies nine,
> Delight themselues with musicke harmonie,
> And from the moisture of the mountaine tops,
> The silent springs daunce downe with murmuring streams,
> And water al the ground with cristal waues.
> (II. i. 36–44)

[2] Cf. the short study by Tucker Brooke, *The Shakespeare Apocrypha*, 1908, Introd., p. xvii.

This piling together of parallel phrases and rhetorical figures, unaccompanied by any essential development of thought, at the same time leads to an all too obvious elucidation of the meaning, and to an irritating tautology which makes many passages sound like a mere jingle:

> If the braue nation of the *Troglodites*,
> If all the coleblacke *Aethiopians*,
> If all the forces of the *Amazons*,
> If all the hostes of the Barbarian lands . . .
> (IV. i. 30–3)

The excessive use of such devices as anaphora and epiphora, often arranged alternately and thus giving rise to a form of patterned speech, is another sign of this craving for rhetorical adornment and cumulative effects. It results, however, in a style which marks time, as it were, or goes round in circles. Nowhere else in pre-Shakespearian drama is this style so clearly exemplified as in *Locrine*.

As has already been intimated, *Locrine* owes something to the chronicle plays in its method of composition and presentation. Action is no longer excluded from the scenes but is allowed to take place in them. The audience is no longer merely given retrospective accounts of the past and foreshadowings of the future while the plot remains at a standstill; on the contrary, there is plenty of stage-business, and the great variety of events enacted in the scenes makes them seem full of life and vigour. However, this has not resulted in a coherent and well-constructed plot; it is merely a loose and inartistically ordered succession of episodes which shows no signs of a conscious attempt at coordination. The new relationship between the subject-matter and the architecture of the scenes, and the more eventful action taking place in the stage, would seem to require that the speeches should be associated more closely with the dramatic movement. Some balance between the two, one would think, must necessarily be established. But this is not the case. In plan and execution the set speeches continue to display the rigid disposition and the patterned style that belong to the classical tragedies modelled on Seneca.

However, there is one motif developed in the set speeches which, by allusions to the historical background of the plot, links them to the actual course of events; this is the 'review of the situation'. At the beginning of a scene the leading characters announce how far they have come, what the state of affairs is and what the locality of the scene, and so on. In doing so they may use a good deal of rhetorical colouring, as for example at the beginning of Act II, Scene i:

> At length the snaile doth clime the highest tops,
> Ascending vp the stately castle walls;
> At length the water with continuall drops,
> Doth penetrate the hardest marble stone;
> At length we are arriued in *Albion*.
> (II. i. 1–5)

Such an opening to a speech[1] giving a 'situation-report', so to speak, and at the same time filling out the exposition, is very common in pre-Shakespearian drama, and indeed Shakespeare continually does the same thing in his history plays.

In other episodes, too, we see that the set speech now admits more narrative than it had in *Gismond* and *The Misfortunes of Arthur*; this is a function which had hitherto been reserved for the report or messenger-speech. On the other hand, the purely didactic element has been reduced; it has been relegated to the prologues which precede the several acts. In these prologues Ate introduces a series of dumb shows which take the form either of a mythological scene (Acts II, IV, V), or of a scene from a beast-fable[2] (Acts I, III).

[1] Cf., among others:

> Thus are we come, victorious conquerors,
> Vnto the flowing currents siluer streames . . .
> (III. ii. 1–2)
>
> Now am I garded with an hoste of men,
> Whose hautie courage is inuincible:
> Now am I hembde with troupes of souldiers . . .
> (III. iv. 1–3)
>
> Thus from the fury of *Bellonas* broiles,
> With sounde of drumme and trumpets melodie,
> The Brittaine king returnes triumphantly . . .
> (IV. i. 1–3)

[2] E.g., Act III: '*A Crocadile sitting on a riuers banke, and a little Snake stinging it. Then both of them fall into the water.*'

Thus the prologue has now partly assumed the function of the Chorus, and no Chorus is therefore needed in this play.

Locrine is not a good play. However, it brings before us the unworked raw material from which the great drama of the English Renaissance was eventually to be developed, when at last a real fusion of foreign and native styles was achieved.[1] In *Locrine* the two elements merely co-exist; there is as yet no organic integration or harmony between them. In this play the structural problems which had still to be solved by English playwrights can be seen with special clarity.

[1] Cf. Tucker Brooke, *The Tudor Drama*, p. 208.

7

Kyd

That Kyd was much more successful in his attempt to reconcile the classical and the native styles of drama is obvious in *The Spanish Tragedy*.[1] In this play we see how a gifted playwright with a strongly marked sense of theatre managed to fuse the heterogeneous and discordant elements of earlier types of play, and from them produced a striking and original composition of his own. With its skilful exploitation and combination of different stylistic levels and different kinds of dramatic artifice and stage-effect, *The Spanish Tragedy* was bound to be a success; moreover, Kyd sensibly took into account the various tendencies of contemporary taste. However, his mastery is grounded in matters of technique rather than in any dramatic urge that took its rise from his own personal experience, and as a result *The Spanish Tragedy* fails to move us today; furthermore, we are offended by the lapses in taste which Schlegel deplored.[2] However, the prodigious success of the play on the Elizabethan stage is evidence that Kyd's contemporaries must have felt otherwise. Its exaggerated theatricality and its combination of a highly emotional rhetoric with an intricate and exciting plot are the very qualities which are likely to have roused their admiration, the qualities which gave the play its exceptional appeal.

What effect has this new skill in the techniques of dramatic com-

[1] This is well studied by P. W. Biesterfeldt, *Die dramatische Technik Thomas Kyds*, Halle, 1936. Cf. also Fischer, *Zur Kunstentwicklung der englischen Tragödie*, p. 94; Tucker Brooke, *The Tudor Drama*, pp. 209 ff.; J. Schick, Introd. to his edition of *The Spanish Tragedy* in the Temple Dramatists, 1898; Philip Edwards, Introd. to the Revels Plays edition (Methuen, 1959).

[2] *August Wilhelm v. Schlegels Vorlesungen über dramatische Kunst und Literatur*, ed. G. V. Amoretti, Bonn, 1923. Vol. II, p. 233.

position on the handling of the set speech? Kyd knew how to pull out all the stops, how to exploit every linguistic and theatrical trick at his disposal in the theatre of the day; naturally he also recognized the potentialities of the declamatory set speech, and he showed some skill in adapting it to his purposes as a whole. In contrast to *Locrine*, *The Spanish Tragedy* offers us a coherent and artistically constructed plot [1] in which the threads of the action are skilfully interwoven and complicated. Although a number of subsidiary episodes are introduced, the course of the main plot remains perfectly clear; with all his tricks of mystification and delayed action and contrast, Kyd shows a conscious virtuosity in his handling of plot, and steadily advances the action through its various stages. Within this framework, the set speeches which periodically occur are strategically placed. Even when, as often happens, their subject-matter goes beyond the requirements of the immediate context, the mere fact that they are part of a coherent plot prevents them from losing touch with the action of the play.

Furthermore, even the *visible* structure of the work, the distribution of the longer speeches through its pages, shows the skill and the conscious artistry with which they have been introduced. There are no longer any scenes in which a number of long set speeches just follow one another without variation. Equally striking is the fact that situations which in the earlier tradition would have been represented entirely by means of long set speeches are now dealt with in other ways. For example, the second part of the second scene (I. ii) corresponds in its outlines to the familiar 'tribunal scene'; it is a scene in which a dispute between two nobles is arbitrated and settled by the King. This settlement is brought about, not by means of long-drawn statements, but in rapid, dramatically exciting dialogue.[2] Where the longer set speeches or monologues do occur, they are generally placed next to passages of stichomythia – concise, quickly-changing single-line dialogue that moves at a great pace. Thus the tempo of the play is speeded up, and by a situation's being consciously worked up to a climax, the relevant phase of the action

[1] On this and later points cf. Biesterfeldt's excellent analyses, op. cit.

[2] Cf. also I. iii. 43 ff., where the news of Balthazar's still being alive is imparted in some dramatically effective dialogue.

is advanced. In the set speeches and monologues, however, this forward movement is checked, and by means of the deliberation upon a course of conduct or the declamatory set piece we are transported to a higher, more universal level, and thus lose contact with the specific situation that is being presented. This rise and fall in the dramatic tempo, and the diversity in the method of presentation – with its claims alike upon the eye and the ear – give rise to a structural pattern which far surpasses anything with a similar tendency up to that time found in English drama.

Even in the structure of the individual scene we may observe, in the distribution of the longer speeches, the deliberate application of a structural principle. In Act II, Scene i, for instance, the two long speeches of Balthazar are placed at the beginning and the end; these are the speeches in which, in his highly rhetorical and antithetic style, he discusses the objects respectively of his love and his hate, Bellimperia and Horatio. The first speech is devoted entirely to Bellimperia; the second, after Pedringano's disclosure of the love-affair between Horatio and Bellimperia, concerns itself with Horatio alone. Thus the two goals of Balthazar's future endeavours are brought into sharp relief, not only in dialogue enlivened by action, but also through the rhetorical emphasis of the set speeches; and the significant new turn given to events in the central part of the scene, in the disclosures made in the exciting, fast-moving dialogue of Lorenzo and Pedringano, is shown for what it is by means of the two corner-posts of the scene, that is, the two set speeches of Balthazar. Comparable corner-posts in Act III, Scene ii, are the long soliloquy of Hieronimo at the beginning of the scene, and the closing soliloquy in which Lorenzo reveals his purposes; by their means we find out all about the two contending forces which, in the course of the ensuing scenes, are to be engaged in intrigue and conflict against each other.

A structural device of another kind may be seen in Act I, Scene iv. In the first part of this scene the meeting between Horatio and Bellimperia takes place. On this occasion Horatio has once more to tell the story of Don Andrea's death. There follows, together with Bellimperia's symbolic action in bestowing Don Andrea's scarf on Horatio, an ambiguous conversation, which is rounded off, on

Horatio's departure, with a soliloquy by Bellimperia. In this first section of the scene the longer speeches impose a slower tempo, and this is in keeping with the situation, in which the recapitulated account of Don Andrea's death gradually draws Horatio and Bellimperia together. Now comes some dialogue employing a very different technique. The encounter between Bellimperia and her future adversaries Lorenzo and Balthazar – shortly to be broken in upon by Horatio – is conducted in a rapid exchange of polished, witty, single-line questions and answers. By means of this rapid cross-fire of questions asked and countered, these tactics of evasion and pointed rejoinder, tension is raised, and the main lines of the conflict are sketched in, its significance being emphasized by the by-play with the glove which Bellimperia drops and Horatio picks up. Both times, therefore, the outward form and the tempo of the dialogue are adapted to the situation, and an impressive sense of contrast is produced by the clash of the two different techniques. As far as concerns the distribution of long and short speeches, of duologue and colloquy divided between several speakers, the same observations might be applied to a number of other scenes.

Even when the speeches disconcert us by their length, as in Act I, Scene ii, suggesting a reversion to the technique of detailed narrative report characteristic of the earlier classical plays,[1] we find on closer study that the long-drawn recapitulation serves a definite dramatic purpose in the complication of the plot. *The Spanish Tragedy* is a tragedy of revenge; [2] it is introduced by an Induction in which Don Andrea appears in the company of Revenge.[3] What Andrea here discloses about his death was not sufficient, however, to establish an urgent revenge-motif; this motif had to be forcibly impressed on the audience by means of a detailed report of the battle in which, at

[1] Cf. Biesterfeldt, op. cit., p. 65. F. S. Boas indeed still sees here an excessive weight of epic elements (Kyd, *Works*, Oxford, 1901, p. xxxii).

[2] Cf. F. T. Bowers, *Elizabethan Revenge Tragedy, 1578–1642*, Princeton U.P., 1940.

[3] Don Andrea's Ghost and Revenge form the Chorus, which comes in after each act and speaks its commentary. But even the Chorus-speeches, which in the classical plays commented on events and gave a didactic exposition of them, have been given some dramatic quality by Kyd. Don Andrea's Ghost and Revenge together constitute the Spirit of Revenge directing events from the background; they are no longer mere anonymous onlookers.

the same time, the true circumstances of Balthazar's capture could be related. As a contrast to this dispassionate report, presented by the Spanish General, the next scene (I. iii) gives us the distortions and misrepresentations of Villuppo, and these are followed again (I. iv) by Horatio's corrective account of the facts. According to the convention hitherto followed, any report-speech in a play had to be accepted as an objective account of what had happened, and it would have been superfluous to give more than one version of the same event. Here, however, we have reports given from several different points of view, and their relative value is of dramatic significance; among them there is even one wholly false report. These varying reports all have their consequences in the events of later scenes; they become mainsprings in the action of the play.[1] Moreover, the retrospective narration in them is to some extent woven into the texture of the plot. Of course Kyd could not have drawn out to such a length the Spanish General's account of the battle, which indeed in its earlier part (up to l. 45) has no real relevance to the plot, had not his audience expected showy and elaborately rhetorical[2] report-speeches of this kind, and valued them as 'good theatre' and as the peculiar glory of a play.

That the set speeches are more closely integrated with the structure of the plot than had up till then been the case does not mean that their speakers are brought into a close relationship with each other. Where the longer speeches are concerned, even in *The Spanish Tragedy* the characters are much more prone to talk at cross purposes than to make contact with one anothers' minds. Only in the genuine dialogue-passages does any interplay develop in which the speakers are delicately attuned to one another and establish a real contact. When the device of 'speaking past one another' is employed in such a context, it is usually done as a deliberate dramatic

[1] Apart from this, the report of the battle in a sense establishes the atmosphere of the tragedy in that it strikes the note, fundamental to the play, of bitter strife and slaughter. The strife here portrayed continues an underground course in the hidden intrigues of the succeeding acts, and comes out into the open again in the final scene. Moreover, in the last part of this battle-report, from l. 63 onwards, a neutral account of the character and role of Horatio as well as of Balthazar is given, and this is important for what happens later.

[2] E.g., ll. 116–20.

artifice; understanding and misunderstanding are by this means deftly and ironically played off against each other, and in such a way as to bring out more subtle contrasts between the speakers.[1] However, scarcely a single one of the longer speeches is fully attuned to the person addressed, except in those few instances where it is a matter of giving instructions or of announcing a decision (e.g., I. ii. 179 ff.); and in any case these are not rhetorical set speeches as we have been using the term. In fact there are no long speeches that could be classified as conventional 'conversion-speeches', 'dissuasion-speeches', or 'instigation-speeches';[2] where an attempt is made to influence a person, it is done in dialogue. The inference may be drawn that Kyd found the long set speech inappropriate for the development of close personal relationships; he assigned this function to his dialogue.

From the early classical tragedies we are familiar with the two ends normally and chiefly served by the long set speech: those of moralizing self-revelation and dissection of the emotions. The novelty of Kyd's method may be illustrated by a couple of examples. The two speeches of the Viceroy at the beginning of Act I, Scene iii, and Act III, Scene i, are not essentially different in theme from that of Gorboduc at the beginning of Act III in *Gorboduc*. The main difference lies in the stronger dramatic quality imparted to the Viceroy's speeches, especially the first one (I. iii), where his throwing himself on the ground and the gesture with which he offers to give away his crown are intended to add to the theatricality. There is a further difference in the effective way in which the climax is worked up in the Viceroy's speech, with all its rhetorical figures and its pointedly antithetic phraseology; for in the place of Gorboduc's dispassionate reflections he gives us an impassioned display of a man reasoning with himself. We get the impression of a mind-probing self-communion, a quasi-psychological soliloquy, as the Viceroy enters into judgement with himself and with the goddess Fortune.[3]

[1] Cf. Biesterfeldt, op. cit., pp. 73–4.

[2] There is, however, the long speech (IV. i. 1–28) in which Bellimperia reproaches Hieronimo for his passivity and thus drives him to act.

[3] The Viceroy's opening speech in III. i lacks this peculiar tone. It might equally well belong to *Gorboduc*, and, with some allied scenes, might serve to exemplify Schücking's view that even the original text of *The Span. Trag.* is

We find the same tendency to break up the thought into antitheses, and to analyse a situation by means of argument and counter-argument, in Balthazar's first speech in Act II, Scene i (ll. 9–28). This speech is actually intended as an answer to Lorenzo's attempt to allay his despair at his repulse by Bellimperia. However, finding a self-sufficing pleasure in the rhetorical development of his theme, he draws out through twenty lines of ingenious antitheses his contrast between his wooing of Bellimperia and her rejection of his advances, as well as his examination of his prospects as a lover.[1] The rhetorical 'type' underlying this effusion is the Senecan 'deliberation-speech'. In Seneca, however, in spite of all the rhetorical colouring, a continuous train of thought emerges, whereas here the thought is split up into a series of symmetrically ordered antitheses for the sake of the rhetorical pattern. By this procedure, which Kyd also follows in other passages, thought and feeling are trimmed and shaped in such a way as to adapt them to the rationalistic see-saw of argument and counter-argument.

Balthazar's speech at the end of the scene (II. i. 113–35), in which all his thoughts are concentrated on Horatio, shows us another form of this verbal ingenuity by means of which the facts of a case are 'dressed up' for the sake of a rhetorical pattern. In this case Horatio's fight with him and his fate as a lover are, by the rhetorical devices of epiploke and climax, given the appearance of a logical chain of cause and effect in which the one circumstance is a necessary consequence of the other. But this logic is of the most superficial kind, and moreover it is only one component of the ingenious verbal byplay which is at this point being carried on. Certainly it cannot have been by accident that Kyd here allows Balthazar in particular to indulge in a pointed, rhetorical turn of speech of just this nature (cf. his speeches at I. ii. 138–44, 161–5; I. iv. 93–7). For the lack of substance in this repetitive style of his, tediously

---

not uniform (Levin L. Schücking, *Die Zusätze zur Spanish Tragedy*, Sächs. Akad. d. Wissenschaften z. Leipzig, phil-hist. Kl., Vol. 90, Heft 2, 1938, p. 37).

[1] Lorenzo's remark, 'My Lord, for my sake leaue this ecstasie', is a criticism of the artificiality of this speech-technique, which employs several of the antithetical figures belonging to 'topics of invention'. Cf. Sister Miriam Joseph, *Shakespeare's Use of the Arts of Language*, p. 322.

amplified by antithesis and other rhetorical figures, is exactly in keeping with the irresolute, dependent, puppet-like role that Balthazar is to sustain in the play. The replies and retorts that his words receive from Lorenzo and Bellimperia seem to provide some hint as to the way in which his manner of speech is to be understood (I. iv. 90, 'Tush, tush, my lord! let goe these ambages'; I. iv. 98, 'Alas, my Lord, these are but words of course'; II. i. 29, 'My Lord, for my sake leaue this extasie'). Although this technique of characterizing a person by his habits of speech is not consistently followed (see, e.g., III. xiv. 95 ff.), the passages that have been referred to may be taken as an attempt to indicate character by the use of overworked or misused rhetorical tricks. This dramatic contrivance was later considerably developed by Shakespeare.

Much more significant of course are Hieronimo's soliloquies and set speeches, which to a large degree determine the peculiar character of *The Spanish Tragedy*, and which helped to give to the famous role of Hieronimo its outstanding success. Not only are they the pith and marrow of this play itself; they also form a kind of core for the whole body of drama that immediately preceded Shakespeare, for they were imitated by many playwrights; and by a few playwrights somewhat later they were also burlesqued.[1] By means of these soliloquies, and of other speeches that are virtually soliloquies, Kyd added to a play already abounding in action and intrigue something which was designed to provide a complement, as it were, to the theatrically effective world of outward event and action, of underhand conspiracies, murders, and tangled enmities; he added the inward drama which is played out in the soul of the protagonist, Hieronimo, and which causes him to lead a solitary existence in the midst of the affairs of this world and drives him to the verge of madness. Hieronimo's emotional and declamatory set speeches, therefore, though they remain strongly indebted to the style of Seneca,[2] acquire a new significance. In the classical tragedies all the leading characters as a rule delivered set speeches and soliloquies in which their deepest thoughts and feelings were

[1] Cf. Schücking, op. cit., p. 25; Schick, op. cit., Introd., p. xxix.

[2] Hieronimo's important speeches in the 'additions' are excluded from our discussion.

brought to the surface and laid bare. In *The Spanish Tragedy* it is especially Hieronimo who does this; only the soliloquy of Isabella which ends in her suicide (IV. ii), and which is to be regarded as a kind of prelude to what is yet to come, might also be named in this connexion. Lorenzo's soliloquies are of a different order; they are not soliloquies in which his deepest feelings are involved, but the self-revelatory soliloquies of a villain in which his scheming is disclosed, together with the explanation of his motives.

In Hieronimo, on the other hand, Kyd has created a figure [1] who, by his singular and eccentric nature, his brooding over his sorrow, his mistrust and vacillation and procrastination, is set apart in a very marked fashion from the other characters. Hieronimo becomes a solitary. He is forced into a lonely isolation by the terrible suffering that falls upon him. He has to keep his own plans secret, and in his reflections on the murder, his tactics of delay, and his investigation of the outrage, he has to act quite alone. Hieronimo's part in the play is therefore planned in terms of soliloquy, and Kyd has thus given his numerous soliloquies a new basis in their function of revealing a type of character and establishing its role in the plot. Already in Seneca, of course, there were the beginnings of such a process, and these might have served as a model; yet Kyd appears to have been the first playwright in the history of English drama who from these beginnings succeeded in creating a convincing character by means of soliloquy.

In spite of the rhetorical commonplaces of classical origin in Hieronimo's utterances of grief and despair, and in spite of Kyd's obvious endeavour wherever possible to out-Seneca Seneca within the framework of classical conventions of rhetoric,[2] a whole range of new qualities emerged in his work. Let us glance at Hieronimo's

[1] He is not of course a fully consistent 'character', but the representation of certain obvious traits in particular situations.

[2] Nashe's disparaging remark in his famous Preface to *Menaphon* (1589) is an attempt to hit off Kyd's borrowings from Seneca; he was of course unwilling to concede that in other ways *The Span. Trag.* was striking out in fresh directions. ('Yet English Seneca, read by candle-light, yields many good sentences. . . . The sea exhaled by drops will in continuance be dry, and Seneca let blood line by line, and page by page, at length must needs die for our stage . . .') Cf. Schick, op. cit., pp. ix–xiii.

first soliloquy (II. v. 1–33). As Schücking has shown with some probability, the second part of this speech, with its conventional apostrophes of lament, may well have been replaced in the later version of the play by the expanded form of it which occurs in lines 46–98.[1] The first part, however, is not in the manner of the soliloquies with which we have so far been familiar:

> What out-cries pluck me from my naked bed,
> And chill my throbbing hart with trembling feare,
> Which neuer danger yet could daunt before?
> Who cals *Hieronimo*? speak, heere I am.
> I did not slumber; therefore twas no dreame.
> No, no, it was some woman cride for helpe;
> And heere within this garden did she crie;
> And in this garden must I rescue her.
> But stay, what murdrous spectacle is this?
> A man hangd vp and all the murderers gone:
> And in my bower, to lay the guilt on me.
> This place was made for pleasure, not for death.
>
> (II. v. 1–12)

This is a soliloquy which is not only spoken, but also acted. Hieronimo comes running into the garden in his night-shirt, Bellimperia's screams still ringing in his ears, so that they cannot have been a dream or a figment of his imagination. In the darkness of the garden he searches for this woman who has cried out for help, and comes upon the body of a dead man hanging from a tree. Up to this point the soliloquy is not a mere passage of emotional rhetoric unaccompanied by action; it is a speech which accurately reflects what Hieronimo is experiencing, at the same time indicating his actions by means of internal stage-directions. We still find this technique used by Shakespeare, though by him it is as a rule more subtly and more covertly managed.

Hieronimo's soliloquies are on several occasions, though not invariably, attended by stage-business; they demand properties or appropriate gesture. At such times we see the hand of the true man of the theatre; declamatory as it may be, the soliloquy is made an

[1] Cf. Schücking, op. cit., p. 31.

integral part of the plot, and at the same time turned into a piece of good theatre. That great cry of grief, 'Oh eies, no eies . . .' (III. ii. 1 ff.),[1] one of the most famous pieces of rhetoric in Elizabethan drama, is given actuality on the stage by the direction, *A Letter falleth.* From this point onwards the soliloquy is carried on in much less rhetorical language, for Hieronimo picks up the letter, reads it, and from its contents draws deductions as to his future course of conduct. In the same way, his soliloquy at the end of Act III, Scene vii, is largely taken up by the reading of the letter handed to him by the Hangman, the information it gives him about the circumstances of Horatio's murder, and the deliberations to which it gives rise. Even the outbursts of grief, 'Woe to the cause of these constrained warres . . .' etc., are associated with direct references to action; only the soliloquy with which the scene opens consists of unmixed lamentation. Similarly, the soliloquy at the beginning of Act III, Scene xii, when Hieronimo enters with a dagger in one hand and a rope in the other to await the arrival of the King, is an 'acted' soliloquy. It is true that it contains that lurid image of the fiery tower of judgement beside the lake of hell; but immediately after this it is again linked with the action, and Hieronimo engages in some stage-business with the properties:

> Downe by the dale that flowes with purple gore,
> Standeth a firie Tower; there sits a iudge
> Vpon a seat of steele and molten brasse,
> And twixt his teeth he holdes a fire-brand,
> That leades vnto the lake where hell doth stand.
> Away, *Hieronimo*; to him be gone:
> Heele doe thee iustice for *Horatios* death.
> Turne downe this path: thou shalt be with him straite;
> Or this, and then thou needst not take thy breth:
> This way, or that way: – soft and faire, not so:
> For if I hang or kill my selfe, lets know
> Who will reuenge *Horatios* murther then?
> No, no; fie, no: pardon me, ile none of that.
> *He flings away the dagger and halter.*
> (III. xii. 7–19)

[1] Treated in Chap. 15 in connexion with the formal lament.

There is nothing of this kind in Seneca. The histrionic quality of the popular drama has here forced its way into the static, declamatory monologue of the classical tradition. Only with regard to the lament at the beginning of Act III, Scene vii, can it be said that the conventional form of the rhetorical lament has been preserved in its entirety. On all other occasions the action of the play is advanced in one way or another in the course of the soliloquies, and the speaking is accompanied by gesture or by stage-business. Even in Isabella's final soliloquy (IV. ii) this histrionic and theatrically effective quality is manifested;[1] for in the form of a soliloquy we are given what is essentially a short 'action-scene', in the course of which Isabella tears down the leaves and branches of the tree on which Horatio was hanged, lays her curse on the garden in which the tree is growing, and finally stabs herself.

What is to be said of the speeches of Hieronimo that are not soliloquies, those which occur in dialogue-scenes? In these scenes his speeches for the most part tend to deviate into monologue, and the use of this type of speech is particularly effective in reinforcing the sense of isolation in Hieronimo's mind. In *Gorboduc* and the tragedies that succeeded it the speech that veers away into monologue had been employed because the playwright needed it as a vehicle for moral reflections or passionate lament. Kyd, however, makes Hieronimo address his words to himself in a fashion that is wholly appropriate to his spiritual condition; he consciously and deliberately isolates him from the other characters present in these dialogues. The grief-stricken old man, who is obsessed by thoughts which remain hidden from the other characters, and who appears distracted (and indeed wants to appear so), must with his very strange manner and speech have produced an uncanny effect on the stage. The set speech deviating into monologue, a mere convention with Kyd's predecessors, is now well on the way to becoming an organic and dramatically significant form of expression, even if it is not yet so on all occasions.[2] Other good examples occur in

[1] The beginning of this monologue is unusual: 'Tell me no more!'

[2] Thus the reflection with which Hieronimo begins his dialogue with the Deputy in III. vi employs the old technique of elucidation. On the other hand, his speeches in the 'additions' show Kyd's approaches to true soliloquy

the twelfth and thirteenth scenes of Act III; both times Hieronimo breaks up a dialogue-sequence. He is so strongly reminded of his grief by a catch-word – 'Horatio' at III. xii. 58, and the Old Man's petition 'for his murdred Sonne' at III. xiii. 78 – that he lets the despair he has with difficulty been holding in check break out into wild and whirling words.[1]

The calculated failure to understand, the talking at cross-purposes, the breaking away from a dialogue-sequence: all these devices, up till now the peculiar property of comic drama, have in this exhibition of Hieronimo's pretended madness been given a new function, which is dramatically effective, and at the same time sound psychology. Here, too, Kyd reveals himself as a master craftsman, one who knew how to make dramatic capital out of the greatest variety of dramatic artifices.

The remaining plays of Kyd, *Soliman and Perseda* and *Cornelia* (a translation of Garnier's *Cornélie*), may in this context be disregarded. On a few occasions, indeed, the speeches in *Soliman and Perseda* show a noticeably stronger tendency to establish and maintain contact with the person addressed (e.g., I. ii. 1 ff.), and the rigidity of the set-speech pattern is relaxed by making the longer speeches part of the dialogue. The style of the work as a whole, however, the method of presentation, and the general dramatic technique, are weaker and less original than those of *The Spanish Tragedy*, where Kyd was quite obviously writing at the height of his powers.

---

developing further and taking on a new psychological realism which, in the later style of the 'additions', opens up new forms of expression for soliloquy. Cf. Schücking, op. cit.

[1] Cf. Biesterfeldt, op. cit., pp. 74–5.

8

Marlowe: I

Tamburlaine

What distinguishes the treatment of the set speech in Marlowe's *Tamburlaine* (c. 1587)[1] from all that came before it will be best understood from a consideration of the play as a whole. In the classical tragedy up to this time such unity as a play possessed was a matter of outward qualities alone; in most of Marlowe's plays, on the other hand, there is an unmistakable focal point, a central issue, to which all subsidiary issues are related. In *Gorboduc* the plot was designed to exemplify a political and moral doctrine, to which there were repeated references, and the central interest of the play is therefore communicated only in a very diluted form. In Marlowe, however, the focal point of the play is an *idea*.[2] This idea impresses itself on us the more insistently because its representative and embodiment is the hero himself, the protagonist, round whom the whole action and all the other characters revolve. *Tamburlaine* represents the earliest stage of this type of drama, for here the central figure, having no one of comparable magnitude to balance him, too powerfully dominates the play and too exclusively determines its plot; he is, moreover, the only unifying factor in a work which is still clumsy and jerky in structure, and in which the same course of events is worked over again and again, climax following upon climax in a series of episodes not greatly differing from one another. For this central figure 'great and thundering speech'[3]

[1] On the date cf. E. K. Chambers, *TLS*, 28 Aug. 1930.

[2] Cf. Una Ellis-Fermor, *Christopher Marlowe*, London, 1927.

[3] *Tamburlaine* opens with a reference to the power of speech:

> *Myc.* Brother Cosroe, I find myself aggriev'd;
> Yet insufficient to express the same,
> For it requires a great and thundering speech. (I. i. 1–3)

M. C. Bradbrook (*Themes and Conventions*, p. 141) interprets these words of Mycetes as 'buffoonery' and as a 'corrective to the high-astounding terms'.

is the entirely appropriate medium of expression – and of existence; indeed it is the one and only form in which he does exist. When *Tamburlaine* the play is mentioned, we immediately think of Tamburlaine's speeches; they are what remains most vividly and enduringly in the memory, and the play would be unthinkable without them.

This in itself is an indication that these speeches are no longer mere 'declamatory insertions', mere purple patches introduced for the sake of immediate effect. Furthermore, the long set speech no longer appears so much a thing apart from the more fast-moving dialogue which occurs with it; on the contrary, some kind of balance is beginning to be struck, so that there are frequent transitions from long to short speeches, and from short speeches to brisk dialogue. As was becoming apparent already in *The Spanish Tragedy*, and in a cruder form even earlier in *Locrine*, speech-drama is gradually being transformed into the drama of action. However, whereas in *The Spanish Tragedy* the longer set speeches for the most part lacked any clear connexion with the passages of dialogue, even when they were immediately next to them, in *Tamburlaine* the disparity has been still further reduced, as is obvious even to the eye if we turn over the pages of the two works.

The characters of the earlier plays gave the impression that they would seize every suitable opportunity for turning a given situation into an occasion for long-winded declamation and the delivery of a set speech. This can no longer be said with regard to Tamburlaine. For Tamburlaine the set speech is a necessary and constant condition of his existence; it is the very stuff and substance of his role in the play. It follows therefore that where Tamburlaine is concerned there is a very much closer relationship between the speaker and his speeches, and that they are very much more characteristic of him personally than had been the case with any previous figure in English drama. However, even with him, it must be admitted, there is not yet any question of the creation of a real *character*; rather we have here the conception of 'a dramatic figure symbolising certain qualities',[1] and this conception is so powerful that it colours every one of Tamburlaine's speeches, and stamps it with the unmistakable

[1] Cf. Bradbrook, op. cit., p. 137.

hall-mark of his utterance. If Elizabethan drama more than the drama of any other time takes its life from speech, from the spoken word, if in a larger measure than any other drama it gains its power from the language it employs,[1] then Marlowe's *Tamburlaine* marks a fresh stage of development, a stage at which this language at last becomes a genuinely dramatic medium of expression and of character-portrayal. For this is the really novel function assumed by Tamburlaine's speeches, that they are self-expression and self-portrayal of an exceptional and dynamic type; and it is this that marks the play, for all its weaknesses, as a work of amazing genius.

Self-portrayal of the kind illustrated in Tamburlaine's speeches is something very different from the 'self-introduction' and 'self-explanation' that were regularly employed as a dramatic convention on the first entry of the characters or personified abstractions in the Miracle and Morality plays. Marlowe has made something entirely new of this device. Instead of the neutral, more or less colourless account of the character's origin, name, and nature, instead of the recital of plans and purposes, he has in Tamburlaine given us a unique self-representation which is informed in every line by the individuality of this mighty figure. In the drama before this time the monologue had usually combined its expository function with that of reinforcing the moral of the whole play; it is now in a much fuller sense a means of self-expression, and for the reason that the 'moral' in *Tamburlaine* is identified with the feelings and desires of the protagonist. Thus the earlier conventions of self-portrayal have in the person of Tamburlaine been turned to new purposes. What had been straightforward self-introduction becomes on his lips self-glorification on the grand scale; what had been the mere statement of purposes becomes the daring anticipation of all future contingencies; and the disclosure of wishes for the future becomes a voluptuous surrender to wishful thinking. All these attitudes, which find their expression in the set speeches of the play, are in a new fashion rooted in Tamburlaine's unique and remarkable personality, in his presumptuous, superhuman aspirations. His hyperbolical way of speaking, for example, his ostentatious boastfulness,

[1] 'The essential structure of Elizabethan drama lies not in the narrative or the character but in the words.' Bradbrook, op. cit., p. 5.

fantastic and exaggerated as it may appear, does not, as Miss Una Ellis-Fermor has pointed out, strike us as absurd.[1] It is not just a mode of behaviour imposed on him as a dramatic type, but a personal style that is in proportion to the man himself.

This style of Tamburlaine's, well as it serves for the expression of a variety of motifs, is remarkably uniform. It is partly achieved by the grandiloquence of the blank verse; however, it is also permeated and coloured throughout by a rich metaphorical quality,[2] and is marked by distinctive syntactical and stylistic patterns and by a distinctive vocabulary.[3] The poetry of Tamburlaine flashes and sparkles and reverberates with sound, as though to dazzle us with its lightnings and deafen us with its thunders; it rings with the names of precious metals and other things of price; immeasurable distances and vast unplumbed depths open before us; the whole universe seems to whirl about us. It is this highly individual quality in Marlowe's imagery[4] that fuses the heterogeneous elements of the poetry into a close harmony; it is this which, together with the dynamic character of the blank verse, constitutes the most important unifying principle of the speeches.

The most characteristic attitude that is revealed in Tamburlaine's speeches is his anticipation of the future. This comes out not only when he is unfolding his plans for the future, and in his threats and his promises, his curses and his protestations, but even in his self-glorification. For the most part this future of his has no existence in the real world, but only in a dream-world of his imagination. Accordingly it is his aspiring imagination which is the true driving-force behind Tamburlaine's speeches. It flares up in every picture he gives of the future, and transmutes it into a golden vision. In consequence his plans for the future lose all concreteness and precision; they become vague, and out of touch with reality. It could

[1] Una Ellis-Fermor, op. cit., p. 27.

[2] H. Levin, *The Overreacher*, p. 42, refers to F. I. Carpenter's statement that there are more than 400 metaphors and images in *Tamburlaine* against 250 in all the later plays.

[3] Cf. Levin's remarks on the use of proper names, op. cit., p. 43.

[4] See Marion B. Smith, *Marlowe's Imagery and the Marlowe Canon*, Philadelphia, 1940. Cf. also Una Ellis-Fermor, *Christopher Marlowe*, p. 49, and W. Clemen, *The Development of Shakespeare's Imagery*, London, 1951.

hardly have been otherwise. Had Marlowe made his hero in declaring his aims for the future confine himself strictly to ideas based on reality, the intrinsic contradiction between wish and fulfilment, between the superhuman, godlike figure, as Marlowe had conceived it, and its inevitable human limitations, would have struck us as grotesque.[1]

In these speeches of Tamburlaine, with their fanciful visions of the future, Marlowe has at the same time tried to give expression to the indomitable will of man. No playwright before Marlowe felt so intensely this power of the human will, or was able to voice it as convincingly as he did in the mighty sweep of his self-conscious, boldly individual blank verse.[2] Practically all of Tamburlaine's utterances are manifestations of a gigantic will which, combining with his fantastic anticipations, is invested with a dynamic quality not previously found in English dramatic speech. His speeches give the impression of having an immense driving-power behind them; for all their lack of touch with reality, they have been transformed into action, and they are like blows from a club – though it must be admitted that some of these blows fall upon the empty air. The deeds which Tamburlaine in fact performs are also essentially lacking in reality, for there is no opposition, no counterforce, such as every kind of reality must give rise to.

This new passion and drive in Tamburlaine's speeches had the effect of thoroughly disrupting the static pattern of the old rhetorical structure and the old methods of rationalistic analysis. The procedure of piling up phrase upon phrase, motif upon motif, balancing verse-paragraph against verse-paragraph in an attempt to build up an obvious symmetry, is resorted to comparatively seldom, indeed only in a handful of the set speeches.[3] Such a formal rhetorical pattern as often occurs in Kyd is certainly very rare. In its place Marlowe, true artist in language as he was, with his new blank verse introduced a new dynamic principle into the dramatic set speech, one which clearly made a profound impression on his contemporaries,

[1] Cf. Bradbrook, op. cit., p. 138.

[2] On Marlowe's verse see C. F. Tucker Brooke, 'Marlowe's Versification and Style', *SP*, XIX, 1922.

[3] Tucker Brooke, op. cit., p. 189.

and not least on Shakespeare. In his use of language form and content entered upon a new alliance. The following lines will serve as an example; they are from one of the many passages in which Tamburlaine announces his future intentions:

Our quivering lances shaking in the air
And bullets like Jove's dreadful thunderbolts
Enrolled in flames and fiery smouldering mists
Shall threat the gods more than Cyclopian wars;
And with our sun-bright armour, as we march,
We'll chase the stars from heaven and dim their eyes
That stand and muse at our admired arms.
(II. iii. 18–24)

The succeeding line, spoken by Theridamas, 'You see, my lord, what working words he hath', no doubt represents the impression that language of this kind made on Marlowe's contemporaries.

Such highly metaphorical language, no less than his habit of working his imagination up to the pitch of a wishful thinking that is utterly remote from reality, is characteristic of the majority of Tamburlaine's speeches, even where there is no question of threats or of warlike projects. When he is wooing Zenocrate, he does so by means of just such promises for the future, promises which develop into increasingly unreal wish-fulfilment dreams:

Thy garments shall be made of Median silk,
Enchas'd with precious jewels of mine own,
More rich and valurous than Zenocrate's.
With milk-white harts upon an ivory sled
Thou shalt be drawn amidst the frozen pools,
And scale the icy mountains' lofty tops,
Which with thy beauty will be soon resolv'd.
(I. ii. 95–101)

What we find illustrated in this and in many other passages is a new principle of structure in the dramatic set speech, one which is no longer based on rhetoric and the rationalization of the subject-matter, but is essentially poetic in character. The imagination of the poet, darting forward to what is remote and in the future, is set aflame by the first idea it seizes upon – often it need only be a name – and bodies forth images which become progressively less tangible until they reach the realms of unreality. The structural principle in this case, therefore, is no longer that of a preconceived rhetorical 'disposition', in which every motif is treated according to the circumscribed conventions laid down for it; on the contrary, Tamburlaine's speeches are actually growing while they are being spoken. They also show, of course, the same fundamental tendency that was apparent in the classical plays, the tendency, that is, towards heightened effects, and towards *amplificatio*. The heightening and the amplification are no longer, however, achieved by the stringing together of rhetorical devices – apostrophes, questions, and the like – but by the process of enlarging on a vision; that is, it is no longer mere rhetoric which is responsible for the heightening effect, but imagination. Even when Tamburlaine speaks to Zenocrate merely to tell her to sit down on the throne beside Zabina, her name and her beauty at once conjure up in his imagination those increasingly fantastic images with which he so voluptuously invests her:

> Zenocrate, the loveliest maid alive,
> Fairer than rocks of pearl and precious stone,
> The only paragon of Tamburlaine;
> Whose eyes are brighter than the lamps of heaven,
> And speech more pleasant than sweet harmony;
> That with thy looks canst clear the darkened sky,
> And calm the rage of thundering Jupiter;
> Sit down by her.
>
> (III. iii. 117–24)

If we ran through all of Tamburlaine's speeches, we should find that the greatest amount of space in them is taken up by wish-fulfilment images of this kind. These images find their most appropriate and characteristic form of expression in Tamburlaine's many formulas of protestation, especially in the more hyperbolical protestations; it is a form of expression which Marlowe nowhere else employs as often as in this play. At the same time, these wish-fulfilment imaginings have a part to play in Tamburlaine's self-portrayal. When he sets his feet on the back of the conquered Turkish emperor Bajazeth, making a footstool of him, and triumpantly proclaims:

> For I, the chiefest lamp of all the earth,
> First rising in the east with mild aspect,
> But fixed now in the meridian line,
> Will send up fire to your turning spheres,
> And cause the sun to borrow light of you;
> (IV. ii. 36–40)

this mixture of self-glorification and vision of the future is typical of what occurs in many other passages.[1] Indeed, even when Tamburlaine knows that his fortunes are at their highest point, expressly avowing this knowledge,[2] even then he cannot bear to remain in the present moment, but at once turns his thoughts to new plans of conquest.[3]

How then does it come about that this constant preoccupation with an imagined future in Tamburlaine's wishes, threats, promises, and protestations does not give the impression of wearisome rhodomontade or mere attitudinizing?[4] The answer to this question is that, especially in Part I, Tamburlaine is impelled by more than merely a naked lust for material conquest and kingly power. As Miss Ellis-Fermor has so convincingly shown, there stands behind this superhuman will the idea of the omnipotence of the human spirit, of the transfiguring power of the aspiring soul of man which can bring the unattainable within his grasp.[5] It is this idea of the youthful Marlowe, typical of the Renaissance in its lofty conception of the human will, and at the same time romantic in its preoccupation with the remote and unattainable, that governs the speeches of Tamburlaine. It is this that sublimates the crude boasting of the bloodthirsty world-conqueror, so that the objects touched by the verse are transmuted into true poetry.

The question of the relationship between the set speech and the

[1] E.g., *2 Tamburlaine*, IV. iii. 97 ff. [2] *2 Tamburlaine*, I. vi. 23 ff.

[3] *2 Tamburlaine*, I. vi. 30 ff.

[4] It must be admitted that this is sometimes the impression given by the repetitions and recapitulations of Part II.

[5] Cf. Ellis-Fermor, op. cit., pp. 28 ff.

person addressed in it has been glanced at only in passing. Tamburlaine himself often begins a speech by addressing some other person, but within a few lines is talking about himself.[1] This happens even in the 'conversion-speeches'. For instance, when Theridamas takes the field against him with a large army and appears before him for a parley, Tamburlaine succeeds by the persuasive power of his tongue in shaking his loyalty to his king and enticing him over to his own side.[2] Yet the core of his speech here is self-portrayal, in the shape of a vision of the future. Again, when he addresses the captive Soldan in order to restore him, as the father of Zenocrate, to his kingly power, it is only a few moments before he goes on to speak of his own power, and the speech develops into a fresh example of his self-glorification (V. ii. 423 ff.). Even in his wooing of Zenocrate, Tamburlaine makes no attempt to attune himself to her and respond to her feelings; his courtship takes the form of boastful promises which, in that they concern solely his own purposes, once again amount to self-glorification (I. ii. 34 ff., 83 ff.). This practice of disregarding the other participant in a dialogue – a frequent practice in the earlier drama, as we have seen – finds its dramatic justification in *Tamburlaine* in the nature of the protagonist. For in his monomania he has eyes for himself alone; he is Marlowe's first sketch of the egocentric attitude to life, an attitude which must in some ways have been that of Marlowe himself.

There are only a few speeches of Tamburlaine to which these remarks do not apply. Among them are his panegyric on Zenocrate as she lies dying and his lament for her (*2 Tam.*, II. iv. 1 ff.), the

[1] E.g., II. iii. 6 ff.; II. vii. 12 ff.; IV. iv. 5 ff. In the first of these three speeches, addressed to the conquered Cosroe, occur those famous lines, 'Nature . . . Doth teach us all to have aspiring minds', lines which, as F. S. Boas remarked, come 'with almost ludicrous inaptness' from Tamburlaine (*Shakespeare and His Predecessors*, p. 42).

[2] Again the effect of this persuasion-speech calls forth comment:

Ther. Not Hermes, prolocutor to the gods,
Could use persuasions more pathetical.
(I. ii. 209–10)

On this speech see also M. Poirier, *Christopher Marlowe*, London, 1951, p. 94. Further passages in which Tamburlaine's ability 'to persuade at such a sudden pinch', and his command of 'working words', are illustrated will be found cited in Levin, *The Overreacher*, pp. 44–5.

lecture on fortification to which he treats his sons (*2 Tamb.*, III. ii. 53 ff.), the long retrospective account of his life that he gives just before he himself dies (*2 Tamb.*, V. iii. 126 ff.), and his actual dying speech (*2 Tamb.*, V. iii. 224 ff.).

The panegyric on Zenocrate shows close affinities with Elizabethan poetic conventions in its structure, in the repetition of the metrically regular lines in which Zenocrate's name is introduced, and in its imagery. It is a highly lyrical description[1] – it is indeed a formal lyric in the style of the contemporary epithalamium. It opens with references to nature's participation in Tamburlaine's feelings, and goes on to speak of Zenocrate's imminent death; it ends with five parallel visions in which we are shown the loving sympathy and grief in turn of the angels, of the heavenly bodies, of nature, and of God himself. This panegyric exemplifies the ease and naturalness with which lyrical forms could be absorbed by the drama; it shows too that Marlowe the playwright is inseparable from Marlowe the poet. Marlowe had the skill, however, to harmonize the lyricism of this passage with the dramatic style of his death-bed scene, and to make it effective in the dramatic sense; this point will be developed later. For the rest, this speech, as are all the speeches addressed to Zenocrate, is an expression of that passionate delight in beauty by which Marlowe himself was moved, and which he wished to bring out also in Tamburlaine, together with his aspirations towards infinite power. This duality might be regarded as an inconsistency by any one who, thinking in terms of psychological types, wanted to look on Tamburlaine as a real-life character, which of course he is not.[2] As for the lecture to his sons[3] and the account of his past life, they are both rather uncharacteristic of the way in which the set speech is normally used in *Tamburlaine*; like

[1] Cf. Tucker Brooke, op. cit., p. 190; see also Allardyce Nicoll on the language of these lines: 'His verses take on a strange iridescence where the marvelling at the loveliness becomes confused with the rich sound of words loved for their own sake' (*British Drama*, London, 1949, p. 82).

[2] Cf. Poirier, op. cit., p. 109.

[3] This speech of instruction is given a place of honour on the title-page of Part II: 'Tamburlaine the Greate. With his impassionate furie, for the death of his Lady and Loue faire Zenocrate: his forme of exhortation and discipline to his three Sonnes, and the manner of his owne death.'

a number of passages in *Faustus* and other later plays of Marlowe, they are examples of traditional set-speech types introduced into a play which otherwise is striking out in new directions in the handling of the set speech. Tamburlaine's lament for Zenocrate and his own death-bed speech will be dealt with in the final chapter of this book.

So far only Tamburlaine's speeches have been discussed. The other characters, who are only conventionally portrayed, and who could easily be interchanged like puppets, appear to derive their manner of speech from Tamburlaine; they give us the same boasts and threats, the same curses, and the same vehement protestations. Moreover, the same formulas occur in their speeches as in his.[1] Bajazeth's dark threats and maledictions are in essence nothing more than a reduplication of Tamburlaine's threats with the speech-headings changed (e.g., V. ii. 151 ff.). However, the speeches of the subsidiary figures[2] do more than those of Tamburlaine in the way of exposition, that is to say, it is they who supply the narrative element of the play. Yet it is important that the impression of Tamburlaine's greatness and might should be constantly kept before us in the speeches of these other characters, so that we may hear about him almost without intermission. This represents a further step in the direction of dramatic unity, and it is at the same time an example of that dramatic device of character-portrayal through the words of other *dramatis personae* which Shakespeare was later to develop in so masterly a fashion. There is, however, less art in the way in which this 'presence' of Tamburlaine in scenes where he does not appear in person is brought out than there is in the sense we have of Richard III's presence in every scene of the play that bears his name. Like everything else in Marlowe's play, this aspect of the hero's portrayal is obvious and obtrusive. In Act II, Scene i, for instance, there is a straightforward *descriptio* devoted to his appearance in the form of a set speech by Menaphon (ll. 7–30).[3] Such a concentrated

[1] E.g., II. vi. 5 ff., II. vi. 25 ff.; III. i. 21 ff.; III. i. 64 ff.; III. iii. 103 ff.; III. iii. 195 ff.; IV. iv. 16 ff.; *2 Tamburlaine*, I. i. 25 ff.

[2] For the laments and dying speeches of Zenocrate, Bajazeth and Zabina, see Chap. 15.

[3] Cf. also III. ii. 66 ff.; *2 Tamburlaine*, III. iv. 45 ff.

treatment of set 'themes' by means of set speeches, not yet broken up into looser units, is typical of the pre-Shakespearian drama. These character-descriptions – and to them we might add the portrayal of Zenocrate in Tamburlaine's speeches – are also typical of the way in which Marlowe himself experienced concrete reality and gave it verbal expression. For we get no precise or concrete impressions from these speeches, and there is nothing in them of the conventional way of describing characters. Anything concrete resolves itself into comparatives and superlatives which rather obscure than clarify the picture; reality is heightened to the point where it ceases to be real. We are given, not the portrait of a person whom it would be possible to imagine, but a dynamic impression which is intended to reflect and enhance the splendour and might of the person described.

It was in the nature of Marlowe that he should thus by-pass concreteness and reality and move about in worlds of ideas and fantasies, and that in his ardent, youthful aspiration towards the highest he should transcend the limitations of the immediately present and actual. This natural bent he imparted to his characters, and gave it expression in the style of their speeches. What we find in an especially pronounced degree in Tamburlaine is in a lesser degree a characteristic of all the Marlovian heroes; for all of them language is, so to speak, a means of existing in another dimension, in that it carries them beyond the bounds of their own real existence and enables them constantly to soar beyond what is actual and present. In the language they use they are able to bring to realization what they 'will' and 'desire', but would not be able to accomplish in a real existence. It is in their language that they have a foretaste and an illusion of things which happen in dreams that never come true.

Tamburlaine's 'great and thundering speech' made a tremendous impression on Marlowe's contemporaries. Obviously it reflected pretty accurately some latent ideal cherished by the men of the English Renaissance. What modern critics may feel to be insufferable bombast[1] must at that time have seemed like a trumpet-call

[1] 'It must be confessed, however, that to a modern ear the uninterrupted flow of this high-pitched and loud-mouthed poetry becomes an intolerable ordeal': Philip Henderson, *Christopher Marlowe*, London, 1952, p. 87.

sounding the advent of an age that was conscious and proud of its own power. For the Elizabethans, who so persistently aimed at strong and vivid effects, quietness and restraint, the subtle point and the veiled hint, had to give place to the blatant and the forceful, to uninhibited emotion and the full-voiced assertion. It would have been easier in any other age than this to tone down the fortissimo of Tamburlaine's speeches. Shakespeare's great achievement must be seen against this background. For although parodies of this bombastic style began to appear soon after Tamburlaine became so well known a figure,[1] Shakespeare is nevertheless the first to have toned down this forcefulness of utterance; he was the first to bring out shades of meaning, and to speak in a quiet voice capable of expressing nuances and half-tones.

The significance attached to the more considerable speeches in *Tamburlaine* might easily mislead us into overlooking the connexion between these speeches and the staging of the play as a whole. Yet the two things go hand in hand. In the classical plays the presentation of an argument by means of a set speech and its explanation in mime ran side by side, but no relationship was established between them; in *Tamburlaine* Marlowe created a highly individual dramatic style in which stage-tableau and stage-business combined with the long speeches to produce a new kind of unity. A good example of this is the scene of Zenocrate's death, the scene that opens with the panegyric on Zenocrate already referred to. The stage-direction reads:

> *The arras is drawn, and* ZENOCRATE *lies in her bed of state;* TAMBURLAINE *sitting by her; three Physicians about her bed, tempering potions;* THERIDAMAS, TECHELLES, USUMCASANE *and the three sons.*
>
> (2 *Tamb.*, II. iv)

When the curtain of the inner stage is drawn a living picture is disclosed, a tableau, the stylized and symbolical grouping of which lends it a peculiar expressiveness and power. In this picture we see

[1] As appears to be the case in Greene's *Orlando Furioso*, which is discussed in Chap. 12. Cf. also Nashe's sarcastic attack on 'the swelling bombast of a bragging blank verse'.

three sets of three characters positioned round the central group, which consists of the grief-stricken Tamburlaine and the dying Zenocrate; apart from one of the Physicians, who speaks two lines at the end of the panegyric, and Theridamas, who speaks six lines near the end of the scene, they stand there in complete silence, like a group of statuary. Marlowe has repeatedly used a three-fold arrangement of this kind in *Tamburlaine*,[1] not only in the construction of individual scenes, but in the composition as a whole, embracing both the first and the second parts. The purely episodic type of structure appears thus to have been replaced by a closely knit, consciously stylized method of construction which aims at a clear system of character-grouping.

In Zenocrate's death-bed scene this set tableau of mutes provides a fitting background for the solemn measure of the deeply moving panegyric and lament, the second half of which also observes the tripartite principle, in that it is divided into six sections, each consisting of three lines followed by a refrain closing with Zenocrate's name. This speech ends abruptly with Tamburlaine's single-line question to the Physicians, which opens the way to dialogue; and a further question to Zenocrate, similarly a single-line question, leads to the final exchange between Zenocrate and her beloved, which again consists of three speeches. Then in Zenocrate's last words,

> Some music, and my fit will cease, my lord,
> (2 *Tamb.*, II. iv. 77)

we have an indirect stage-direction, which is given effect by the formal stage-direction, *They call music.* The three succeeding speeches in which Tamburlaine gives way to his grief and despair are set like frames about the death of Zenocrate, which occurs during a short pause, to the sound of music. The last of these three speeches, ending with the name of the dearly-loved Zenocrate, brings the whole scene to a close, and at its conclusion there is the final stage-direction, *The arras is drawn.* The scene is built up as a strictly organized dramatic sequence, where the speeches, like massive pillars, both frame and support the statuesque tableau, in

[1] Cf. Levin, *The Overreacher*, pp. 35, 46.

which meanwhile only a single slight movement takes place. The grand, monumental style of the speeches, with their lyricism and their strong appeal to the emotions, has found its counterpart in a stage-tableau and a stage-action which are attended by the same ritual solemnity and grandeur. Thus the question asked earlier, whether the set speech is a mere 'insertion', leading us away from the action proper and holding it up, is not here to the point.

The last scene of the Second Part of *Tamburlaine* is also a death-bed scene, at the end of which the protagonist himself dies. In its construction this scene again illustrates Marlowe's development of a 'monumental' style of presentation, a style which no longer leaves the set speech in a vacuum, but relates it organically to the scene pictured on the stage, to the economical yet expressive and symbolic use of properties, and not least of all to the significance of the action. The solemn introductory passage is shared out between the three viceroys with their choric lament on the imminent death of Tamburlaine; and then comes Tamburlaine's triumphal entry on the ceremonial car drawn by the captive kings. The episode that follows, with its more vigorous action, is cut short and brought to a standstill by Tamburlaine's long retrospect over his past life, which stands at the mid-point of the scene. With the help of a map of the world that is brought to him, Tamburlaine describes the course of his extensive conquests, and thus at the very end of his life he at last leaves the vague realms of wishful thinking and makes contact with reality by the exactness of his topographical references. There follows the crowning of the prince Amyras, set between a speech by Tamburlaine and the answer from his newly crowned son, which develops into a lament. After a final exchange of dialogue between Tamburlaine and his trusty lieutenants, there comes the great dying speech of the world-conqueror, symbolically introduced by the bringing in of the hearse holding the body of Zenocrate. Thus in this scene all the more substantial speeches are placed at important focal points and are appropriately supported by stage-tableau or stage-business – for to all intents and purposes the group of the three mourning viceroys at the beginning is a tableau. In the main speeches the action is continually being held up or brought to a standstill, but this process is consciously and deliberately integrated with the slow forward movement of the plot, relaxed only at carefully regulated intervals.

Finally, while we are dealing with scenes of mourning and death, we should consider the way in which, in the last scene of Part I, the mourning and dying speeches of Bajazeth and Zabina and Zenocrate's contribution are made to form a natural sequence, and in which they are set off against one another and contrasted, and adjusted to the action taking place on the stage.[1] First there is the exchange, once again divided into three pairs of speeches, between Bajazeth and Zabina, the climax of which is the two parallel speeches of execration uttered by the two as 'pendants', so to speak (V. ii. 176 ff., 192 ff.). Then, as the first part of a second trilogy, comes the dying speech of Bajazeth. This ends with his self-destruction, and it is both contrasted and outdone by its successor, which, tailing off into prose, presents the madness and death of Zabina. Both kill themselves by dashing out their brains against the iron bars of Bajazeth's cage.[2] Hard upon this follows Zenocrate's lament, in which the blank verse is resumed, and which with Bajazeth's speech frames Zabina's prose speech and 'spotlights' it as the climax of the whole episode. This speech of Zenocrate's harks back to the bloody execution of the virgins of Damascus, and thus is made to achieve a carefully designed cumulative effect in that, to the reasons for grief that we have just beheld with our own eyes, it adds a third reason which is merely reported. Only at the very end does Zenocrate's lament refer to the calamity which has taken place a few moments earlier and which her eyes all at once take in. Thus the third of this series of laments works up a remarkable dramatic suspense. For while the spectators are every moment expecting Zenocrate to catch sight of the two bodies, the disaster that has just occurred is outweighed in her speech by her grief for an outrage that was committed earlier. Anippe's short speech of three lines which follows once more concentrates the interest of the audience directly upon the scene on the stage; and now Zenocrate embarks on

[1] See Chap. 15.

[2] '*He brains himself against the cage*' (V. ii. 241); '*She runs against the cage, and brains herself*' (V. ii. 256).

another long speech in which this last frightful deed is anathematized and its ruthless author Tamburlaine is apostrophized.

If we examine this series of important speeches at the end of Part I of *Tamburlaine* solely from the point of view of the language they employ, we cannot avoid the conclusion that here, as in other episodes, Marlowe's starting-point was the epic style, and not the dramatic. However, he always succeeded in combining these epic forms of expression with a dramatic setting. Indeed he created for himself a dramatic style of presentation which was capable of absorbing a very large proportion of epic language.

In Tamburlaine's showy parades, in the set tableaux, and in the impressive way in which symbolic gesture, stage-business and properties are brought into prominence,[1] it is quite easy to point to the various influences operating on the play: those of the pageants,[2] of the spectacular elements in the masques, and of the Italian *trionfi*—just as, on the other side, the 'Renaissance style' of the sixteenth-century Continental theatre exhibits many features corresponding to those of *Tamburlaine*, as may be illustrated from the style of production of the Rederijke Drama in Holland, which also employed tableaux logically correlated with the grand style of declamation.[3]

That Marlowe in his *Tamburlaine* consciously coordinated the set speech and the stage-tableau, the spoken word and stage-business, can, it is true, be maintained only with regard to a few scenes. For in many other episodes sudden alarums and battles are scattered indiscriminately among passages of speech, or are introduced by means of awkwardly explanatory lines of prose. The scuffling and the running hither and thither that are designed to cater for the eyes remain, as it were, self-contained; they are not yet related to an artistic control of language. It is with a full knowledge of this fact that the scenes in which Marlowe achieved a successful combination of language, stage-tableau, and action have been singled out for special comment.

[1] Levin (op. cit., pp. 39 ff., 49 ff.) refers to the symbolic use of the crown in the language as well as the action.

[2] Cf. Alice S. Venezky, *Pageantry on the Elizabethan Stage.*

[3] Cf. H. H. Borcherdt, *Das europäische Theater im Mittelalter und in der Renaissance*, Leipzig, 1935, pp. 142 and passim; also Kernodle, *From Art to Theatre*, Chap. III.

9

Imitations of Marlowe's *Tamburlaine*

Selimus and *The Wounds of Civil War*

The various derivatives of *Tamburlaine* that appeared within the next few years show how ill the highly original genius manifested in Marlowe's dramatic first-fruits lent itself to imitation.[1] These plays may be divided into two classes: either they are paltry, misguided attempts at straightforward imitation, or they are obvious parodies like Greene's *Orlando Furioso*. Tamburlaine's hyberbolical speeches continually hovered close to the dividing-line where passionate utterance may topple over into extravagance and absurdity; this quality in them was soon seized on by writers antagonistic to Marlowe or by the champions of other stylistic ideals.[2] Within Marlowe's play these speeches were justified in the dramatic sense by Tamburlaine's character, which had its roots deep down in Marlowe's own nature and in his creative imagination. Where these prerequisites were lacking such a style of utterance was bound to degenerate into mere hollow show and empty bombast, into a ludicrous posturing which had no backing in human experience. Unless it was matched by powers of expression of a commensurate grandeur, any attempt to reproduce the proportions of this titanic figure and of his mighty struggles to master the world could only succeed in widening the gap between subject-matter and presentation, between lifelike character-portrayal and mere verbiage.

Selimus and Lodge's *The Wounds of Civil War* have been chosen here as examples of derivatives of *Tamburlaine* because they illustrate various of the difficulties and dangers inherent in ill-advised

[1] Cf. Tucker Brooke, *Tudor Drama*, p. 245.

[2] Cf. Ben Jonson's opinion of Tamburlaine's 'furious vociferation', and Shakespeare's parody of the style in Pistol.

attempts at imitation.[1] The whole of pre-Shakespearian drama yields no better example than *Selimus* (after 1591) of a play that is bogged down in set speeches.[2] In no other play are there so many long speeches with so little bearing on the dramatic requirements of the situations presented. Yet *Selimus* is not by any means a pure 'speech-drama' in the same sense as the classical tragedies were, for its author tries to give it life by introducing a great many incidents. These, however, take the banal form of sudden murders, atrocities, and warlike parades, clumsily dragged in and showing very little connexion with the speeches. This is true even of the comic prose scene in which the shepherd Bullithrumble figures (ll. 1783–2096). The dilemma facing the playwrights who were still under the influence of Seneca, but who wanted to create what would be at one and the same time a speech-drama and a drama of action, is brought before us in an extreme form in this disjointed juxtaposition of long set speeches and violent actions.

Selimus illustrates well the fact that a play cannot be made from a variety of elements gleaned from a variety of sources and merely pieced together by an author apparently little versed in the principles of dramatic composition. It reveals with especial clarity the defective sense of proportion that marks so many branches of early Elizabethan literature, the utter lack of balance and harmony between the various component parts of a work. This deficiency is emphasized by the tendency to run from one extreme to another, and by the lack of restraint shown in bringing the most violently incompatible elements into close association with one another. Yet Shakespearian drama could never have come into existence but for the diversity, the luxuriance, and the unfettered licence of this earlier period. The miraculous development of Shakespeare's art could not have taken place within strictly limited and closely preserved conventions of form and style according to which every-

[1] Greene's *Alphonsus of Aragon* is discussed in Chap. 12. *Locrine* shows only occasional echoes of *Tamburlaine* and was therefore treated independently. Existing studies of the influence of *Tamburlaine* on contemporary drama are not very helpful (e.g., A. W. Verity, *The Influence of Christopher Marlowe on Shakespeare's Earlier Style*, Cambridge, 1886).

[2] On *Selimus* see Jean Jacquot, *MLR*, XLVIII, 1953; Irving Ribner, *SP*, LII, 1955; Inga-Stina Ekeblad, *NQ*, May 1957.

thing, as in the French classical drama, had to conform to a clearly defined framework; it needed such a wilderness in order to thrive. And this is what justifies some consideration of so very poor a piece of work as *Selimus*.

In *Selimus* we soon see that the undramatic treatment of the set speeches is to some extent conditioned and prescribed by the abrupt and schematic manipulation of the characters' entrances and exits. The commonest way in which the scenes are constructed is that one of the groups into which the *dramatis personae* are divided marches on to the stage, where a few long speeches are exchanged, to be followed by the departure of the whole group. Only on rare occasions are there entrances and exits that bring about any change in the grouping within the scene; where this happens (e.g., ll. 831–1120, 1150–1248), these scenes are the exceptions that prove the rule. The static and schematic nature of the action is further revealed in the fact that the opposing parties are only a very few times brought face to face. This is true, of course, of a great many pre-Shakespearian plays, of the chronicle plays in particular; we might call it the 'technique of isolation'. For this reason the set speeches very seldom find their way into situations that are dramatically exciting. And indeed, where they do so, as in the encounter of Bajazet and his rebellious son Selimus (ll. 579–659), the sense of dramatic contrast is quickly swallowed up in the pedantic detail of the exposition. Most of the speeches, however, are not in any way related to the characters whom they ostensibly affect; they are reflections, explanations, complaints, or arguments addressed to the audience, and often the other characters concerned are remembered only in the last few lines.[1] In scarcely any other play of the early Elizabethan period is the tendency for the speeches

[1] At the beginning of the play Bajazet at least sends his followers away before delivering his soliloquy ('For I am heauie and disconsolate'), and recalls them when, after 120 lines, he has finished it ('Come, bashaws enter, Bajazet hath done'). But when a hundred lines later Selimus comes in with his retinue, he does not show the same respect for the type of situation, and at once, in the presence of the others, embarks on his self-revelation of more than 150 lines, in which there are arguments suggesting the mistaken English notion of Machiavelli's 'policy of irreligion', and other themes partly recalling *Tamburlaine*.

to drift into monologue carried to such extremes as here; nor are there many other plays in which this use of monologue has a slighter basis in the state of mind of the speakers. Here in its crudest and most obvious form is the soliloquy designed for the enlightenment of the audience and as a mouthpiece for the promulgation of the author's own opinions.[1]

What was in connexion with *Locrine* described as the 'situation-report' is of course found also in this play, which in the Prologue is explicitly named a *historie*;[2] it often, indeed usually, occurs at the beginning of speeches. The ineptitude with which the narrative material is introduced is very striking, and betrays the author's utter lack of experience as a playwright.

Selimus illustrates, among other things, that the most obtrusive element in the less gifted imitations of *Tamburlaine* is the habit of reporting and explaining, of interrupting the dramatic flow and choking it with passages of didactic exposition and comment; thus the indirect approach is continually being used instead of the direct. One of the things pre-Shakespearian drama had to learn was that this lack of directness must give way to a type of language that was direct, immediate, and closely relevant to its context and to the character concerned. Even Shakespeare did not always manage this in his early plays.

The diction of *Selimus* shows what a considerable falling-off in intensity attended its author's attempt to reproduce the idiom of Tamburlaine. Instead of Tamburlaine's dynamic imagery we have a mere handful of long-drawn epic similes,[3] and instead of the urgent forward thrust of the Marlovian blank verse a largely insipid versification. The verse is occasionally coloured by the use of unfamiliar words,[4] and here and there it falls into verse-paragraphs bound

[1] For the use of this convention in several Shakespearian soliloquies see Schücking, *Character Problems in Shakespeare's Plays.*

[2] No fained toy nor forged Tragedie,
Gentles we here present vnto your view,
But a most lamentable historie
Which this last age acknowledgeth for true.

[3] Cf. 441, 1011.

[4] See A. B. Grosart's Introduction to *Selimus* in the Temple Dramatists.

together either by consecutive or by alternate rhyme[1] (e.g., ll. 1–120, 770–91, 831–59, and elsewhere); but we get the feeling that these devices are merely being used arbitrarily, and they produce an impression of artificiality. Although there are some borrowings from Seneca's *Thyestes*,[2] the diction as a whole has none of the compactness or the rhetorical texture of Seneca's language. In a few passages, especially in the speeches of lament and execration and the dying speeches of Bajazet, Aga, and Corcut near the end of the play, attempts are made to build up a patterned speech,[3] but they do not amount to much; the procedure of drawing out a statement by piling together variations on a theme in a series of parallel clauses is nothing more here than the monotonous repetition of a device borrowed from earlier plays. Although the language is freely sprinkled with imagery referring to beasts of prey, and towards the end with images of death, vengeance, and the afterlife, it does not give the impression of an organic growth, and on the whole it misses its effects; we cannot in this play speak of any unifying factors in the language such as we found in *Tamburlaine*.

In Thomas Lodge's *The Wounds of Civil War* (1587/8),[4] another play in the line of *Tamburlaine*, the set speech again plays a considerable part in the dramatic structure, although the stirring, eventful plot of this work, the earliest Roman play in English literature, brings it nearer than *Selimus* to the typical chronicle

[1] M. C. Bradbrook, *Themes and Conventions*, p. 102.

[2] Cf. Cunliffe, *The Influence of Seneca on Elizabethan Tragedy*.

[3] Cf. 1495, Bajazet speaking:

> Ah *Aga*, *Baiazeth* faine would speak to thee
> But sodaine sorrow eateth vp my words.
> *Baiazeth Aga*, faine would weepe for thee,
> But cruell sorrow drieth vp my teares.
> *Baiazeth Aga*, faine would die for thee,
> But griefe hath weakned my poore aged hands.
> How can he speak, whose tongue sorrow hath tide?
> How can he mourne, that cannot shead a teare?
> How shall he liue, that full of miserie
> Calleth for death, which will not let him die?

[4] On the dating cf. N. B. Paradise, *Thomas Lodge*, Yale U.P., 1931, pp. 129–37. E. K. Chambers dates it c. 1588, following Ward and Fleay, but an earlier date appears possible.

play. Even in this play, however, there is not yet any mutual interplay between speech and action. Many of the episodes seem to have been conceived as pure 'set-speech scenes', while others are pure 'action-scenes'; no mixing of the two techniques begins to take place until the later acts. Nevertheless we now do find *scenes* of action, and not a mere wordless hustle and bustle, as in *Selimus*.

Already in the first act there are examples of the juxtaposition of static set-speech sequences with intermittent bursts of activity.[1] At the same time this act shows quite clearly that the speech episodes which follow one another so closely are always based on conventional situations of the kind that prescribe the use of stereotyped set speeches. Thus the scene in the Senate with its series of typical 'counsel-speeches' is followed by the 'provocation', in the form of Sylla's boastful threats (ll. 227 ff.); this, after an interlude of action, is succeeded by a situation which calls for dissuasion, and Anthony thereupon delivers a 'dissuasion-speech' (ll. 267 ff.). Then comes the typical 'complaint-situation', made up of three speeches of lament and commentary which are of approximately equal length, and which are used in the manner of a chorus (ll. 302 ff.); and finally, after a further battle-interlude in which not a single word is spoken the sequence is brought to a conclusion by Sylla's 'instigation-speech' (ll. 341 ff.) to his desponding soldiers. The same thing happens in the following acts, in which it is possible to pick out several 'set-speech situations' of this kind pressing hard upon one another's heels; and indeed the structure of the whole play, scene by scene, is in the long run determined by such situations. These examples enable us to see clearly the mechanics of this method of composition, which is continually governed by stereotyped speeches and situations.

[1] The Council of Senators on the Capitol is to make a decision on Marius's appointment as General. The Senators discuss the matter at great length, and then Marius himself rises to 'pleade his cause'. Now Sylla, who is being replaced, appears, and a 'challenge-situation' develops between him and Marius. Sylla's boastful and threatening speech at 221 ff. shows clear echoes of *Tamburlaine*. The general departure of the Senators and that of Sylla and his party are indicated in detailed stage-directions, and not in speech. The departing Sylla is called back by Anthony, who tries to dissuade him from war against Marius.

A new feature, however, is that the speeches are much more closely attuned to the interlocutor than in *Selimus*, even more so, indeed, than in *Tamburlaine*. Often he is addressed quite directly, and the fact that he is intended to be influenced by the speech and brought round to a different outlook is borne in mind. The set speech is no longer felt to be a mere 'declamatory insertion'; it is now a means by which something is actually set in motion.

Lodge was convinced that dramatic speech must possess 'eloquence', that the most important business of a speech was to produce some effect on its recipient. In the replies and reactions of the persons addressed he continually introduces references to such things as 'honey'd words', or 'cunning eloquence', in other words, to the impression that the speech makes on the hearer.[1] The questions put to the other participant in a dialogue are no longer, therefore, merely rhetorical questions, but are intended to apply to him

[1] Thus Sylla says, before Anthony's speech of dissuasion:

> Anthony, thou knowst thy hony words doo pierce,
> And moue the minde of Scilla to remorse.
> (262–3)

And later he says:

> Inough my Anthony, for thy honied tongue
> Washt in a sirrop of sweete Conseruatiues,
> Driueth confused thoughts through Scillas minde.
> (296–8)

After Sylla's speech to the soldiers Pompey declares:

> I Scilla, these are words of mickle worth,
> Fit for the master of so great a minde.
> (407–8)

Then there is Granius to Sylla:

> Thy tongue adornde with flowing eloquence . . .
> (460)

Cinna speaks of Anthony's 'sugar'd lips' and 'cunning eloquence'. The Jailer describes the effect of Marius's words on his heart (975 ff.). However, the clearest acknowledgement of the persuasive power of words is to be seen in the remarks of the soldiers after Anthony's speech:

> *1 soul.* Why what enchanting termes of arte are these?
> That force my hart to pitie his distresse . . .
> *3 soul.* So sweet his words that now of late me seemes
> His art doth draw my soule from out my lips.
> (1839–44)

directly. The arguments he might use in reply are anticipated and countered in advance. The result is a more varied mode of expression, which makes use of quite different means of persuasion. This can be illustrated by quoting some lines from Anthony's first speech to Sylla:

> For Scillas hast, O whither wilt thou flie?
> Tell me my Scilla what dost thou take in hand?
> What warres are these thou stirrest vp in Rome?
> What fire is this is kindled by thy wrath?
> A fire that must be quencht by Romaines blood,
> A warre that will confound our Emperie,
> And last an Act of fowle impietie.
> Brute beasts nill breake the mutuall law of loue,
> And birds affection will not violate,
> The senceles trees haue concord mongst themselues,
> And stones agree in linkes of amitie,
> If they my Scilla brooke not to haue iarre,
> What then are men that gainst themselues doo warre?
> Thoult say my Scilla honour stirres thee vp:
> Ist honor to infringe the lawes of Rome?
> Thoult say perhaps the titles thou hast wonne,
> It were dishonor for thee to forgoe . . .
>
> (267–83)

The use of the four examples drawn from nature, here introduced as arguments reinforcing the persuasive power of the speech, follows a pattern that is found in other passages elsewhere in the play.[1] In the same way sententious maxims, proverbs, and parables are made to serve the purposes of the argumentative speech – just as they are often used by Shakespeare in his early plays. In Lyly the method of advancing an argument by means of illustrations from nature became a regular mannerism, and it is also used by Kyd.[2] It is not unlikely that playwrights were influenced and confirmed in their use of the device by Lyly's example.

In addition to the speeches and episodes in which *persuasio* is

[1] E.g., Anthony's speech, 1814 ff.

[2] Cf., e.g., *Span. Trag.*, II. i. 3–9.

applied to individuals,[1] there are some speeches of the same kind which are intended to influence a larger number of people. Sylla's 'instigation-speech' to his soldiers has already been referred to. To the same type of *exhortatio* belong the speech of the young Marius to his retinue (II. iii), those of Cinna and Anthony to the Senators (III. i), of Marius to the Senators (IV. i), and of Sylla to the Roman people (V. i). Then the conventional episode of the triumphal entry, which Lodge several times makes use of in this play, brings out speeches which might have been written in imitation of Tamburlaine's effusions of triumph and self-glorification – those, for instance, of Sylla in II. i and V. i, and of Marius in IV. i.

These speeches, however, represent only one side of the play. Also very common are the familiar types of the reflective speech with a didactic purpose and the formal lament accompanied by moralizing comment. In numerous passages the characters refer to the fact that Fortune cannot be gainsaid, that this life of ours is precarious and transitory, that the moment of our highest prosperity and power is the moment when we should most fear a fall.[2] The medieval theme of the fickleness of the goddess Fortune, which Willard Farnham has traced right through the Morality Plays and up to the beginnings of English tragedy,[3] also permeates

[1] The most important is the episode in which the three soldiers sent by Marius to kill Anthony are addressed by him and forthwith give up their design (cf. p. 136, note 1). Anthony calls on the Muse to make his words so persuasive that the soldiers will be turned from their purpose:

> And thou sweet neece of Atlas on whose lips
> And tender tongue, the pliant Muses sit,
> Let gentle course of sweet aspiring speech,
> Let honnie flowing tearmes of wearie woe,
> Let frutefull figures and delightfull lines
> Enforce a spring of pitie from their eyes . . .
> (1818–23)

[2] Thus towards the end of the play, without our being prepared for it, Sylla reports the 'sodaine change' that has come about in him. This change from blind and haughty tyranny to wise discernment is expounded in the same speech (2309–35), in which there is a whole series of moral *dicta* on the lot of kings, contentment in a simple country life, and the mutability of fortune.

[3] Farnham, *The Medieval Heritage of Elizabethan Tragedy*.

the play, and is the basis of many of the didactic reflections in its speeches.

In Marius's long soliloquy (ll. 1189 ff.) an artificial lyricism depending on references to nature is grafted on to his complaints against the times and the ways of the world, for he likens his miserable solitude to the mountains and invokes the nymph Echo. Here the naturalistic effect of the regularly returning echo is made the means of imposing order on what he says, and turning it into a species of 'patterned speech'.[1] In Marius's closing speech there is an obvious attempt on Lodge's part to make the mood of nature chime in with that of the speaker; this is a rare device in pre-Shakespearian drama, and is therefore worthy of remark here in spite of the undeveloped technique by which everything is described from the outside.[2]

The taste for experiment that is revealed in this bringing together of so many different forms of expression – in this respect providing a strong contrast to *Tamburlaine* – can also be seen in the variety of stylistic techniques employed. But they are used in an amateur way, without system and without discrimination, and they cannot therefore give either individual speeches or the play as a whole a decided character of their own.[3]

[1] Cf. Bradbrook, *Themes and Conventions*, p. 104.

[2] This melancholy desart where we meete,
Resembleth well yong Marius restles thoughts.
Here dreadfull silence, solitarie caues,
No chirping birds with solace singing sweetlie,
Are harbored for delight: but from the oake
Leaueles and saples through decaying age,
The scritch-owle chants her fatall boding layes.
Within my brest, care, danger, sorrow dwells . . .
(1247–55)

[3] A special favourite is the parallelism (common also in *Locrine*) of lines with the same beginnings or endings, sometimes a combination of the two, as in 1845–5, 1820–2; 2083 ff., 2095 ff. E.g.,

Thy coloured wings steeped in purple blood,
Thy blinding wreath distainde in purple blood,
Thy royall Robes washt in my purple blood,
Shall witnes to the world thy thirst of blood . . .
(2095–8)

Like the author of *Locrine*, Lodge has a very wide range of linguistic artifices at his disposal. He is like a painter who knows how to mix the various colours on his palette, and can paint the minutest details with them, but is incapable of blending them into a composition. Language and the handling of individual motifs were given earlier consideration in Elizabethan tragedy than the conduct of plot, the portrayal of character, or unity of idea. To follow the further development of these important components of drama, and the fuller absorption of the set speech into the texture of the play that accompanied it, we must return to Marlowe.

There is another form of parallelism:

> Goe thou as fortunate as Greekes to Troy,
> As glorious as Alcides in thy toiles,
> As happie as Sertorius in thy fight,
> As valiant as Achilles in thy might.
> (1552–5)

A combination of various figures:

> Rome shall repent, babe, mother, shall repent,
> Aire weeping clowdie sorrowes shall repent,
> Wind breathing many sighings shall repent . . .
> (1112–4)

There are also experiments with alliteration:

> Thogh swolne with sighs my hart for sorrow burst,
> And tongue with teares and plaints be choaked vp,
> Yet will I furrow forth with forced breath
> A speedie passage to my pensiue speech.
> (1900–3)

10

Marlowe: II

The Jew of Malta

The Jew of Malta belongs, with *Doctor Faustus* and *Dido*, to those plays of Marlowe which, in W. W. Greg's words, 'are or appear to be only in part Marlowe's'.[1] The state of their texts makes it difficult to criticize these plays satisfactorily, and comment on their style and artistry must therefore be somewhat tentative. However, if we are to trace the development of Marlowe's dramatic art in general and of his handling of dramatic speech in particular, such important plays as *The Jew of Malta* and *Doctor Faustus* can certainly not be left out of account.

Even if we could assume that *The Jew of Malta* originally contained more long set speeches than the three to be found in the extant version, there can be no doubt that it has a very great deal more in the way of short dialogue than *Tamburlaine*,[2] and that it represents an entirely different method of dramatic composition. Our safest way of approaching the play will be to begin by comparing its structure and plot with those of *Tamburlaine*, for these are the things least likely to have been affected by any cuts or alterations that may have taken place during the transmission of the text.

Tamburlaine is made up of a series of clearly defined episodes in the course of which single groups of characters appear and exchange speeches. *The Jew of Malta*, on the other hand, has a plot which is full of incident, and which includes a variety of swiftly developing and skilfully interwoven subsidiary episodes.[3] This plot is no longer,

[1] Cf. W. W. Greg, *Marlowe's Doctor Faustus, 1604–1616*, Parallel Texts, Oxford, 1950, p. 10.

[2] Cf. the statistical comparison of speech-lengths in Marlowe's plays in Levin, *The Overreacher*, p. 187.

[3] Cf. Fischer, *Zur Kunstentwicklung der englischen Tragödie*, p. 119.

like that of *Tamburlaine*, entirely dependent on the protagonist, nor does it, like that of *Faustus*, mirror symbolically the temptations and spiritual conflicts of the principal character. It is much more like a piece of everyday life in that it unfolds independently of its hero Barabas; it reacts on him and obliges him too to act and react, and with its constant interchange of movement and countermovement, stroke and counterstroke, it makes possible a new kind of dramatic interplay in which the hero is set against a background of continually changing situations, these situations being what determines whether he is to resolve upon action or refrain from it. In many respects, therefore, the architecture of the plot is reminiscent of Kyd's *Spanish Tragedy*. However, in spite of Kyd's greater virtuosity in the handling of the intrigue, the plot of *The Spanish Tragedy* has something contrived and artificial about it; the strings on which the puppets are made to dance are all too obviously visible. The highly melodramatic tone produced in *The Spanish Tragedy* by the declamatory character of the set speeches reappears in *The Jew of Malta* only as an undercurrent. In its place we catch, even in Barabas's long soliloquies, a new note which is much closer to the idiom of everyday speech – an unusually well modulated poetic diction, constantly varying its tempo, and capable of being adapted with a dramatic vividness to the changing subject-matter.

Marlowe's play contains no such emotional set-piece or lament, detaching us altogether from the concrete circumstances of the plot, as we find, for instance, at the beginning of Act III, Scene vii, in *The Spanish Tragedy*. Only on rare occasions does the language make us lose touch with the reality and immediacy of the events that are taking place. Nevertheless, even in *The Jew of Malta* we are still faced by the familiar discrepancy between the lyricism of the emotional outbursts and the prosaic realism with which the events of the play are reported, whether in the speeches or in the dialogue.[1] For although these passages of lyrical emotionalism

[1] 'Few playwrights have ever shown such power in conceiving states of intense feeling, and surely none of comparable greatness has ever been less skilful than Marlowe in blending this lyric fabric with the structural framework of a tragedy' (*The Works of Christopher Marlowe*, ed. C. F. Tucker Brooke, p. 233). We must remember, of course, that the last three acts of *The*

have become both shorter and fewer than those of *Tamburlaine*, they are not yet so perfectly fused with the structure and the overall stylistic impression of the play that the transition from the one level of style to the other is not perceptible. However, generally speaking this is true of Elizabethan drama as a whole, and even of the early plays of Shakespeare. Thus, for example, in Barabas's long soliloquy at the beginning of Act II, Scene i, the simile of 'the sad presaging raven, that . . . in the shadow of the silent night Doth shake contagion from her sable wings', creates a lyrical atmosphere which forms a curious contrast with the cool and calculating terms in which Barabas elsewhere lays bare his policy. The language of the *dramatis personae* is not yet in any consistent fashion determined by their characters; this is to be found for the first time in Shakespeare.

We have seen that Marlowe was already well on the way to writing 'character-drama' in *Tamburlaine* (as also later in *Doctor Faustus*), in that he used the set speech for the self-portrayal of his characters and the reflection of their spiritual processes. Following up this side of his dramatic development, we find that in *The Jew of Malta* Barabas's longer speeches and soliloquies also serve this purpose of establishing his character; his character and personality are revealed to at least the same extent, however, in the dialogue, in the plots he devises, and in his actions and reactions generally. This method of characterization plays but a small part in *Tamburlaine* and *Doctor Faustus*; it is more finely developed here, and gives an impression of greater richness, especially in the earlier acts. In the second half of the play, which is evidently only a crude, unpolished draft, Marlowe again neglects this means of portraying character, in the third and fourth acts in particular.

While Faustus's longer speeches and soliloquies are intended to reflect his intellectual and spiritual conflicts, in Barabas's self-portrayal the emphasis is to a very large extent laid on the unfolding of his stratagems and descriptions of the circumstances in which he finds himself. Yet this self-characterization of his has a

---

Jew of Malta give evidence of a very faulty transmission of the text. 'In the last three acts of *The Jew* there are not many signs that Marlowe is at work' (F. P. Wilson, *Marlowe and the Early Shakespeare*).

thoroughly original ring, with its thrillingly dramatic use of language and the vividness with which it conveys his actions and environment, continually intermingling the stately dignity of the poetry with the idiom of everyday speech, and even including a certain amount of colloquialism.[1]

This form of self-revelation is the more necessary in establishing the figure of Barabas because Marlowe has endowed him with a duplicity which to a large extent derives from the fact that he is here giving dramatic embodiment to the 'policy' of the English perversions of Machiavelli.[2] The Prologue, which is spoken by Machiavelli in person, puts the connexion beyond dispute. The extent of Machiavelli's influence on the composition, the subject-matter and the action of *The Jew of Malta* and *The Massacre at Paris* has with reason been judged so considerable, that these two plays are often spoken of as the 'Machiavellian plays'[3] or the 'plays of policy'.[4] The role of Barabas consists in this, that he almost constantly practises dissimulation towards his fellows and is a very different person from what he appears to be, and that, with a view to securing his rights or encompassing vengeance or gaining his nefarious ends, he devises dark intrigues, sets unsuspecting persons at one another's throats, and, calling 'policy' to his aid, stealthily lays traps in which his opponents, and finally even his own daughter, are to be brought to their downfall.

Barabas's numerous soliloquies are continually used to throw light on this duplicity of his. The two soliloquies at the very beginning of the play have the function of revealing to the audience the peculiar nature of the man which would account for such behaviour. The first, spoken by Barabas in his counting-house as he tells over his riches, is intended with its highly-coloured enumeration of precious stones and distant lands to give us a picture of the

[1] See the excellent discussion of the opening soliloquy in F. P. Wilson, op. cit., pp. 58 ff.

[2] Cf. Mario Praz, 'Machiavelli and the Elizabethans' (*Proc. British Academy*, XIII).

[3] Poirier, *Christopher Marlowe*, pp. 146 ff.

[4] Una Ellis-Fermor, *Christopher Marlowe*, pp. 88 ff. Cf. also Tucker Brooke: 'We are dealing confessedly with a unique form of drama governed by rules of its own – the Machiavellian tragedy' (*The Works*, p. 232).

wealthy Jewish merchant wallowing among his treasures and awaiting the return of his argosies.[1] The second brings into close relationship the blessings represented by this wealth and the lot of the Jew in a Christian world:

> Rather had I, a Jew, be hated thus,
> Than pitied in a Christian poverty.
> (I. i. 112–13)

Thus both soliloquies have a purely expository purpose. They furnish no glimpses of an inner life, nor do they represent philosophic self-questioning or disclose what the speaker's plans are for the future; in a thoroughly concrete fashion, and without any details of what has gone before, they give a picture of the present and as yet unthreatened standing of Barabas, bringing into relief the two leading motifs that are to be so important in the future action, that is, his riches and his situation as a member of the Jewish nation. No longer are these two soliloquies mere 'footlight-soliloquies'; the first in particular is attended by visible activity – the counting of the money and the stowing away of the treasures – which has a dramatic effect much more to the purpose than the passionate gestures by which soliloquies were accompanied in the earlier drama. Equally remarkable is the extent to which both soliloquies derive their substance solely from the present moment, reducing to a minimum the retrospect which elsewhere is drawn out to such great length.

However, this technique by which so much of the expository material is packed into two long soliloquies is later in the play replaced by a form of representation which makes increasingly greater use of carefully organized dialogue. All the soliloquies that follow these two are shorter; very often they are nothing more than indications of action that is going forward, combined with a brief account of the present state of affairs and intended to prepare us for future events by showing us the speaker's motives and designs. In these soliloquies, therefore, it is much less important that depth should be added to the character-study than that the audience should be provided with pointers to what is going on; thus they will not misunderstand the double game being played by Barabas,

[1] Cf. Wilson, op. cit., pp. 58 ff.

but will get some idea how his future intrigues are to be carried on. This type of soliloquy, which is very common in pre-Shakespearian drama, is almost always associated with villains and schemers. Lorenzo's soliloquies in *The Spanish Tragedy* are of the same kind, and those of Shakespeare's Richard III and Iago are also in this tradition.[1] It is a part of the convention that the principles which are at issue should be clearly expounded, and this is illustrated in one of Barabas's soliloquies in the fifth act:

> Thus hast thou gotten, by thy policy,
> No simple place, no small authority;
> I now am governor of Malta; true,
> But Malta hates me, and, in hating me,
> My life's in danger; and what boots it thee,
> Poor Barabas, to be the governor,
> Whenas thy life shall be at their command?
> No, Barabas, this must be look'd into;
> And, since by wrong thou gott'st authority,
> Maintain it bravely by firm policy;
> At least, unprofitably lose it not:
> For he that liveth by authority,
> And neither gets him friends, nor fills his bags,
> Lives like the ass that Aesop speaketh of,
> That labours with a load of bread and wine,
> And leaves it off to snap on thistle tops:
> But Barabas will be more circumspect.
> Begin betimes; Occasion's bald behind:
> Slip not thine opportunity, for fear too late
> Thou seek'st for much, but canst not compass it.
> (V. ii. 27–46)

At the same time remarks dropped in dialogue are taking over the functions of self-characterization and self-explanation. The various structural forms of the play are no longer sharply differentiated, therefore, like those of earlier days; they can be interchanged, and a balance between them is beginning to be struck.

Only once in *The Jew of Malta* is there a set speech which, by

[1] Cf. Schücking, *Character Problems*, esp. Chaps. I and V.

reason both of its length and its subject-matter, quite obviously falls outside the bounds of dialogue; this is when Barabas tells his newly-acquired slave Ithamore about his criminal dealings (II. iii. 175 ff.). And this speech happens to be one of the weakest and least convincingly motivated in the whole play;[1] it shows clearly the break in the portrayal of Barabas which becomes so strongly evident in the third and fourth acts.

In *The Massacre at Paris*, which has come down to us in a badly mutilated text offering little satisfactory basis for criticism,[2] there is nothing that can be called a real set speech, although at the beginning Guise delivers a rather long expository and self-revelatory soliloquy to which the comments just made might well be applied. Quite apart from the poor state of its text, the whole play was obviously written hastily and without care, and moreover without any particular inspiration. Not only is the plot muddled, obscure, and entirely lacking in urgency; even the vigour of the language, the weight and energy of expression which are so noteworthy in all of Marlowe's other plays, has deteriorated so much that Marlowe's authorship seems to be assured only for parts of the work, and it may therefore be left out of account in the present study.

Doctor Faustus

Marlowe's *Doctor Faustus*[3] signalizes a new stage in the history of English drama in so far as here for the first time a playwright embodied in dramatic form a symbolic representation of his own spiritual wrestlings. A spiritual conflict had, it is true, been dramatized in the Morality Plays – in *Everyman*, for example. There, however, it had been the universal human conflict between good and evil, entirely divorced from the individual standpoint of the playwright. In contrast to this, although to some extent he employs the same technique as the Moralities, Marlowe endows Faustus with his own personal problems, and dramatizes his own conflicting

[1] Cf. Poirier, op. cit., pp. 158 ff.

[2] Cf. Greg, *Marlowe's Doctor Faustus, 1604–1616*, p. 10.

[3] Greg is followed in placing *Faustus* late in Marlowe's development, though not later than *Edward II*.

ideas about the fundamental issues of human life.[1] Thus *Doctor Faustus* develops into a spiritual tragedy, in the sense that the external circumstances and events of the play no longer have any intrinsic value, but are significant only in so far as they enable us to understand Faustus's spiritual state and to see what goes on inside his mind. In this context we may disregard the interpolated episodes, which were provided partly as comic relief and partly to pander to the audience's fondness for spectacle; Marlowe's authorship of these episodes is very questionable, and in any case they do not represent the core of the play.[2] *Doctor Faustus* is, like *Tamburlaine*, a single-character play, in that the action proceeds entirely from the central figure and is entirely dependent on him; with the difference, however, that this action is not kept in motion, as in *Tamburlaine*, by the 'acting' and willing of the hero, but represents, as in *Everyman*, the temptations, conflicts, and inner struggles by which Faustus himself is beset. The other characters have therefore very little existence of their own; Faustus's antagonists are not human beings, but ultimately supernatural powers which ally themselves with the forces in his own soul.[3]

This specific pattern is responsible for some of the essential qualities in Faustus's speeches. Although his soliloquies and longer speeches do not by any means take up the greatest amount of space in the play, for it abounds in dialogue, they are nevertheless its lifeblood, and the most important part of what it has to say.

These speeches are the natural vehicle for the expression of the spiritual warfare and the conflicts of ideas that take place in Faustus himself, the successive stages of which also determine the external structure of the play. This no longer takes the form of parallel

[1] Here and later, cf. Ellis-Fermor, op. cit., Chap. V.

[2] Even in the other parts the state of the text makes judgement of the play difficult; however, as far as the thesis of this book is concerned, the comments made above can be justified in the face of all textual uncertainties. Cf. Greg, *The Tragical History of the Life and Death of Dr. Faustus: A Conjectural Reconstruction*, Oxford, 1950; *Marlowe's Doctor Faustus, 1604–1616* (esp. pp. 97 ff. for detailed discussion of the problem); Wilson, *Marlowe and the Early Shakespeare*.

[3] Cf. Poirier, op. cit., p. 114. Fischer, op. cit., p. 134, adopts a different standpoint.

scenes presenting contrasts or variations on a theme,[1] but is a true sequence of scenes which have their basis entirely in Faustus's own development. Thus Marlowe in this play advances a further step towards dramatic unity, towards a full internal coherence in the dramatic structure.[2] Not only is Faustus himself on the stage during the greater part of the play, not only does he sustain its spirit from beginning to end, but his speeches and soliloquies open before us a path of spiritual experience the different stages of which are organically related to one another. This was not the case in *Tamburlaine*. There the longer speeches merely represented variously stated expressions of the same mental attitude and of the same determination on the protagonist's part to impose his will on others; they cannot be said to give us any feeling of development in him.

The internal conflict which we see going on through all of Faustus's speeches and soliloquies may affect their structure and diction. This is to be seen happening already in the opening soliloquy, with which Goethe's presentation of Faust has so often been compared. Here is a short excerpt:

> '*Stipendium peccati mors est.*' Ha! '*Stipendium*,' *etc.*
> The reward of sin is death: that's hard. [*Reads.*
> '*Si pecasse negamus, fallimur*
> *Et nulla est in nobis veritas.*'
> If we say that we have no sin,
> We deceive ourselves, and there is no truth in us.
> Why, then, belike we must sin,
> And so consequently die;
> Ay, we must die an everlasting death.
> (I. i. 39–47)[3]

In this, as in many other passages, Latin or English sayings in the form of moral maxims and *dicta* are introduced, and at first sight it might seem that the same thing is being done here as was done by Seneca and his direct imitators in England, namely, that epigrams

[1] Cf. Schirmer, *Geschichte der englischen Literatur*, Vol. I 1954, p. 251.

[2] With the reservations applied to the text, however; see p. 148, note 2. Cf. also Wilson, op. cit., pp. 70 ff.

[3] This speech should probably be printed as prose; cf. Greg's *Conjectural Reconstruction*, p. 3.

and sententious maxims are being dragged in at every conceivable opportunity. But in *Faustus* these sayings have an entirely different function, both in the text of the play and in the train of thought. They are not just rhetorical adornments imposed on the speeches; they are judgements that Faustus arrives at for himself, truths that he lays out before himself for examination, and which call out in him new questions or contradictions. There is serious meaning in these maxims of his; they represent for him the heads round which his thoughts revolve.

Analysis of this soliloquy as a whole, as of the majority of Faustus's speeches and soliloquies, shows that in this play we have got away from the form of set speech which deals successively, according to a plan prescribed in advance, with stereotyped themes and motifs; in its place we have self-communion, which evolves according to the promptings of the moment. Up till this time the practice of systematizing the set speech and tricking it out with rhetorical devices had stifled and deadened the processes of real thought and feeling. Here, however, Faustus is actually thinking at the same time as he is speaking; the speech grows step by step, keeping pace with the progress of his thoughts, and this is a very significant fact for the future development of dramatic speech. The voicing of genuine doubt and irresolution has taken the place here of the old see-saw of argument and counter-argument, and instead of a character talking to himself, using his speech as a means of self-revelation for the benefit of the audience, we have true soliloquy; instead of quotations and maxims with a purely decorative function, we have personal judgements which the speaker has painfully arrived at by puzzling them out for himself.

There are some exceptions, of course. A few of Faustus's speeches follow the earlier method of providing internal directions for stage-business (e.g., I. iii. 1–15) or merely reporting action (e.g., III. i. 1–24). Others again are reminiscent of the wishful thinking that was so characteristic of Tamburlaine's speeches, for Faustus shares with Tamburlaine his aspirations towards the remote, the fabulous, and the unattainable.[1] In a good many passages, however, it is evident that a new language has been created to express hesitation

[1] Cf. I. i. 79–97; I. iii. 104–16.

and irresolution and the fluctuations of a mind torn by changing moods – for the expression, in short, of spiritual conflict. Thus the handling of the soliloquy in such a way that for the first time in English drama it reproduces the actual inner experience of a soliloquy has led in this play to the development of a new type of speech, and one that is unmistakably different from anything that had been heard before. This is illustrated in the following two short soliloquies, neither of which expresses any particular 'point of view', any 'plan', any *ad hoc* form of self-revelation; on the other hand, they both mirror exactly what goes on in Faustus's mind in those moments when he is alone:

> Now, Faustus, must
> Thou needs be damn'd, and canst thou not be sav'd.
> What boots it, then, to think on God or heaven?
> Away with such vain fancies, and despair;
> Despair in God, and trust in Belzebub:
> Now go not backward; Faustus, be resolute:
> Why waver'st thou? O, something soundeth in mine ear,
> 'Abjure this magic, turn to God again!'
> Ay, and Faustus will turn to God again.
> To God? he loves thee not;
> The God thou serv'st is thine own appetite,
> Wherein is fix'd the love of Belzebub:
> To him I'll build an altar and a church,
> And offer lukewarm blood of new-born babes.
>
> (II. i. 1–14)

> What might the staying of my blood portend?
> Is it unwilling I should write this bill?
> Why streams it not, that I may write afresh?
> *Faustus gives to thee his soul:* oh, there it stay'd!
> Why shouldst thou not? is not thy soul thine own?
> Then write again, *Faustus gives to thee his soul.*
>
> (II. i. 64–9)

It is not only in the soliloquies that we are made aware of these fluctuations and conflicts in Faustus's mind; this also happens in some of the speeches that he utters in the presence of others. These often have a passionate intensity which must suggest that Marlowe was translating into dramatic speech his own personal and most deeply experienced spiritual struggles (cf. II. ii. 18–32).[1] And this is a very remarkable, indeed astonishing, thing to find in the drama of this period, not excluding Shakespeare's.

Faustus's famous last soliloquy shows how these processes of thought and feeling may be given a setting in time, and here too the irrevocability of the fleeting time is emphasized by the stage-device of the clock that strikes the half-hours from eleven o'clock to midnight. This is one of the outstanding passages of pre-Shakespearian drama; W. W. Greg describes it as 'spiritual drama keyed to its highest pitch'.[2] Here are the first twenty lines or so:

[*The clock strikes eleven.*

Ah, Faustus,
Now hast thou but one bare hour to live,
And then thou must be damn'd perpetually.
Stand still, you ever moving spheres of heaven,
That time may cease, and midnight never come;
Fair Nature's eye, rise, rise again, and make
Perpetual day; or let this hour be but
A year, a month, a week, a natural day,
That Faustus may repent and save his soul!
O lente, lente currite, noctis equi!
The stars move still, time runs, the clock will strike,
The devil will come, and Faustus must be damn'd.
O, I'll leap up to my God! – Who pulls me down? –
See, see, where Christ's blood streams in the firmament!
One drop would save my soul, half a drop: ah, my Christ! –
Ah, rend not my heart for naming of my Christ!

[1] In the same way Tamburlaine's self-obsessed monologues might be regarded as a reflection of Marlowe's own personal preoccupations. However, the consciousness of two souls within his breast, the need to grapple with two alternatives, makes Faustus's speeches a species of dialogue with himself, a theatre of conflict.

[2] *Marlowe's Doctor Faustus, 1604–1616*, p. 10.

Yet will I call on him: O, spare me, Lucifer! –
Where is it now? 'tis gone: and see, where God
Stretcheth out his arm, and bends his ireful brows!
Mountains and hills, come, come, and fall on me,
And hide me from the heavy wrath of God!
No, no!
Then will I headlong run into the earth:
Earth, gape! O, no, it will not harbour me!

(V. ii. 136–60)

It is a very long way from this to the rhetorical rant of the common run of pre-Shakespearian tragic heroes when they are at the point of death. Here it is deep spiritual experience that is being transmuted into drama, reproduced with unexampled immediacy and verisimilitude in the diction and imagery, and, too, in the exclamatory character of the soliloquy.[1] This is a true soliloquy, the utterance of a tragic hero who is overcome by a sense of desertion in the agony of his returning self-knowledge and his realization that he must carry on his struggle completely unaided. The tendency towards abstract thinking which elsewhere marks Faustus's speeches has been replaced here by the capacity to see spiritual abstractions in concrete terms as visible figures and actions, so that the spiritual conflict is transformed into something that happens before our eyes. It impresses itself on us so strongly as 'happening' for the further reason that here, probably for the first time in pre-Shakespearian drama, time is made a part of the very substance of the speech; the swift and irresistible passing of that final hour before midnight is conveyed by the unrealistic but in the dramatic sense unusually effective compression of this period of time into a speech of fifty-eight lines.[2] It is true that the soliloquy opens with the conventional apostrophe to the heavenly spheres to stand still and the appeal to the sun to go on shining through the night. However, in this instance both appeals have their rise in Faustus's horror at the unstayable passing of time. They are not just dragged in from outside, and then immediately forgotten; the image is kept alive, so that a few lines later we read, 'The stars move still . . .' The same is

[1] Cf. Ellis-Fermor, op. cit., p. 68.

[2] Cf. Levin, op. cit., p. 128.

true of the later invocation to the stars (ll. 160 ff.) and the images of heaven and the clouds, which are instinct with the agonized impotence of the soul that is shut off from all hope of salvation and is 'damn'd perpetually'. Desire and the frustration of desire, aspiration and its violent disappointment, here affect the character of the language itself, down to the very movement of the sentence and the choice of diction. The thrusting together within a single line of two short statements, the second of which negatives the first and despairingly acknowledges it as something impossible of fulfilment, may be classed as a form of antithesis, but it is antithesis which has ceased to be a mere rhetorical trick, because in this case it has been overlaid with reality. The tendency in the language towards a lapidary conciseness and direct simplicity, already apparent in a few of the dialogue-passages, but also to the fore in the present speech, suggests that a new type of subject-matter and a remarkable intensification of experience have forced the playwright to seek out new forms of expression and style. In passages like this we find Marlowe's most mature dramatic writing, and the power with which Faustus's spiritual experience is conveyed in certain scenes of the play places *Doctor Faustus*, for all its deficiencies, at the very summit of Marlowe's achievement.

Edward II

In *Edward II* we encounter the same artistic problem as faced us in *The Jew of Malta*. For here is a play which on the one hand shows close structural affinities with the chronicle plays, in that it has a stirring plot with a rapid flow of incident and plenty of variety, while on the other hand it has points of contact with tragedy in its attempts to bring on to the stage heart-rending scenes filled with passionate utterances, deep pathos, and high tragic dignity.[1] Another striking thing about the play is that the kinds of situation which, at an earlier stage in the evolution of English drama, would have been turned into entirely static episodes or declamatory show-

[1] Much has been written about the novel features of this play as a tragedy of character and a tragic history, and about its structure, its characterization, and its content. See, e.g., Ellis-Fermor, Levin, Poirier, Boas, Wilson, Briggs.

pieces by a series of long and exaggeratedly rhetorical set speeches, here take the form of swiftly unfolding scenes of action containing a good deal of well-developed dialogue. Examples of this are the baiting of the King by the Barons (I. i. 74–133, I. iv. 8–93), the King's parting from Gaveston (I. iv. 106–69), his grief and mourning at Gaveston's departure (I. iv. 304 ff.), and his triumph at the defeat of the rebellious Barons (IV. iii. 1 ff.). The new dramatic technique employed in these and certain other episodes brings into prominence a whole variety of changing motive forces in the play; it enables us to apprehend all these episodes with great vividness as real actions carried out by the characters with and against one another. Moreover, we no longer find odd moments singled out from the course of events and raised to an artificial intensity by means of set declamations – mere pictures, so to speak, though given the illusion of life; instead, we seem ourselves to be participating in what is taking place.

In *Edward II* it is made quite clear that the characters not only carry the emotional burden of the play, but also sustain its plot; on the other hand, it is equally clear that the plot is not solely dependent on what they do. Marlowe has struck a balance between a plot whose events are directed by its hero and one which develops independently of him and reacts upon him. It is true that the King sets certain events in motion, but he has also to maintain a passive role in the plot. This plot is broken up into a great many separate episodes, most of them quite short, but we can follow it as a close-knit, coherent and logical chain of cause and effect, for in all the episodes the person and character of the King are in some way involved. Thus Marlowe made an appreciable advance towards what is commonly described as 'character-drama', but he was not equally successful all along the line. He was so intent on creating a fast-moving plot, especially in the earlier part of the play, that he did not leave himself enough room to develop the emotional significance of particular moments and to work out his situations in an unhurried way. The scenes follow one another much too quickly, and there are too many of them; they do not take root in our memory, as do the scenes in Shakespeare's histories from *Richard III* onwards, which by themselves form pictures with a symbolic impact and remain unforgettably in our minds as miniature plays in their own right. For all his skill in complicating the plot, the composition, especially in the first two-thirds of the play, is hurried and breathless, and nothing is carried through to its proper conclusion. For long stretches the language is entirely factual and its choice is determined by the practical consideration of keeping the plot moving; it supplies information, instruction, explanation, question and answer, and is all the time concerned solely with externalities. There are moments, indeed, when the emotional atmosphere begins to grow more intense, but the poetic power which is necessary to translate it into words almost at once fades away. We get no further than isolated outbursts of feeling, which are too abruptly handled and do not impart their tone to the accompanying dialogue in the scene. Thus Marlowe's new dramatic technique conveyed too little of what the set speech had earlier given us too much of. He had not yet found for himself a language which, like that of Shakespearian tragedy, was capable of representing every kind of incident concretely, and which was at one and the same time succinct, emotionally satisfying, and forceful in expression. Even in *Edward II* he was still hovering uncertainly between two different levels of style; he could not reconcile his poet's command of language with his capabilities as a dramatist.[1]

This discrepancy is particularly noticeable in scenes in which some approach is made towards the expression of emotion but is not sufficiently followed up. An example of this occurs in Act I, Scene iv, where Edward falls into a monologue as he is grieving over Gaveston's departure, and will not pay any attention to the Queen and the other persons on the stage:

[*Re-enter the* KING, *mourning.*

K.Edw. He's gone, and for his absence thus I mourn.
Did never sorrow go so near my heart
As doth the want of my sweet Gaveston;
And could my crown's revenue bring him back,
I would freely give it to his enemies,
And think I gain'd, having bought so dear a friend.

[1] Cf. Tucker Brooke, *The Works*, p. 309.

Q.Isab. Hark, how he harps upon his minion.
K.Edw. My heart is as an anvil unto sorrow,
Which beats upon it like the Cyclops' hammers,
And with the noise turns up my giddy brain,
And makes me frantic for my Gaveston.
Ah, had some bloodless Fury rose from hell,
And with my kingly sceptre struck me dead,
When I was forc'd to leave my Gaveston.
Lan. *Diablo!* What passions call you these.
Q.Isab. My gracious lord, I come to bring you news.
K.Edw. That you have parled with your Mortimer.
Q.Isab. That Gaveston, my lord, shall be repeal'd.
(I. iv. 304 ff.)

Here is a formal lament of the familiar type, but it is cut short, and we are immediately plunged into matter-of-fact dialogue. The earlier lament of the Queen when Edward repulses her is even more abruptly cut short (I. iv. 163 ff.), as is that of the younger Spencer when Edward is led away (IV. vi. 99 ff.).

Just the same kind of discrepancy may be observed in the soliloquies, especially those in the early part of the play. In these soliloquies the mythological imagery and classical parallels and the rhetorical exaggeration of the curses and protestations seem to be based on the stylistic pattern of the earlier classical tragedies, and they are curiously at variance with the very different language of their context.[1]

On one occasion, in the second half of the play, the Queen embarks on a speech of welcome to her friends on their return to England; this quickly gives place to mournful reflections on the state of affairs then prevailing, and then she goes on to appeal to the absent Edward. At this point the younger Mortimer interrupts her:

Nay, madam, if you be a warrior,
You must not grow so passionate in speeches.
(IV. iv. 15–16)

[1] Cf. Gaveston, I. i. 50–72; Queen, I. iv. 170–86; also the dialogue between the two Mortimers, I. iv. 384–418.

This interruption of Mortimer's seems to be symptomatic of what Marlowe himself did on more than one occasion when 'passionate speeches' showed signs of breaking into his play. He was sensible that long-drawn set speeches in the manner of Tamburlaine would act as clogs on his new technique of rapid movement.[1] But apart from this consideration, he must have felt that for King Edward, whom he put into the play more as a passive than an active character, an entirely different style of speech must be adopted from Tamburlaine's passionate, highly eloquent declarations of his purposes, which stand as substitutes for action. The speech-technique especially of the later scenes enables us to see that active emotion has resolved itself into a tragic passivity, to correspond with which new forms of expression have had to be created.

It is not until the second half of the play that the set speech once more comes into its own as a legitimate feature of the dramatic architecture. Marlowe now deliberately employs this medium in order to make it clear that Edward's role is that of a martyr, and in order to awaken our sympathies for him in his suffering and to invest his figure with pathos, dignity and a measure of splendour. In the first half Edward's role is to a larger extent that of an active participant in the action; in this second part he comes to the fore much more as a sensitive and suffering soul, and not the least effective means of creating this impression is the entirely different language, much more intense than that of the first part, by which he is made to reveal himself. In about the middle of the play Edward's awakening to the necessity of resisting the Barons and the change in him from apathy to activity are indicated by means of a set speech containing the great vow of vengeance that he utters on his knees (III. i. 128 ff.); so now, after the reversal of his fortunes, his new role as a passive sufferer is also inaugurated by means of speeches that are given special prominence. However, it is noteworthy that what would earlier have been a speech of self-revelation in the form of outright monologue is now addressed to another person and is accompanied by stage-business. As far as subject-matter is concerned, the words that Edward addresses to the Abbot are the same as those which princes who had fallen from prosperity

[1] See Briggs's note on IV. iv. 41, in his edn. of *Edward II.*

into misfortune had been in the habit of repeating in English tragedy from the time of *Gorboduc* onwards. This time, however, it is not the sympathy of the audience that is indirectly being invited, as in earlier examples, but that of the Abbot; and since various of the other persons present are addressed in turn, the whole speech gives an effect of dramatic compression, and of belonging naturally to the dialogue-sequence of which it forms a part:

> Father, thy face should harbour no deceit.
> O, hadst thou ever been a king, thy heart,
> Pierced deeply with sense of my distress,
> Could not but take compassion of my state.
> Stately and proud, in riches and in train,
> Whilom I was, powerful, and full of pomp:
> But what is he whom rule and empery
> Have not in life or death made miserable?
> Come, Spencer; come, Baldock, come, sit down by me;
> Make trial now of that philosophy,
> That in our famous nurseries of arts
> Thou suckedst from Plato and from Aristotle.
> Father, this life contemplative is heaven.
> O that I might this life in quiet lead.
> But we, alas, are chas'd; and you, my friends,
> Your lives and my dishonour they pursue.
> Yet, gentle monks, for treasure, gold nor fee,
> Do you betray us and our company.
>
> (IV. vi. 8–25)

Whereas in this scene there are only comparatively short self-revelatory speeches of this kind (cf. 37 ff., 61 ff.), the central interest of the next scene, the scene which represents the abdication of the King, lies in two long set speeches, the longest in the whole play. The way in which Marlowe uses these two speeches brings out once more his powerful sense of drama; they add depth to the symbolic procedure of handing over the crown, and in them the figure of the King is endued with a genuine pathos very different from the impression he gave at the beginning of the play. Here Marlowe has contrived one of those great situations, packed with significance, which would be sure to call out the deepest sympathy and interest in the audience of his day. And at this moment he deliberately slows down the tempo, and makes of this episode a profoundly moving spectacle which, like the penultimate scene in the dungeon, is thrown into relief, by means of its concentration and the detail with which it is developed, against the rapidity of movement that marks the other scenes.

These abdication-speeches, which have often been compared with the great abdication-speech in Shakespeare's *Richard II* (IV. i),[1] show how Marlowe set about the task of creating a form of self-revelation which should reflect both past and present circumstances, and thereby make this episode the focal point of the plot; and also of bringing out the vehemence with which the King's passions are torn between conflicting impulses – an effect which is much more vividly produced here than in Shakespeare's play. Once again, as in *Doctor Faustus*, we see the attempt to portray a spiritual conflict through the medium of the set speech. Moreover, the various elements that form the subject-matter, the review of the situation, the self-contemplation, the inner conflict, and the epigrammatic summing-up of the moral, all these things, together with the stage-business and the way in which the speaker interrupts his own reflections to address the bystanders, combine to produce a new form of set speech; and it is one which, even if some of its motifs remind us of the declamation and emotionalism of past days, is much more successful than the earlier type as dramatic self-expression, and is at the same time more closely in tune with the situation presented on the stage. Even now we have not completely got away from sententious maxims, such as

> But what are kings, when regiment is gone,
> But perfect shadows in a sunshine day?
>
> (V. i. 26–7)

However, passages of this nature, in their very versification emphasizing the independence of the single line, are very much in the minority. The speeches now display a greater homogeneity of structure and a subordination of the individual parts to the total

[1] Cf. Briggs, op. cit., 182–3.

effect, and this is reflected even in the verse-structure, in contradistinction to that of *Tamburlaine.*[1] Just as he does in *Faustus*, Marlowe succeeds here in making the speeches express what is at that very moment going on in the speaker's mind, but this time he adds external action as well in the gestures of the King and the reactions of the other characters (e.g., V. i. 96–111).Thus we are now well on the way towards the dramatized and fully dramatic set speech which Shakespeare was to handle with such consummate mastery, and which he was to endow with new profundities of thought and feeling.

Dido, Queen of Carthage

Marlowe's *Tragedy of Dido, Queen of Carthage* remains to be dealt with, and it has designedly been taken last, at the very end of this survey of the development of the set speech in Marlovian drama. The majority of critics regard this as the earliest of Marlowe's plays. In its original version it undoubtedly dates from his Cambridge days; but if we examine the way in which he handles the speeches in certain passages, we must accept as probable the conjecture put forward by Tucker Brooke that he revised it very much later, perhaps even at the time when he was writing *Edward II.*[2] Aeneas's long narrative account of the fall of Troy is still typical of the circumstantial report-speech, while Dido's extravagant promises, rising to their climax in alluring wish-fulfilment dreams, are close to those of Tamburlaine both in content and in style of utterance (e.g., III. i. 112–32; IV. iv. 44–54; IV. iv. 93 ff.). On the other hand, we may extract from the parting-scene one of the farewell-speeches of Dido in which she passionately woos Aeneas when he is straining to be off; here the movingly dramatic language has very little in common with the style of the earlier period, and it presupposes just those

[1] Cf. Tucker Brooke, 'Marlowe's Versification and Style', *SP*, XIX, pp. 186–205.

[2] Tucker Brooke, *The Works*, pp. 387–8. However, in his account of Renaissance literature in *Literary History of England*, ed. A. C. Baugh (New York, 1948, p. 515), Tucker Brooke expresses the view that *Dido* is Marlowe's first play.

developments that were discussed in the last section in relation to *Edward II*:

Aen. Then let me go, and never say farewell.
Did. 'Let me go; farewell; I must from hence.'
These words are poison to poor Dido's soul:
O, speak like my Aeneas, like my love!
Why look'st thou toward the sea? the time hath been
When Dido's beauty chain'd thine eyes to her.
Am I less fair than when thou saw'st me first?
O, then, Aeneas, 'tis for grief of thee!
Say thou wilt stay in Carthage with thy queen,
And Dido's beauty will return again.
Aeneas, say, how canst thou take thy leave?
Wilt thou kiss Dido? O, thy lips have sworn
To stay with Dido! canst thou take her hand?
(V. i. 109–121)

This is no longer mere set declamation, divorced from the situation that is being enacted and losing itself in a torrent of emotional verbiage; these words of Dido's rise immediately out of the situation, and the fact of Aeneas's presence is conveyed in every emotion and every movement implied by her speech. The same thing may be observed in the final speech of farewell (V. i. 155–92), and in Dido's speech from the walls of Carthage, where she displays such a highly dramatic agitation as she follows Aeneas's departure with her eyes and thinks she sees him turning about to come back to her. The very free handling of the richly modulated blank verse, the diction which is likewise freed from all constraint by the force of passion and the exploitation of the telling moment, the partial renunciation of metaphorical ornament in favour of a greater directness: all these things point to the fact that we are here faced with a style of set speech very far removed from the melodramatic tirades of Tamburlaine.

11

Peele

Compared with the plays of Marlowe, the work of George Peele marks a retrogression as far as the process of 'dramatizing' the set speech and making it an integral part of the dramatic composition is concerned. Peele had no talent for dramatic structure,[1] for consistency in the handling of plot and the portayal of character, for the harmonious interdependence of the various elements that make up the whole play; he had no sense of proportion, of order, of dramatic architecture. On the other hand, he possessed strongly marked powers of expression and a real gift for the effective presentation of individual episodes and situations. To do justice to Peele's plays, we must not judge them according to the normally accepted standards of dramatic unity and structure; they must be judged by criteria that are appropriate to their special character.

The Arraignment of Paris

Peele's very first play, *The Arraignment of Paris* (before 1584), gives a good idea of the diversity of types that could at that time come under the heading of drama. The work is a pastoral drama with a mythological basis which adopts essential features from the *genres* both of the masque and of the pageant. It is a pleasant mixture of mythological pageantry,[2] symbolic and allegorical representation

[1] Cf. the informative discussion of structure and plotting in Peele's plays by A. M. Sampley, 'Plot Structure in Peele's Plays', *PMLA*, LI, 1936. On the chronology see H. M. Dowling, 'The Date and Order of Peele's Plays', *NQ*, Series 2, 1933, p. 164; D. Horne in *The Life and Minor Works of George Peele*, ed. C. T. Prouty, 1952.

[2] 'This is not so much a play as a pastoral pageant' – T. M. Parrott and R. H. Ball, *A Short View of Elizabethan Drama*, p. 67.

by means both of mute and of vigorous 'speaking' tableaux, songs, lyrical interludes, and set speeches; and in furnishing so agreeable a feast for both eye and ear, it was bound to be a success with audiences of its time. Such a loose combination of spectacular scenes with lyrical interludes and purely decorative episodes at once suggests comparisons with the modern revue. There is indeed, as in all Peele's plays, a thread of plot running through the whole thing, but it is so often interrupted, and so many distracting episodes are grafted on to it, that it cannot by any means be regarded as the most important element in the play, nor can it serve as a starting-point for criticism.

The various episodes must in fact be judged as independent tableaux. The looseness of the connexion between them allows of and at times even prompts a use of the set speech that comes close to what were earlier described as 'self-sufficient declamatory insertions'. In this play, however, the emphasis is laid, not on the rhetorical quality of the declamation, but on its lyrical decorativeness. This is illustrated in the very first scene, when Flora enters and in the presence of Pan, Faunus, Silvanus and Pomona delivers a set speech extolling the beauty of the flowers:

> ... The water-flowers and lilies on the banks,
> Like blazing comets, burgen all in ranks;
> Under the hawthorn and the poplar-tree,
> Where sacred Phoebe may delight to be,
> The primerose, and the purple hyacinth,
> The dainty violet, and the wholesome minth,
> The double daisy, and the cowslip, queen
> Of summer flowers, do overpeer the green;
> And round about the valley as ye pass,
> Ye may ne see for peeping flowers the grass.
>
> (I. i. 57–66)

Even as here a glorious carpet of flowers is spread before us, so in a later passage this world of flowers is peopled with the appropriate birds and beasts (I. i. 112 ff.), in the next scene fables are recounted from classical mythology (I. ii. 16 ff.), and in Act II we are regaled with the story of Echo. However, it would be beside the point here to look for dramatic relevance, consistency of background with character, and things of that kind. Like the songs, these passages are delightfully decorative and full of charm, and they are worthy of note for their euphonious rhymed couplets and their felicitous, richly-coloured diction; according to their nature they represent the grafting of purely lyrical or of lyrical narrative buds on to the original stock of the play, but they are not in any sense assimilated, nor are the changes of tone prepared for.

Even where there are genuine speech-episodes which develop the actual theme of the play, the contest of the three goddesses and the judgement of Paris, there is nothing in the nature of dramatic tension in the speeches. There is the same gracious leisureliness in the style, the same decorativeness and elegance in the diction, though for the most part it has also a limpid clarity. The dispute of the goddesses, which has enabled Peele to return to the long-standing tradition of the dramatic debate, does not work up to any sort of dramatic situation; indeed Peele was less interested here in dramatic climaxes than he was in the beauty of his diction and the euphony of his speeches, which are interchanged like formal addresses on a ceremonial occasion. In Paris's long speech for the defence before the council of the gods in Act IV we have of course a typical 'oration', and it is actually designated as such in the text.[1] Here too we see how the 'judicial speech' which belongs traditionally to the 'tribunal scene' is adapted to the sphere of mythological pastoral drama. Peele has abandoned all rhetorical flourishes and metaphorical adornments, as well as learned allusions, and the speech is an example of his ability to write in a language that is not only mellifluous, but uninflated, crystal clear, and absolutely pure; it illustrates also his confident handling of a supple blank verse – and this too before Marlowe. Paris defends himself with grace, self-assurance, and conviction; his arguments are as judiciously chosen as they are unforced in their orderly sequence. The elegant blank verse with its frequent enjambement and extended periods gives his speech an entirely natural flow. In other words, this is a conventional 'rhetorical' set speech without the rhetoric; it has eloquence without the

[1] 'PARIS' oration to the Council of the Gods.'

usual string of tropes and figures.[1] Gone are the carefully balanced clauses of the pleading-speeches in *Gorboduc*, the ordered accumulation of arguments, appeals, and sententious observations; in their place we now have fluent, straightforward exposition which carries conviction more by reason of the ideas put forward than of the language employed, and yet does so without any lowering in its dignity of expression. Peele seems in fact to have attained to a new ease in the technique of the set speech, an ease which shines through even so essentially 'rhetorical' a passage as this.

But it would be wrong to use what Peele achieved on this single occasion as a standard by which to measure his handling of the set speech in other plays. This style of writing was well within his powers, but he showed no special preference for it. He experiments with language in just the same way as he experiments with the various dramatic *genres* and techniques and combines them with one another. The '*Atlas* of Poetrie and *primus verborum artifex*',[2] as Peele was called by his contemporaries, was up to all the tricks of the trade as they were understood in his day. Yet it is just from the point of view of their language that his plays have so far failed to receive serious consideration. A study of this side of them would show that the 'manifold varietie of inuention'[3] that Nashe so warmly applauded is revealed even more pronouncedly in Peele's infinite variety of language and the bold transitions between the different levels of style and diction than in the features on which the critics have concentrated, and as a rule with disapproval:[4] that is, the incoherent succession of heterogeneous episodes, where tragic and comic incidents jostle one another, and scenes relevant to the plot are mingled with wholly irrelevant interludes. For it is the language that not only heightens the interest of what is from the point of view of plot an unsatisfactory hotch-potch, but also invests it with a special charm of its own. This command over so wide a range of

[1] Instead of 'word-figures' Peele uses 'thought-figures', such as anticipation of the arguments that an opponent might use.

[2] Nashe, Preface to Greene's *Menaphon*, 1589.

[3] Nashe, loc. cit.

[4] Cf. already A. W. Ward, *English Dramatic Literature*, London, 1889, Vol. I, pp. 366 ff.; Creizenach, *Das englische Drama im Zeitalter Shakespeares*, Halle, 1916, Vol. I, pp. 570–87.

tone and style must have contributed substantially to the great esteem in which Peele's plays were held.

Edward I

This mastery is especially apparent in *Edward I* (before 1593), a play which ought to be of interest not only for the position it holds in the history of the chronicle play – so far it has usually been this aspect of it that has been treated[1] – but also and chiefly for the language it employs. We have already seen in *Locrine* how the linguistic unity of the English Senecan drama was shattered when in a single scene realistic prose dialogue stood cheek by jowl with set declamation. In *Edward I* this intermingling of styles is carried a stage further. In *Locrine* the prose had been reserved for the low-life characters, especially the clowns; the two levels of style had been kept distinct, without any cross-influence between them. In *Edward I*, on the other hand, this rigid distinction has very largely been done away with, and in one and the same speech we may pass from dignified, highly decorated diction to colloquial prose, as for example in Longshanks's speech at X. 264 ff., and Elinor's at X. 180 ff. Exalted personages such as these at one moment use stilted, bombastic, and generally rhetorical language and deliver 'orations' that run true to type, and the next moment, often within the same scene, they drop into speech that is natural, familiar, and realistic. As a result the language of the play as a whole lacks uniformity; it has a variegated texture in which soaring, passionate blank verse in the manner of Marlowe, speeches in a pedantically regular measure, lyrical passages, vehement dialogue in realistic prose, and an extravagantly fanciful manner of speech jostle one another quite indiscriminately. The intermingling of different metres adds to and emphasizes the diversity of the style. However, Peele does not use all this manifold variety in his language as a means of differentiating his *dramatis personae*. There are no signs yet of the association of a particular way of speaking with a particular character, such as we are later to find in Shakespeare and such as was constantly aimed

[1] Cf. F. Schelling, *The English Chronicle Play*, New York, 1902, passim.

at in the idiom of Tamburlaine. Peele, as we have already seen, is always very much more interested in the effect of the individual episode, and he pays no regard to anything that precedes or follows it. It is in the episode that he displays his sense of drama, and according to the requirements of the episode that he moulds his diction. Many of these episodes involve pageants of one kind or another, splendid processions of royal personages with their retinues, triumphal entries, official receptions, coronation-scenes, and the like.[1] The stage-directions at the beginnings of the scenes, often long and detailed, make it clear enough how closely these scenes approximate to set tableaux. The set speeches take their place within this framework as the most important part of the ritual; they belong to the ceremoniousness of the court life that is depicted. They are a representational and impersonal means of heightening the effect of the tableau or of the events being enacted, which are similarly representational. Thus the *genus demonstrativum* is the commonest of the rhetorical species represented in the set speeches: the speech of salutation[2] for instance, the panegyric,[3] the speech of incitement,[4] or the speech of homage.[5] In the very first scene there are examples of such speeches which, like descriptive titles on oil-paintings, fill out what has already before this been pictured on the stage. The patriotic lines on England that are put into the mouth of the Queen Mother provide a good illustration:

> Illustrious England, ancient seat of Kings,
> Whose chivalry hath royalised thy fame,
> That sounding bravely through terrestrial vale,
> Proclaiming conquests, spoils and victories,
> Rings glorious echoes through the farthest world; . . .
>
> (I. 11 ff.)

Alternatively the set speech may serve as a kind of representational introduction to the stately pageantry which immediately follows it. For instance, the lines just quoted from the Queen Mother's speech run straight on into a description of how the King will return in

[1] On the pageantry see Venezky, *Pageantry on the Elizabethan Stage.*
[2] Cf. Scenes I and III.
[3] III. 74 ff.
[4] Scenes XIII and XIV.
[5] Scene III.

triumph from his crusade (ll. 27 ff.). And the speech is scarcely ended when to the sounding of trumpets the King himself enters in great state attended by a large retinue, as we are informed in some detail in the stage-direction. A little later occurs the following passage, which exemplifies the use of the set speech as the 'word-illustration', so to speak, to the stage tableau previously set for us by means of the stage-direction:

> *The Queen-Mother being set on the one side, and Queen Elinor on the other, the King sitteth in the midst, mounted highest, and at his feet the ensign underneath him.*
>
> O glorious Capitol! beauteous senate-house!
> Triumphant Edward, how, like sturdy oaks,
> Do these thy soldiers circle thee about,
> To shield and shelter thee from winter's storms! . . .
>
> (I. 101 ff.)

In the great coronation scene (Sc. III), after the crowning of the Scottish king Baliol, Queen Elinor addresses a few gracious words of greeting and felicitation to him; and then, without any preparation beyond the direction 'QUEEN ELINOR'S *speech*', she embarks in highly poetic terms on a panegyric of the King and herself:

> The welkin, spangled through with golden spots,
> Reflects no finer in a frosty night
> Than lovely Longshanks in his Elinor's eye:
> So, Ned, thy Nell in every part of thee,
> Thy person's guarded with a troop of queens,
> And every queen as brave as Elinor.
>
> (III. 74 ff.)

Here her homage is expressed in the form of a lyrical poem transplanted bodily into the play; it is labelled indeed as a 'speech', but it is not in any way a dramatic speech. Nor is it a speech that is especially characteristic of the Queen, or one that takes into account the part she plays elsewhere, for her anti-English attitude has already been clearly established in the first scene (I. 229 ff.). That fact, however, is entirely forgotten here, for it was in accordance with convention that the Queen should deliver a formal panegyric on a ceremonial occasion of this nature.[1]

The surprising thing, however, is that this same Queen Elinor, who is capable of delivering such well composed and elaborately lyrical speeches, should in another place, even though she is making a triumphal entry with her full train, drop into a totally different idiom:

> Give me my pantables.
> Fie, this hot weather, how it makes me sweat!
> Heigh-ho, my heart! ah, I am passing faint!
> Give me my fan that I may cool my face.
> Hold, take my mask, but see you rumple it not.
> This wind and dust, see how it smolders me!
> Some drink, good Gloucester, or I die for drink!
> (VI. 1 ff.)

Here Elinor uses a colloquial, realistic diction accompanied by animated movements and lively play of the features; the conventional, stylized speech of a queen has given place to the impatient, irritable language of an imperious and temperamental woman. Here palpably is an idiom which carries us into the world of comedy; and this is done even more obviously in the extremely fast-moving, vigorous dialogue in the later part of the scene, and reaches its climax when the capricious Elinor boxes her husband's ears (note especially ll. 85 ff.).

Such a mixture of styles brings about some surprising and occasionally abrupt transitions, and this at times within a single speech. In the following passage, for example, Longshanks and Elinor are talking about the newly born prince:

Longsh. In good time, madam; he is your own; lap him as you list: but I promise thee, Nell, I would not for ten thousand pounds the country should take unkindness at thy words.

Elin. 'Tis no marvel, sure; you have been royally received at their hands.
No, Ned, but that thy Nell doth want her will,

[1] Cf. E. M. W. Tillyard, *Shakespeare's History Plays*, London, 1948, pp. 103–4.

Her boy should glister like the summer's sun,
In robes as rich as Jove when he triumphs.
His pap should be of precious nectar made,
His food ambrosia – no earthly woman's milk,
(X. 175 ff.)

Here certain conventional features of the declamatory set speech – the crescendo of comparisons attached to the various things that are associated with the baby prince – are employed by way of *amplificatio* to add both to the decorativeness and to the dignity of the dialogue. Peele was of course thoroughly familiar with all the tricks of style, the comparison that adds dignity,[1] the epic simile,[2] anaphora,[3] the apostrophe,[4] synonyms,[5] alliteration, and many other rhetorical figures. He did not make an immoderate use of them, but employed them sparingly. It cannot be said, however, that he uses them with discrimination, or with a conscious functional purpose. While it is true that he knew his way about the whole keyboard of language, he had not yet the ability to create with this instrument a dramatic orchestration capable of expressing inner connexions and effecting subtle transitions. Whenever the opportunity presented itself, he surrendered himself to the beauty of word-music, or to special effects whether of language or situation. Lyrical poet and word-artist as he was, he did not allow his gifts in these directions to be held in check by the dramatist in him.

The Battle of Alcazar

Beside the rich variety of style and language in *Edward I*, *The Battle of Alcazar* (1588/9) makes a retrograde step, and it offers little that is new.[6] Although Peele's other plays show that he had already developed far beyond such methods, in this clumsy and unsophisticated piece he is obviously applying to certain clearly

[1] X. 182, 235, 266.
[2] XXV. 20.
[3] E.g., XXXIII. 27; XXV. 118.
[4] E.g., II. 342; XXIV. 202, 208.
[5] E.g., III. 11.
[6] Criticism of the play is made difficult by the fact that the text is an abridgement, which has affected the style for the worse. Cf. W. W. Greg, *Two Elizabethan Stage Abridgments*, 1922; Horne, op. cit., pp. 77 ff.

defined themes the familiar technique of scene-structure and set speeches that is characteristic of early Elizabethan tragedies such as *Gorboduc*. Peele tried his hand at plays of every type, and with *The Battle of Alcazar*, which in some points shows the influence also of *Tamburlaine* and *The Spanish Tragedy*, he adopted the manner of the classical tragedy. The various acts are introduced by a Presenter, and the first and last also by dumb shows, and very little movement takes place within the scenes, so that no interaction is developed between the characters, who for the most part merely confront one another with long, static set speeches. There is a notable lack of dramatic suspense and of variety in the episodes, except in the last act; in most scenes we are shown representatives of only one of the parties, and as they are in agreement on principles, they merely exchange their views. There are scarcely any encounters of opposites, and no real dramatic conflicts, although the plot offers opportunities for them. As in the classical drama, all genuinely dramatic motives and occurrences have been left outside the play, so that the scenes enacted before us consist very largely of episodes with a minimum of suspense – of such matter as the exchange of greetings and of information, or the concluding of decisions. And for these purposes the set speech is a suitable medium. Naturally the characters have no properly sustained roles; they are paraded before us in a series of separate, clearly differentiated situations: before their fall, at the zenith of their fortunes, after their fall. How these situations arise out of one another is not, however, made clear. The play gives the impression therefore of a succession of tableaux in which merely static situations are presented. All the actions that ought to proceed from the plot, or be shown as incidental to it, are clumsily relegated to the speeches. In addition to the speeches which provide explanation or information, there are a few passages of high-flown emotional rhetoric, and the disparity between the two styles and the absence of transitional matter are strongly marked. The Moor, Muly Mahamet, is the principal mouthpiece for these flights of passion, and they take the form of outbursts of despair or execration (e.g., II. iii. 1 ff.; V. i. 74 ff.). With the help of such devices as the repetition and sheer accumulation of words, thrown into glaring relief by means of alliteration, a blood-curdling effect is intended to be produced by these outbursts, which are characterized by Muly's consort (II. iii. 16) as 'these huge exclaims':

> Cursed mayst thou be for such a cursed son!
> Cursed be thy son with every curse thou hast!
> Ye elements of whom consists this clay,
> This mass of flesh, this cursed crazed corpse,
> Destroy, dissolve, disturb, and dissipate,
> What water, earth, and air congeal'd.
>
> (V. i. 87–92)

The piling together of verbal artifices in this way, reminiscent as it is of *The Spanish Tragedy*, was not a thing that Peele excelled in; his talent lay rather in the lyricism and the dignity that he imparted to the set speech, and *The Battle of Alcazar* therefore displays but little of his artistry in language at its best.

David and Bethsabe

Much the same may be said of *The Love of King David and Fair Bethsabe* (1592–4),[1] probably the only dramatized version in that period of a Bible story. Here too declamation takes up far the greatest part of the play, and dialogue of a more natural type appears in only a few places, as in the drinking episode (III. 248–309). However, there is much more lyricism in the speeches, and practically every opportunity is seized of giving rhapsodic descriptions of both human and natural beauty.[2] In order to provide occasions for lyrical descriptions of this kind, the characters are kept in a sort of artificial isolation from one another; instead of speaking directly to one

[1] On the date cf. Horne, op. cit., p. 92; I. Ekeblad, *English Stud.*, 1958. Earlier critics preferred a date between 1587 and 1592.

[2] Cf. from the first scene Bethsabe's song and her speech to Zephyr (I. i ff.; I. 11 ff.), and David's speech (I. 26 ff.); also and especially Absalon's invitation to David to spend the 'sheep-feast on the plain of Hazor' with him (III. 158 ff.):

> The time of year is pleasant for your grace;
> And gladsome summer in her shady robes,
> Crowned with roses and with painted flowers,
> With all her nymphs, shall entertain my lord,
> That, from the thicket of my verdant groves,
> Will sprinkle honey dews about his breast . . .

another, they stand there side by side but without much apparent contact, and instead of a colloquy we find a couple of lyrical speeches placed formally one after the other. Thus Bethsabe is introduced to us in the first scene, where she provides in her 'song' a fine specimen of the Elizabethan lyric; she goes on to apostrophize Zephyr, while David, sitting apart ('*sits above viewing her*'), for his part provides a complement to her speech by extolling her beauty in some rich and melodious lines:

> May that sweet plain that bears her pleasant weight
> Be still enamelled with discoloured flowers;
> That precious fount bear sand of purest gold;
> And, for the pebble, let the silver streams
> That pierce earth's bowels to maintain the source,
> Play upon rubies, sapphires, chrysolites;
> The brims let be embraced with golden curls
> Of moss that sleeps with sound the waters make
> For joy to feed the fount with their recourse; . . .
>
> (I. 35 ff.)

The diction here is typical of Peele in that it associates the loveliness of natural objects with precious jewels, gold, and silver; this type of diction is to be found in many other passages.[1] The very structure of the first episodes in the play makes it perfectly obvious that the actual 'incident' of what is being enacted, that is, Cusay's being sent off to fetch Bethsabe, is cut short purely for the sake of such a display of lyricism, for in the meantime David's glorification of Bethsabe gives rise to one lyrical outburst after another; he embarks on this theme in the speech just quoted from, takes it up again in his words with Cusay (ll. 51 ff.), devotes two soliloquies to it on Cusay's departure (ll. 64. ff.; 92 ff.), and then, in greeting Bethsabe, he falls once more into raptures over her beauty (ll. 105 ff.).

In the same way, a large number of incidental soliloquies, set against the background of otherwise conversational scenes, provide continual opportunities for enlarging upon the states of mind induced by earlier events, or of commenting on them in passages of moralizing verse. On top of this, Peele is fond of developing certain

[1] On the influence of the Ovidian mythological tradition on this kind of lyricism in *David and Bethsabe*, cf. Ekeblad, op. cit.

themes for their own sakes, even within a speech forming part of a dialogue-sequence; so that here too he shows the same tendency to employ monologue-speeches unrelated to their immediate context as we observed in the classical drama. Thus Absalon appears before David to acquaint him with Ammon's transgression, and David's answer runs as follows:

> Hath Ammon brought this evil on my house
> And suffered sin to smite his father's bones?
> Smite, David, deadlier than the voice of heaven,
> And let hate's fire be kindled in thy heart:
> Frame in the arches of thy angry brows,
> Making thy forehead, like a comet, shine,
> To force false Ammon tremble at thy looks.
> Sin, with his sevenfold crown and purple robe,
> Begins his triumph in my guilty throne;
> There sits he watching . . .
>
> (III. 133 ff.)

This is an obvious and typical example of the set speech isolated from its setting, just as it was used in the rhetorical tragedies. Opening with a rhetorical question followed by an exhortation to himself, David goes on to develop a full-length portrait of Sin in epic terms.[1] Then he announces his resolve to destroy the guilty man (ll. 145–8), and only in the last two lines of the speech does he directly address Absalon. This tendency of the set speech to fall into several clearly differentiated sections, often beginning with a whole series of parallel rhetorical questions,[2] corresponds to the schematic patterns that have already been dealt with in earlier chapters in connexion with the classical plays. Similarly in the other types of set speech, the speech of incitement,[3] the instruction-speech,[4] and especially the lament,[5] there are numerous parallels with earlier stages in the development of the set speech. It may be said, therefore, that as far as the structure of dramatic speech is concerned, Peele made no real innovations. By reason of the lyrical and pictorial qualities in his diction, however, he contributed significantly in other ways to the evolution of dramatic style, in that he

[1] Cf. the portrayal of Jehova, 251 ff. [2] Cf., e.g., 1641–54.
[3] Cf. 157 ff. [4] Cf. 1726 ff. [5] See the analysis in Chap. 15.

replaced the predominantly abstract diction of the classical plays by an extraordinarily rich and sensuous vocabulary from which even Shakespeare drew inspiration.

One last point. As one might expect, it is especially revealing to compare the style of the set speeches in this play with the succinct and unpretentious language of the Miracle Plays,[1] for like them it treats of Biblical matter. Where in the Miracles we might read, 'Why look'st thou pale?' in Peele we find

> What means my lord, the king's beloved son,
> That wears upon his right triumphant arm
> The power of Israel for a royal favour,
> That holds upon the tables of his hands
> Banquets of honour and all thought's content,
> To suffer pale and grisly abstinence
> To sit and feed upon his fainting cheeks,
> And suck away the blood that cheers his looks?
> (III. 1–8)

In this passage, not only is the question itself artistically embroidered with a number of metaphors, but the opportunity is taken of investing Ammon himself with a whole variety of attributes.

The Old Wives' Tale

Peele's most original and attractive work, the comedy of *The Old Wives' Tale* (1591–4?), shows the movement towards a more natural handling of dialogue, apparent already in *Edward I*, being carried forward a further stage; it shows too how the juxtaposing of different styles of speech might lead to an extremely effective use of contrast. It is worthy of remark that this happy blending of styles found its beginnings in comedy, which in so many respects kept a step ahead of tragedy.[2] Thus, by a fine stroke of irony, the

[1] 'The old realism of the Miracles is lost in a flood of Elizabethan declamatory rhetoric' – Parrott and Ball, op. cit., p. 67.

[2] Cf. A. P. Rossiter, *English Drama from Early Times to the Elizabethans*; C. M. Gayley, Introduction to *Representative English Comedies*, New York, 1903–14.

characteristic forms of the emotional set speech, though they had had their roots in the tragedies of declamation, are employed in this play to differentiate shades of character. After the homely prattle at the old wife's fireside of the three clowns who have lost their way in the wood, the play within the play begins, and from the mouth of the Second Brother we are treated to the conventional apostrophes in combination with anadiplosis:[1]

> O fortune cruel, cruel and unkind!
> Unkind in that we cannot find our sister,
> Our sister, hapless in her cruel chance.
>
> (142–4)

This is reminiscent of the ingenious burlesque in the Pyramus and Thisbe scenes of *A Midsummer Night's Dream*. Even more obvious is the burlesque of the grand style of declamation in the hexameters spoken by Huanebango, who is probably intended as a mocking representation of Gabriel Harvey, although in the verse itself it is the hexameters of Richard Stanyhurst that are parodied:

> Philida, phileridos, pamphilida, florida, flortos;
> Dub dub-a-dub, bounce, quoth the guns, with a
> sulphurous huff-snuff:
> Waked with a wench, pretty peat, pretty love, and
> my sweet pretty pigsnie,
> Just by thy side shall sit surnamed great Huanebango:
> Safe in my arms will I keep thee, threat Mars, or
> thunder Olympus.
>
> (667–71)

When a particular style is burlesqued, the inference may be drawn that it is no longer generally acceptable, usually indeed that it is almost played out. That the high seriousness of the declamatory set speech could be turned to comic effect is a sign that its limitations and its artificiality were recognized. This is illustrated for us not only in this work of Peele's, but also in Greene's plays, such as *Orlando Furioso*.

[1] The rhetorical device whereby the end of one clause or phrase is repeated at the beginning of the next.

12

Greene

Robert Greene was a more highly skilled playwright than Peele, and had a better knowledge of the theatre of his day. The first 'man of letters' of the English Renaissance, he was as versatile in the field of drama as he was in his other literary activities.[1] Moreover, he was just as much of an innovator as an accomplished imitator both of contemporary and of bygone types of drama. The ability to blend dramatic *genres* and styles of the most heterogeneous character – that tendency in the drama of the 1580s that contributed so very materially to the advances made by Shakespeare – can be studied better in Greene than in any other playwright. His dramatic work brings together the greatest variety and diversity of elements in its structure and language and in the themes it treats. This wide range in his capabilities makes it very difficult to lay a finger on anything that can be called his own personal style, and it has resulted in his being credited with a number of plays whose authorship is undecided. Since he could with such ease, recklessness almost, assume so great a variety of dramatic manners and make them his own, scholars have felt justified in picking upon him first as the author of these plays of doubtful origin.[2] This is no place to embark on a full-scale debate on this question; as a basis for our discussion we shall deal only with those four plays of which Greene's authorship is tolerably certain, *Alphonsus, King of Arragon*, *Orlando Furioso*, *Friar Bacon and Friar Bungay*, and *James the Fourth*.

In some respects these four plays, which belong to the years 1587–91, recapitulate in brief the course of development which has

[1] Cf. John Clark Jordan, *Robert Greene*, New York, 1915.

[2] Cf. T. H. Dickinson's Introduction to the Mermaid Edition of Greene's plays.

been laid down in previous chapters with regard to the nature and function of the set speech. Greene begins with a technique of cumbersome, high-flown declamation, governed by the conventions of formal rhetoric; he finally achieves a type of speech which approaches the tone of conversation, and is natural and at times realistic, though it is true that we encounter this only in occasional passages in his last two plays. But over and above this, his work brings to the fore a whole series of new potentialities, not only for the development of dramatic style, but also for the mutual interrelationship between the set speech and dramatic technique.

Alphonsus, King of Arragon

In *Alphonsus, King of Arragon* (c. 1587)[1] Greene is quite clearly submitting himself to the authority of *Tamburlaine*, which he sets himself to imitate by concentrating the interest of his own play upon one central figure, as well as in style and in his use of the set speech. Here, however, we may see, as we have already observed in *Selimus*, how rapidly the style of Tamburlaine can degenerate in the hands of a less talented playwright when his work is not informed by the poetic fire of the original creation and the grandeur of its underlying conception. Thus the long set speeches in this play are no longer effective as the expression of a powerful will and personality; they are no longer filled with the mighty visions of a mind aspiring to embrace the very universe. They have taken over merely the outward features of this style, the loud assertiveness, the threats, and the boasts – what, in short, may be described as the rant and the bombast. For the rest, Greene tries in his set speeches to find room for very much more in the way of narrative, of sheer reporting, than Marlowe did, so that many speeches, entirely detached as they are from the personality of the speaker, have the effect of interpolated action-reports or situation-reports, from which a clumsy attempt is made to change over to dialogue – note, for example, Belinus's speeches at I. ii. 286 ff. and II. i. 458 ff. The

[1] A new edition of *Alphonsus*, with introduction, commentary and notes, has been prepared by N. J. Sanders (Ph.D. thesis, Birmingham, 1957, MS.).

Prologues of Venus prefacing the several acts are also employed in this way as a means of exposition, as a vehicle for incidental report and comment. Furthermore, Greene is trying in this play to present far more visible action and incident than Marlowe did in *Tamburlaine*. The impression given, however, is that of a confusing flurry of movement, of a plot lacking both in unity and in anything like an organic relationship with the speeches. Yet there is some interest in the attempt Greene made, with the help of certain properties and stage-effects, to convey his meaning and intentions more satisfactorily than he apparently found himself able to do by means of speech and the movements of his characters. The stage-direction at the beginning of the fourth act, *Let there be a brazen Head set in the middle of the place behind the Stage, out of the which cast flames of fire, drums rumble within*, inaugurates a succession of stage-effects which make great play with magic, and which in the other plays are even more spectacular than in this.[1] Resourceful man of the theatre that he was, Greene was able to devise new stage-effects to run side by side with the set speech, dialogue, and physical movement.

Orlando Furioso

Orlando Furioso also stands in the line of Marlowe's *Tamburlaine*; in this play, however, *Tamburlaine* is no longer admiringly imitated, but deliberately parodied.[2] Within a comparatively short time, it seems, the high declamatory style of Marlowe's first play could be examined in a critical light and turned to ridicule by means of burlesque, and this is a sure sign that the way was being prepared for a change of taste in the matter of style, and that conflicting ideas about taste were already in the air. The parody of contemporaries is always of interest to the literary historian because what has at the time been seen as especially typical of a particular style is

[1] Parrott (op. cit., p. 71) believes that *The Span. Trag.* is also being parodied here. Cf. Tucker Brooke in *A Literary History of England*, ed. Baugh, p. 458. Jordan (op. cit.) puts forward the thesis that there is no parody in *Orlando*, merely an unsuccessful attempt to represent madness on the stage.

[2] Cf. also Dickinson's Introduction, p. lx.

exaggerated and caricatured, and hence often stands out more obviously in the parody than in the original. In *Orlando* it is once again the outward features of the style and diction of *Tamburlaine* that Greene has parodied: the string of apostrophes, the protestations and execrations, the hyperbole, the profusion of mythological names and classical parallels, the swaggering and the bumptiousness (here burlesqued by being transferred to courting scenes), and the provocative threats. In the opening scene Greene has worked up a typical 'rhetorical situation' in the form of a wooing-contest: set speeches are delivered in turn by the five suitors for the hand of the Princess Angelica, all similar in structure, and all brought to an identical conclusion in their closing lines. All this is merely stilted speechifying, as in *Gorboduc*, and it is not relieved by any movement; the device by which the suitors stand up one after the other, make their speeches, and then fall silent, has obviously been adopted for the purposes of parody. And there is reason to believe that in certain other particulars, too, Marlowe is being parodied. For instance, Sacripant's lament immediately before his death (V. i. 1272 ff.), with its formal appeal for the annihilation of the universe, is written in imitation of the corresponding laments in *Tamburlaine*, especially that of Bajazeth (*1 Tamb.* V. ii. 223 ff.); and it is also possible that the list of recapitulatory words in the last line but one ('Heauen, earth, men, beasts, and euerie liuing thing') is an imitation of the penultimate line of Hieronimo's famous rhetorical lament, 'Oh eies, no eies . . .' ('Eies, life, world, heauens, hel, night, and day,' *Span. Trag.* III. ii. 22).

In his next two plays Greene no longer shows any influence from Marlowe. He might by now have been expected to be developing his own dramatic technique and his own style. That he never really cultivated a style that was personal to himself alone, but was content with mere experiments and beginnings, must be put down to the fact that his abilities lay too much on the surface, that they were wanting in substance, in genuinely creative dramatic and poetic qualities. His talent is seen in the skill with which he brought together and blended the various styles and *genres*. However, he had not the skill to fuse them into harmonious works of art and to inform them with a unifying spirit of their own. The originality for which he has been so highly praised[1] is therefore to be sought rather in external features – in his skill in blending his materials, his invention of new theatrical effects and his production of new dramatic *genres* – than in any strikingly dramatic qualities in his plots, his characterization and his language. What he did is of course of some importance in the history of drama, for he was able by this talent for combining such heterogeneous elements (even though it largely played itself out in matters of outward technique, in a host of small-scale effects) to provide a not inconsiderable stimulus for other playwrights, as is seen in the subsequent development of tragicomedy.[2] By his own practice he demonstrated clearly to his contemporaries what manifold potentialities lay ready to be exploited by anyone who refused to be bound by the conventions of existing *genres*, and who set out in a new spirit of freedom to interweave dramatic types of the greatest diversity and to associate them with varieties of theme and subject-matter that had not up till that time been turned to account. As far as Greene himself is concerned, this combinative art still consisted to a large extent in the simple juxtaposition of his dramatic ingredients, and not in the creation of essentially new forms; and this may be exemplified by an analysis of his dramatic language such as is now to be undertaken in connexion with *Friar Bacon and Friar Bungay* (c. 1589).

Friar Bacon and Friar Bungay

For this purpose some comparison between the various longer speeches of Margaret may be instructive. She makes her appearance for the first time at the beginning of the third scene:

> *Thom.* By my troth, *Margret*, heeres a wether is able to make a man call his father whorson; if this wether hold, we shall haue hay good cheape, and butter and cheese at *Harlston* will beare no price.

[1] E.g., Ward, op. cit., Vol. I, pp. 379 ff.; later also F. H. Ristine, *English Tragicomedy: Its Origin and History*, New York, 1910, p. 81. But see Tucker Brooke, *The Tudor Drama*, p. 267, and Parrott and Ball, op. cit., pp. 69 ff.

[2] Cf. Eugene M. Waith, *The Pattern of Tragicomedy in Beaumont and Fletcher*, New Haven, 1952.

Marg. *Thomas*, maides when they come to see the faire
Count not to make a cope for dearth of hay;
When we haue turned our butter to the salt,
And set our cheese safely vpon the rackes,
Then let our fathers price it as they please.
We countrie sluts of merry *Fresingfield*
Come to buy needlesse noughts to make vs fine,
And looke that young-men should be francke this day,
And court vs with such fairings as they can.
Phoebus is blythe, and frolicke lookes from heauen,
As when he courted louely *Semele*,
Swearing the pedlers shall haue emptie packs
If that faire wether may make chapmen buy.
(I. III. 346–62)

Here Margaret, the Keeper's daughter, is talking to a rustic (described as a *clown*). In this speech she introduces herself to us, and gives a sketch of her setting in which we are told of the village fair, the cheese and butter-making of the village maidens, and their desire to attract the young men, and lastly of the fair weather, with which in fact Thomas has already opened the conversation. The realistic village slang put into Thomas's mouth is not used by Margaret, although the subjects she touches upon follow quite naturally from his remarks and bring a certain earthiness into the play, carrying on the tone suggested already in the first scene. When this village girl comes in her turn to speak of the weather, she does so with the help of classical parallels, and is thus made to speak entirely out of character. Her long *aside* at the end of the scene, in which she talks about Paris and Oenone, is in no way different in its diction from any corresponding passage in a tragedy. The same must be said of her conventional eulogy of her new lover ('like the pride of vaunting *Troy*' . . . II. iii. 646 ff.); of her assertion, in which she drags in the names of Jove, Danae, Phoebus, Latona, and Mercury, that she will never forsake Lacy (III. i. 990 ff.); of her ridiculous apostrophe to 'Fond *Atae*, doomer of bad boading fates', after she has received the letter in which Lacy casts her off (III. iii. 1497); of the speeches in which, in highly moral, didactic, purposeful terms, she announces her intention of immediately entering a convent and renouncing the world (III. iii. 1515 ff.; V. i. 1860 ff.); and of the pathetic farewell-speech in which she takes leave of the wordly life she has so far led ('Now farewell, world, the engin of all woe.' V. i. 1880 ff.). On all these occasions Margaret uses the old commonplaces that had been served up for corresponding situations in the rhetorical tragedies. We cannot therefore speak of any consistency in her manner of speech, or of any adaptation of the diction to the entirely different, more free and easy comic world of tragi-comedy. Every now and then what can in fact be described as a more free and easy style does make an appearance, both in the dialogue and in the more formal speeches, but it always breaks down in the early stages. The language is not dictated by any consistent approach to the style of the play as a whole, much less by the condition of the persons using it. On the contrary, as is often the case in Elizabethan drama, it is the specific situation and the theme that is being treated that govern the choice of style and language. When in the first scene of the play Prince Edward wishes to express his admiration for his new darling, Margaret, he does so by the time-honoured device, taken straight out of the poetry of the day, of a systematic enumeration of her charms, a mere development of the formal eulogy (I. i. 51 ff.).[1] Again, when at the beginning of Act II the Kings and the Emperor of Germany meet at Hampton House, we have the usual quite conventional speeches of salutation and welcome; and when Prince Edward in his wrath confronts the faithless Lacy, we are treated, in the string of parallel rhetorical questions, to the familiar set-speech forms of the threat and the challenge (III. i). When Vandermast and Bungay stand up to each other in a disputation on their magic arts – one of the completely irrelevant digressions in the play – it is done by the method of long formal 'instruction-speeches' (III. ii). We should hardly expect anything else.

It is only in the diction of the two clowns, Miles and Ralph, that we find a completely unconventional, robust and realistic prose, which affords a powerful contrast to the blank verse used by the

[1] Cf. also Lacy's praise of Margaret, II. iii, and Edward's words about Elinor, III. ii, and IV. ii.

Prince, the King, Margaret, and those about them. However, their appearances are as a rule only incidental, and the spirit of their language and their humour does not affect those who move in higher circles.

Critics have often drawn attention to the presence in this play, and in *James IV* also, of an entirely new element, an atmosphere of country breezes and natural beauty, a 'woodland air'. When looked at more closely, however, this is seen as something that does not go below the surface; it adds a touch of colour only to a handful of scenes and passages, and far the greater part of the play is wholly untouched by it.

Even as the language of the play is a patchwork of commonplaces, stitched together without any intermediate shading, so also the plot and characterization are mere mosaics of individual effects. There is never anything that prepares us for the moments of crisis, or leads up to them, nor are their potentialities fully exploited; moreover, there is no overriding central interest to serve as a connecting thread throughout the work.[1] Greene's play is built up out of small units, and it can scarcely have presented itself to his mind as a complete whole. However, he has the ability to please and entertain us with his handling of these isolated units and with his frolic and pell-mell assortment of variegated themes,[2] not to mention his striking stage-effects; and he so powerfully engages the interest, that even today many a reader, carried away by the charm of individual episodes, will fail to notice how slight is the thread of dramatic and psychological probability, how inadequate both the links between the different themes and the continuity of the whole piece, how puppet-like and lacking in individuality the characters, how glaring and preposterous the inconsistencies.

[1] Parrott's judgement, 'the first well-planned and skilfully executed romantic comedy in England', is exaggerated (op. cit., p. 71).

[2] Cf. P. Z. Round, 'Greene's Materials for *Friar Bacon and Friar Bungay*', *MLR*, XXI, 1926.

James the Fourth

Much the same must be said of *James IV* (before 1592),[1] which has met with even more admiration from the critics. In this play too one is at first bewildered by the mixture of the most widely differing dramatic types. Tragedy, Morality, pageant, romantic fairy-tale, farce, and comedy: all of these actually appear, or are suggested; but they are not fused into a new and close unity in which the separate elements drawn from these various *genres* surrender some of their own individuality in order to produce something entirely original, and, in adapting themselves to the new hybrid form, come to partake of its spirit. One need only turn for a moment to Shakespeare and ask oneself how he conceived of tragi-comedy to realize that Greene's play is at best a tragi-comedy in intention, but not in execution. For Shakespeare's artistry in casting the glow of an all-embracing goodness and serenity over tragic complications which he does not allow to be carried through to their final consequences is a very different thing from Greene's reluctance to present any really deeply felt tragic emotion, and his failure to draw his emotional conflicts through to a satisfactory conclusion. This is not the place for detailed illustration of these points. However, it is relevant to our present purposes to point out in this connexion that whenever the plot gives rise to situations in which any agitation of the mind has to be translated into words,[2] whether it be vacillation, intense mental conflict, despair, forgiveness, or determination, we find nothing but the worn-out formulas of rhetorical tragedy or impersonal, insipid platitudes of a moral and didactic cast.

If we go systematically through the utterances of the leading characters, and especially all their longer speeches, the claims so often put forward as to their life-like portrayal are brought very much in question. For these characters tell us very little about

[1] On *James IV* see Waldo F. McNeir, *MLN*, LXII, 1947; J. C. Maxwell, *MLR*, XLIV, 1949.

[2] E.g., the King's transfer of his affections from Dorothea to Ida (I. i). Dorothea sees her husband's order for her death (III. iii). She resolves to forgive him (V. ii). James hears of the supposed death of his wife (V. vi). Dorothea is reconciled with the King (V. vi).

themselves; on the other hand, far the largest amount of space in their speeches is given to the expression of moral principles of universal application and to other similarly impersonal topics. The persistent tendency towards moral platitudes which runs through all of Greene's work is not, in *James IV*, over-borne by the desire to invest the characters with an individuality of their own; on the contrary, it is everywhere very much to the fore. It is not by any means confined to the scene (V. iv) where the three anonymous representatives of the professional classes, the Lawyer, the Merchant, and the Divine, comment chorus-wise on the 'present state', where in true Morality fashion the private backsliding of the King is held up as a symbol of the common depravity of mankind, and where at the same time many other faults which have nothing to do with the occasion of their censure are glanced at merely in order to give each speaker in turn an opportunity of airing the complaints about the prevailing corruptness of the world that were so common in the drama of the age.[1] This scene, in which the set speech is employed in its function of didactic moral commentary, as in *Gorboduc*, is only the most obvious example of the depersonalized voicing of moral clichés in *James IV*, which, we must remember too, consists of the play within the play that Bohan causes to be performed before King Oberon to show him, 'by demonstration', 'why I hate the world' (Induction). Moreover, it is obvious that the Bishop of St Andrews is dragged into the play for the express purpose of allowing him, in Act II, Scene ii, to deliver two long moral disquisitions, his warning to Queen Dorothea and the attempt at dissuasion interlarded with reproaches that he addresses to the King. All this shows that there is no real connexion between the roles of the characters in the play and their utterances; the more so if we glance also at the moralizing final soliloquies of Andrew (IV. v) and Ateukin (V. ii). It is merely grotesque that Ateukin, of

[1] Conventional complaint of 'the hapless ruins of this realm', appropriate to the moral play or the history, is also given to the minor characters, such as the Purveyor and Andrew, who refer to the topsy-turvy state of the world; e.g., 'The world is at a wise pass when nobility is afraid of a flatterer' (III. ii); 'O what a trim world is this!' (IV. iii); 'Was never such a world, I think, before, When sinners seem to dance within a net' (IV. v).

all people, the Machiavellian villain and the seducer of the King, should in the end, after he has been responsible for all this wretchedness, be moved to moral indignation and exclaim,

> Oh cursed race of men, that traficque guile,
> And in the end, themselues and kings beguile.
> (V. ii. 1963–64)

The discrepancy between a character's role in the play and his pronouncements which is so well illustrated in Ateukin corresponds to the relationship between these passages of moralizing and the spirit of the play as a whole. For the actual plot is almost entirely lacking in real moral purpose. The perpetual moralizing in *Gorboduc* and many of the other plays we have been discussing was to this extent more in place than it is here, that the whole tenor and purpose of these plays was moral and didactic. In Greene there is no such connexion as this; the moralizing has become a mere gesture, and has no intrinsic bearing on the plot as a whole.[1]

Regarding the utterances of the characters in *James IV*, it might be said that the moral judgements of the onlooking 'Chorus', entirely in keeping as they are with the outer framework in which Oberon and Bohan figure, have made an unwarrantable intrusion into the play proper. The characters act as mouthpieces for the playwright's general reflections on life or for his attempts to explain the course of events. For they do not speak as their real selves; instead they pass remarks on the general situation, and comment on their own conduct and actions as outside observers, and in this way they too play the part of a Chorus.[2] This is true indeed of a great many pre-Shakespearian plays, but it is especially conspicuous in Greene. It means that all vital conflict between the characters such as should prompt them to self-expression is reduced to a minimum or altogether suppressed. It means too that throughout the play indirect rather than direct methods of representation are employed. In these circumstances the critic must exercise the utmost caution in speaking of the 'characterization'. This applies even to the two heroines, who are so often praised for the conviction and truth to

[1] Cf. Doran, *Endeavors of Art*, pp. 97–8.
[2] Cf. Parrott and Ball, op. cit., p. 73.

life of their portrayal. In the first scene Ida is spoken to in loving terms by the Scottish King, who has just married the Princess Dorothea, and she at once embarks on a discussion of moral principles. A few scenes later (II. i. 692–705), with a wisdom beyond her years, she uses her needlework as a means of developing for her mother's benefit a parable about God's operations in the world of men. Then there is Dorothea. At the very beginning of the play the English King's admonitions had drawn attention to the exemplary behaviour that would be expected of her; when in the final act she hears of the perils that have lately been gathering about her faithless husband's head, she is at first seized with faintness, and then, announcing her intention of forgiving him, she opens her speech in the following terms:

> Ah, *Nano*, trees liue not without their sap,
> And *Clitie* cannot blush but on the sunne;
> The thirstie earth is broke with many a gap,
> And lands are leane where riuers do not runne:
> Where soule is reft from that it loueth best,
> How can it thriue or boast of quiet rest?
> (V. i. 1906–11)

This sententious preamble with its string of clichés[1] is not merely a prefatory flourish; for Greene it serves also as a fitting substitute for the words that Dorothea ought to have spoken to express her tumult of spirit directly and unmistakably.

Only in a very few scenes does Greene achieve a genuinely new manner, one which in the very sound of the words reproduces something of that melancholy serenity which ought to be one of the properties of tragi-comedy. He does so with particular success in Act IV, Scene iv, the scene that has often been spoken of as having provided the pattern for Shakespeare's *As You Like It*; here Queen Dorothea, dressed as a man and attended by her dwarf, is wandering about in the woods near Edinburgh, and she opens the scene with a short speech which is given a certain rhetorical colouring by the use

[1] Cf. also the conventional formulas of lament in Dorothea's speeches in III. ii.

of anaphora, and which ends with an apostrophe in the form of a rhymed couplet:

> Ah, *Nano*, I am wearie of these weedes,
> Wearie to weeld this weapon that I bare,
> Wearie of loue from whom my woe proceedes,
> Wearie of toyle, since I haue lost my deare.
> O wearie life, where wanteth no distresse,
> But euery thought is paide with heauinesse.
> (IV. iv. 1646–51)

This is immediately followed by Nano's laconic and humorous rejoinder:

> Too much of wearie, madame: if you please,
> Sit downe, let wearie dye, and take your ease.
> (1652–3)

Here the dwarf's cheerful and witty reply acts as a corrective to the plaintiveness of the Queen. Greene makes use of a rhetorical pattern borrowed from the style of tragedy, and subtly transforms it to produce a lightly ironical effect.

In this last play of his Greene has on the whole, at any rate in comparison with Peele, reduced the number of long set speeches, and has shown a certain skill and versatility in his development of a brisk and easily-flowing dialogue and of a conversational manner. Where he does employ longer speeches in *James IV* they obviously, apart from the instances mentioned, serve his dramatic ends much more successfully than do those of Peele, who, as we saw, uses the set speech in a more static manner, and dwells on his lyrical effects and his background colouring. In *James IV* the speeches in which Ateukin[1] sets out to talk the still-wavering King over to the plan of doing away with his wife, and later, when he has agreed, makes him regard his course of action as quite justifiable, are particularly good examples of set speeches which are made an integral part of the plot and help to carry it forward.[2] What is more, these are 'conver-

[1] The eloquent persuasiveness of the cunning intriguer Ateukin is described by his servant as a gift bestowed on him at his birth: 'melle dulcior fluit oratio' (IV. v).

[2] E.g., I. i; II. ii.

sion-speeches' in the true sense of the term; the speaker keeps a sharp eye on his dupe and estimates the effect of his words upon him; he does not merely proceed according to a preconceived rhetorical pattern.[1]

But when all is said and done, these too are advances that lie largely on the outer fringes of dramatic technique. With his sure instinct both for the potentialities and the exigencies of the theatre, Greene recognized the advantages of a more relaxed dramatic structure, a higher tempo in the action, and an easy flow of dialogue, and he broke through the tradition of the long set-speech scene. That much yet remained to be done before dramatic technique could develop into dramatic art it has been one of the objects of this chapter to show, with its analysis of Greene's handling of individual utterances of his characters and his practice in general with regard to the set speech.

[1] Cf., e.g., I. i. 186 ff.

13

Popular Drama and History Plays

Cambises; The Famous Victories of Henry the Fifth; Jack Straw; The Troublesome Raigne of King John; The True Tragedie of Richard the Third; King Leir and his Three Daughters; Woodstock.

The plays so far reviewed have either found a place within the tradition of classical tragedy based on Seneca, or they have been the work of academic authors, the University Wits. In these circles the techniques of rhetoric, both as theory and in practice, were mastered as a matter of course. Even where the path of the national and popular dramatic tradition crossed that of the learned and academic, dramatic speech tended in one respect or another to reflect the influence of the rhetorical set speech whose various forms and stages of development we have been examining in some detail. If we go on now to study the set speeches in plays which preserve pretty closely the characteristic features of the popular drama, we shall find, especially in the early chronicle plays, a dramatic technique that is fundamentally different from that of the more formal English tragedies contemporary with them. Shakespeare's English history plays draw on the popular tradition no less than on that of the early classical tragedy,[1] and as far as the set speech and its role in our drama are concerned, we shall probably learn a good deal from a consideration of this popular trend. For a good many of these plays, of course, the critic is faced by the problem of uncertain and probably seriously corrupted texts; *The Famous Victories of Henry the Fifth* is a case in point. Whether these texts represent inaccurate memorial reconstructions at the hands of unauthorized reporters, or whether the textual corruption

[1] Cf. Walter F. Schirmer, 'Über das Historiendrama in der englischen Renaissance' (*Kleine Schriften*, Tübingen, 1950).

is due to other causes, remains an open question.[1] In any case, such conclusions as are to be drawn here about the use of the set speech in several plays of this type can only be put forward with reservations.

Cambises

While *Gorboduc* represents classical tragedy in its pure form, Thomas Preston's *Cambises*, which belongs to the 1560s,[2] is a hybrid in which the popular element predominates; in many respects the play carries forward the manner of the Moralities, while in its multiplicity of characters and scenes, its wealth of incident, and its liveliness, it displays a technique which looks forward to the early chronicle plays. All the colours are laid on a shade more thickly, everything is cruder and clumsier, than in the contemporary classical plays; and the want of art is further testified by an obvious relish for coarse jests and violence of expression and for graceless stage-effects – for what, in short, is best calculated to appeal to the popular mind.[3] Even here, however, there are speeches that conform closely to type. At the very beginning of the play Cambises opens the business of the Council with a long set speech, reminiscent in its matter of *Gorboduc* I. ii, asking his Lords for their advice, which they then proceed to give him. Like the 'counsel-speeches' that follow, this speech (ll. 126 ff.) is artless in its structure. A few pages later, however, we find in Otian's *lamentatio* at his father's death all the well-worn rhetorical apostrophes and other stylistic devices of the formal lament:

The greeuous greefes and strained sighes my hart doth breake in
    twaine,
And I deplore, most woful childe, that I should see you slaine.
O false and fickle frowning dame, that turneth as the winde,
Is this the ioy in fathers age thou me assignest to finde?

[1] Cf. W. W. Greg, *The Editorial Problem in Shakespeare*, Oxford, 1951; Leo Kirschbaum, 'A Census of Bad Quartos', *RES*, XIV, 1938.

[2] Cf. W. A. Armstrong in *English Studies* XXXI, 1950; XXXVI, 1955.

[3] Cf. Rossiter, *English Drama*, p. 142.

O dolefull day, unhappy houre, that louing child should see
His father deer before his face thus put to death should be!
(447–52)

The use of rhymed heptameter couplets, which tends somewhat to over-emphasize the pathos of these lines, has the effect throughout the play of isolating the pathetic passages from the more comic episodes, which are composed in loose four-stressed couplets; this is a development of the attempt made in almost all the Interludes – and in the historical sense *Cambises* may be reckoned among the Interludes[1] – to achieve some differentiation in style by means of variations in metre and the interchange of prose and verse.[2] *Cambises* has then its share of emotional set speeches,[3] of which the majority are naturally laments, in accordance with the description on the title-page, 'A lamentable Tragedie mixed full of plesant mirth'.

The Famous Victories of Henry the Fifth

But what of the early chronicle plays? One of the earliest is *The Famous Victories of Henry the Fifth*,[4] which belongs to 1588, or even earlier.[5] This is a play which has clearly not fallen under the influence of the other dramatic *genres*, and which therefore offers potentialities for an entirely different course of development. It is written throughout in prose, in a prose moreover which is forceful

[1] Cf. Tucker Brooke, *The Tudor Drama*, pp. 138 ff.

[2] Cf. J. E. Bernard, *The Prosody of the Tudor Interlude*, New Haven, 1939; Traudl Eichhorn, 'Prosa und Vers im vorshakespeareschen Drama', *Shakespeare-Jahrbuch*, 84/86, 1950.

[3] Cf. Tucker Brooke, *The Tudor Drama*, p. 306; Briggs's Introduction to *Edward II*. The same is true of the plays usually named in connexion with *Cambises*, *Horestes* by Pickering (1567), and *Appius and Virginia* by R. Bower.

[4] On *The Famous Victories* see B. M. Ward, *RES*, IV, 1928; Ribner, *The English History Play in the Age of Shakespeare*, p. 71. (This book, published after the German original of the present work, can be referred to only in passing in footnotes.)

[5] On the redating of the chronicle plays see F. P. Wilson, *Marlowe and the Early Shakespeare*.

and straightforward, close to the language of the common folk, and easy and conversational in tone, at its most effective in the terse dialogue of which so much of it is composed. This eminently simple diction and the apparent artlessness of the composition have generally been held against the play in the histories of literature.[1] Such a judgement, however, fails to take sufficient account of the virtues inherent in the very qualities that have been mentioned, that is, the closely knit and entirely unaffected manner of presentation and the vigorous, unpretentious diction. Where else in the drama of the period do we find dialogue in which people talk in so matter-of-fact a way and so naturally and directly of matters of common interest, which is so fast-moving and adaptable, and which employs the language of everyday life so little touched by literary precedents? Even if some of these colloquial features should be due to corruption in a reported text, this would scarcely account for all of them or for the completely different impression that the diction and style as a whole leave on a reader who is used to the typical language of pre-Shakespearian tragedy. For this dialogue is capable of representing even such things as hesitation and evasion on the part of a speaker, and it can also convey the implied gestures and the accompanying action.[2] Moreover, an astonishingly rapid tempo is maintained. There is no circumlocution and no emotional padding; what is eventful and of central interest is apprehended and communicated quite directly, and the plot is carried forward by means of the brisk dialogue in a rapid interchange of question and answer and of information supplied and orders given. This is a very significant fact at a stage of development in the drama when, as we have seen, a great deal of space was still devoted to introspection, to the expression of feeling, to anticipation and retrospect, and to epic narrative.

That the dramatic methods used in this play left but little room for long set speeches is obvious enough, and in fact long-drawn episodes of any kind are exceptional. As an example of an episode in which an attempt is made to give some depth to the emotional side

[1] Cf. Tucker Brooke, *The Tudor Drama*, p. 306, or Briggs, Introduction to *Edward II*, p. cxxii, 'These dramas represent depths as low, artistically speaking, as any to which our stage has descended'.

[2] Cf., e.g., 66 ff., 479 ff., 1006 ff., 1230 ff.

of an incident, there is the scene which was later developed so finely in Shakespeare's *1 Henry IV* (III. ii); this is the scene in which Prince Henry has to render an account of his recent way of life to his father, who is on his sick-bed, and asks for his forgiveness. The Prince makes a long speech in prose which offers the strongest imaginable contrast to everything that has so far been established as characteristic of the dramatic set speech:

> *Hen. 5* [*Aside*]. My conscience accuseth me. [*He kneels.*] Most soueraign lord, and welbeloued father, to answere first to the last point, that is, whereas you coniecture that this hand and this dagger shall be armde against your life, no! Know, my beloued father, far be the thoughts of your sonne – 'sonne,' said I? an vnworthie sonne for so good a father! – but farre be the thoughts of any such pretended mischiefe. And I most humbly render it to your Maiesties hand. And liue, my lord and soueraigne, for euer! And with your dagger-arme show like vengeance vpon the bodie of – 'that, your sonne', I was about to say, and dare not; ah, woe is me therefore! – that, your wilde slaue. Tis not the crowne that I come for, sweete father, because I am vnworthie. And those vilde and reprobate companions – I abandon and vtterly abolish their company for euer! Pardon, sweete father! pardon! the least thing and most desire. And this ruffianly cloake I here teare from my backe, and sacrifice it to the diuel, which is maister of al mischiefe. Pardon me, sweet father! pardon me! . . .
>
> (769–91)

The whole speech is charged with a human feeling that rings absolutely true. The way in which, after the brief *aside* which reveals the depth of his distress, the Prince awkwardly and falteringly brings out his explanations, keeps on interrupting his own words, corrects himself, asks his father's forgiveness with heartfelt affection, and with painful agitation and contrition forswears the company of his low associates, and finally as a token of his change of heart tears the 'ruffianly cloake' from his shoulders: all this carries the fullest conviction. The language of the play as a whole is thoroughly practical in tone; here it is suffused with the warmth of real feeling. This speech, together with the King's death-bed scene (ll. 858–957) which succeeds it after a comic interlude, is one of the very few passages in the drama of the late 1580s in which an incident with a moving human appeal affects us by the very spontaneity and unpretentiousness of the language in which it is presented – in speeches which do not rely for their effect on rhetorical elevation or adornment, and which conform to no preconceived rhetorical pattern.[1]

Jack Straw

While *The Famous Victories of Henry the Fifth* is the only chronicle play entirely in prose written before 1590, *The Life and Death of Jack Straw* (c. 1592),[2] a play which also belongs to an early stage in the evolution of the *genre*, is a mixture of prose and verse, which does not in itself mean, of course, that we shall find rhetorical set speeches in it. This play is much less impressive than *The Famous Victories*, and its author[3] has worked out no particular style of his own. The dialogues are for the most part wooden and lacking in vitality, while the structure and the conduct of the action, with its mechanical alternation of the various sets of characters in successive scenes, not to mention the lack of tension, are evidence of a but slightly developed dramatic sense. The author has, however, been more strongly influenced by the rhetorical drama than was the author of *The Famous Victories*. This statement is borne out by reference to several conventional situations in the play,[4] and a certain number of set speeches also that conform to established

[1] This judgement is of course subject to the reservation at the beginning of this chapter on the uncertain state of the text of this play.

[2] Ed. by Hugo Schütt, Heidelberg, 1901, and by J. S. Farmer, Tudor Facsimile Texts, 1911. See also Ribner, op. cit., p. 71, and Mary G. M. Adkins, *Univ. of Texas Stud. in English*, XXVIII, 1949.

[3] On the grounds of some remote classical allusions, Schütt believes that the author was a university man.

[4] The conference-scene (I. ii), the siege-scene (II. iv), the council- and tribunal-scene (IV. i).

types.[1] Similarly there are links with the earlier Morality Plays. It is evident that this is the work of a dramatic craftsman of very mediocre talent who has made use of reminiscences and stylistic features from a variety of models; and no kind of uniformity could have resulted from such a process as this.[2]

For our present purposes one passage is especially revealing. This is where Tom Miller, one of the rebels, delivers a long prose harangue in the presence of the Queen, and her reaction is the question, in tones of amused surprise, 'What meanes the fellow by all this eloquence?' Here an inoffensive and doltish man of the people is trying to assume the ceremonious style of courtly speech, and fails lamentably in his attempt.[3] He cannot get through his long periods; the long relative clause at the end has a particularly comic effect, and the legal and Biblical terms are like stilts on which he finds himself unable to struggle along. This is a good illustration of the fact that the dignified set speech was the property solely of the higher orders, as indeed Scaliger and others had expressly affirmed. The differentiation of high- and low-life characters by means of verse and prose[4] goes back to an earlier period than this, of course; in *Jack Straw*, however, it is not yet done with any consistency.

Turning to the other chronicle plays which are thought to have been written round about the year 1590, we find that the dramatization of chronicle material creates very different conditions for the use of the set speech from those that obtain in pure tragedy. The amount of material that confronted the author of a historical play in the chronicles and that had to be worked over to give it dramatic shape was very extensive. It was full of incident, and his first consideration was to bring as much of this into his play as possible. For, as has been convincingly argued,[5] the history plays depended

[1] Cf., e.g., Parson Ball's warning homily, which includes typical lament on the evils of the times (I. i. 46 ff.); or the King's opening speech in the Council in which he informs the lords of his decision (IV. i. 1 ff.). Ball's sermon, of course, also shows the influence of the Moralities.

[2] Considering the style as a whole, the view expressed by Fleay, Schütt and Robertson, that the play is entirely or partly by Peele, is not tenable.

[3] Cf. Schütt's note on this passage, p. 152.

[4] Cf. Traudl Eichhorn, op. cit.

[5] Cf. Schirmer, op. cit.; Briggs, op. cit., p. ii.

for their interest much more on the events, the physical action displayed, and the narrative content, than on the characters and the psychological action. In their earliest stages what mattered most in these plays was the dramatization of events that had actually taken place; their plots were a medley of exciting and ever-changing incidents drawn from the national story, and little attention was paid to characterization or spiritual conflicts. It was not until Marlowe's *Edward II* and Shakespeare's English history plays that this type of play came within the province of the tragedy of character; such a treatment was a long way from its original *raison d'être*.

As far as the handling of the set speech is concerned, this means that the expression of feelings, the reflection of passions, and introspection give way to matter of a more factual and practical nature; the report-speech comes much more to the fore, and much more space than hitherto is given to the exposition of plans and purposes, to explanation of the historical or political background, and to arrangements made for particular courses of action to be pursued in the future. In proportion as more of the actual incident is incorporated in the dramatic representation, so inevitably must formal speech-making fall into the background. On the other hand, as we have already seen, the history play by its very nature gives rise to certain conventional situations in which the set speech has an established position, and in these it is regularly used: in the exchange of greetings, for example, in the uttering of challenges, in scenes of triumph, in death-bed scenes, and the like.

The Troublesome Raigne of King John

These conventional type-speeches, however, now appear in a condensed form. The opening lines of the chronicle play *The Troublesome Raigne of King John* (1587–91?)[1] are an example of this. Here

[1] It is assumed here that *The Troublesome Raigne* is earlier than Shakespeare's *King John*; cf. J. Dover Wilson in his edition of *King John* (The New Shakespeare, Cambridge, 1936). Peter Alexander (*Shakespeare Primer*, 1951, p. 63) and E. A. J. Honigmann (New Arden *King John*, 1954) argue that *King John* is the earlier work. On this issue see also J. Elson, 'Studies in the King John Plays', *Adams Memorial Studies*; Robert Adger Law, *SP*, 1957; Matthew P. McDiarmid, *NQ*, 1957.

the Queen's speech of greeting is only eight lines long, whereas in a contemporary tragedy it would have been drawn out to a much greater length. In *The Troublesome Raigne* the emphasis, both in the set speeches and the dialogues, is laid largely on the reporting of facts and occurrences, but here and there a more human note is struck with the expression of moods and feelings and spiritual turmoil. However, these things are no longer presented, as in the early tragedies, by means of passionate set speeches, but in a much more incidental manner, and as a feature that is subordinated to the imparting of facts. This point may be illustrated from a variety of passages: in the first part the conversation between the Bastard Philip Falconbridge and his mother (I. 323 ff.), the Bastard's challenge to the Austrian Duke (II. 135 ff.),[1] Constance's speech to Arthur (IV. 207 ff.), and at the end of this first part King John's speech in the presence of Hubert (XIII. 227 ff.); in Part II there are Essex's speech to the Lords on the discovery of the body of young Prince Arthur, who has just leaped to his death from the castle walls (I. 39 ff.), King John's utterances of despair in the following scene (II. 88 ff., 113 ff., 154 ff.), and the speech in which the dying Meloun reveals Lewis's treacherous designs to the English nobles (V. 1 ff.). In all these speeches a strong element of excitement or agitation is implied, but it no longer finds expression in the preconceived, carefully disposed and stylized forms of set speech with which we have become familiar in the early tragedies – although even here there are certain stylistic usages that betray their origin in this particular tradition.[2] But such instances notwithstanding, the expressions of feeling no longer stand out from the body of the speeches as isolated and self-contained units; on the contrary, there is often, if not always, some inter-play, some interlinking, between the domains of feeling and of purely factual communication. For

[1] Here the Bastard's inward promptings are explained in the short aside by which the speech is prefaced.

[2] E.g., Essex's speech after Arthur's death:

> . . . If waterfloods could fetch his life again,
> My eyes should conduit forth a sea of tears;
> If sobs would help, or sorrows serve the turn,
> My heart should volley out deep piercing plaints.
>
> (Part II, I. 40–3)

the development of Shakespeare's word-artistry and his command of the set speech in his English history plays, this gradual convergence of the emotional and the informative speech was of the highest significance.

The straightforward expression of feeling, presented in terse, unadorned prose, is, as we have seen, a characteristic of *The Famous Victories of Henry the Fifth.* There is nothing like this in *The Troublesome Raigne.* Yet there are some passages in which, even though emotional situations of a conventional kind are involved, the language employed makes only a comparatively slight use of rhetoric and of diction above the everyday level. A good example comes to hand in the words spoken by the young Prince Arthur as he lies dying after his leap from the walls:

> Ho! who is nigh? somebody take me up!
> Where is my mother? let me speak with her.
> Who hurts me thus? Speak, ho! where are you gone?
> Ah me, poor Arthur! I am here alone.
> Why call'd I Mother? how did I forget?
> My fall, my fall, hath kill'd my mother's son.
> How will she weep at tidings of my death!
> My death indeed! O God, my bones are burst.
> Sweet Jesu, save my soul; forgive my rash attempt;
> Comfort my mother; shield her from despair . . .
>
> (2 *Tr. Raigne*, I. 12–21)

In the very artlessness of this speech, its broken, faltering phrases, there resides a quality which has potentialities for development in the future. The high finish acquired by the emotional rhetoric of tragedy precluded the possibility of any significant innovations on this level of diction. A fresh start had to be made at quite a low level before a playwright of the stature of Shakespeare could achieve a style which, as a comparison between *King John* and *The Troublesome Raigne* shows, carries high poetic quality and at the same time rings true as the language of real life.

Since the greatest amount of space in *The Troublesome Raigne* is devoted to question and answer and the giving of information and instructions, most of the dialogue-passages and longer speeches are directly related to the persons addressed. In comparison with Shakespeare's *King John* there are more speeches with that tendency to tail off into monologue that was so very pronounced in the classical tragedies. It is worthy of remark, however, that on several occasions this tendency for a speech to become a monologue can be accounted for quite naturally by the situation to which it belongs, and that it has a psychological basis. There is an example of this in the first scene, when Philip Falconbridge is asked who his father was. At first he does not answer, but stands as if in a dream, in a kind of trance.[1] And if the speech that follows is in fact a monologue, the beginning of which is given a special emphasis by two lines of Latin,[2] that is plausible enough in the circumstances.

Similarly, in Part II the soliloquizing sections in the King's speeches – on which the Bastard's comment is, 'These motions are as passions of a madman' (II. 112) – are explicable on the score that, in his distress and despair at his wretched plight, the King forgets the bystanders and unbosoms himself of his pent-up sorrows.[3] So that here again we meet with an innovation which is of some significance in relation to the handling of the set speech in Shakespeare's plays.

The True Tragedie of Richard the Third

In *The True Tragedie of Richard the Third* (1591?)[4] we can follow still further the processes which have been rendering the set speech more informal and more appropriate to the characters concerned.

[1] *Essex.* Philip, speak, I say; who was thy father?
K. John. Young man, how now? What! art thou in a trance?
Qu. Elin. Philip, awake! The man is in a dream.
Phil. *Philippus, atavis edite Regibus.*
What say'st thou, Philip, 'sprung of ancient Kings'?
Quo me rapit tempestas? . . .
(Part I, I. 247–52)

[2] Cf. the Latin lines in the King's soliloquizing speeches in Part II, I. 20, 132.

[3] Cf. esp. Part II, II. 1–23, 88–104, 113–43; cf. also VI. 1–13, where there is a monologue spoken in the presence of other characters.

[4] Peter Alexander believes *The True Tragedie* to be a bad quarto of Shakespeare's *Richard III.* On this question see also Clayton A. Greer, *SP*, XXIX, 1932; Edleen Begg, *SP*, XXXII, 1935.

The play is a mixture of prose and somewhat undeveloped blank verse, the prose predominating very strongly; and there are also a few passages of rhymed couplets. However, the verse and prose are not confined at all closely to separate and independent sections, nor in any systematic way differentiated according to the standing of the speakers, so that we continually find ourselves passing from an unsophisticated everyday speech to a diction which aims at greater dignity and therefore slips here and there into verse. Verse and prose are continually running up against each other. This fact may of course be partly accounted for by the supposition that a good part of the prose is 'the ruins of half-remembered verse',[1] that in fact it was originally verse. However, it may be taken for granted that this is not always the case, and that even in the authentic text which has not come down to us prose and verse were used side by side. It seems probable that already in the original version prose had been employed for a certain number of topics and states of mind that were more properly the province of verse.

In addition to soliloquies which show that the author was acquainted with the Senecan style and was trying systematically but without much success to reproduce it,[2] there are soliloquies and set speeches in *The True Tragedie* which are entirely in prose. In these there is an obvious and individual attempt to impart some intensity of expression to the colloquial language of everyday life. Quite early in the play the young King has to stand by and see Lord Grey arrested at the order of his uncle, Richard of Gloucester, and he complains in the following terms:

> A Gods, and is it iustice without my consent? Am I a King and beare no authoritie? My louing kindred committed to prison as traytors in my presence, and I stand to giue aime at them. A Edward, would thou laist by thy fathers side, or else he had liued till thou hadst bin better able to rule. If my neere kindred be committed to prison, what remains for me, a crowne? A but how? so beset with sorrows, that the care & grief wil kil me ere I shal

[1] Cf. J. D. Wilson, 'Shakespeare's *Richard III* and *The True Tragedy of Richard the Third, 1594*', *Shak. Quarterly*, III, 1952, p. 300.

[2] Cf. the monologues at V. 1873, and 1398.

> enioy my kingdome. Well since I cannot command, I wil intreat. Good vnkle of Gloster, for all I can say little, but for my vnkle Lord Gray, what need he be a theef . . .
>
> (747 ff.)

This is a dialogue-speech which turns into a soliloquy. It begins with the questions addressed to the bystanders, and then we have the familiar process by which the speaker turns to his own preoccupations. The King goes on to meditate upon his own situation as a king, with all the cares of his office but none of its powers, and then at the end of the speech turns once more to address his uncle. Though this introspection of the King's is presented in unadorned prose instead of verse, in some regards it is more successful in catching the tone of soliloquy,[1] even though a diction of this type must inevitably be deficient in imaginative qualities and poetic dignity. The same may be said of Richard's soliloquies and set speeches,[2] and in this particular his last three speeches are especially revealing. The way in which he speaks to his two accomplices, Catesby and Lovell, half fawning on them and half in loathing, and the excited and precipitate way in which he jumps from one subject to another, show an attempt on the dramatist's part, for all his lack of skill, to bring out in his speeches even the histrionic quality in the figure of Richard.[3]

[1] Naturally the reservation expressed at the beginning of the chapter also applies to this judgement.

[2] E.g., the short monologue at 442 ff., his speech to Buckingham at 665 ff., and his speech at 1624 ff.

[3] *King*. . . . Louell, Catesby, lets ioyne louingly and deuoutly togither, and I will diuide my whole kingdome amongst you.

Both. We will my Lord.

King. We will my lord, a Catesbie, thou lookest like a dog, and thou Louell too, but you will runne away with them that be gone, and the diuel go with you all, God I hope, God, what talke I of God, that haue serued the diuell all this while. No, fortune and courage for mee, and ioyne England against mee with England, Ioyne Europe with Europe, come Christendome, and with Christendome the whole world, and yet I will neuer yeeld but by death onely . . .

(1963 ff.)

King Leir and his Three Daughters

The chronicle plays so far noticed have illustrated the importance that had come to be attached to the plot in comparison with its role in the early tragedies. In the tragedies the plot had merely provided occasions for the development of emotional situations and the working up of set speeches, and from the whole chain of cause and effect only those links had been singled out which lent themselves to this purpose. Emotion and rhetoric embodied in set speeches had acquired importance for their own sake, and the impulse to which they originally owed their existence came to be forgotten altogether. In the chronicle plays the relationship is reversed; the actual staging of the fullest possible amount of the story is now of first importance. Not only is all the action brought on to the stage, but as a result of this the emphasising or expansion of a theme by means of set speeches is very largely done away with. The events played out on the stage must gain their own effects. Plot and the spoken word share the task of producing the main dramatic effects, and at times the plot even surpasses the spoken word in importance.

The True Chronicle History of King Leir and his Three Daughters (c. 1590?) is another play which illustrates these new trends. Here we are confronted by a closely woven network of events in a plot which is full of incident and which is broken up into no fewer than thirty-two interlocking episodes.[1] Moreover, this plot is very skilfully put together, and is comprehensive and logical in its development; the course of events throughout the play is given concreteness and held firmly before us by the movements of the characters, which appear to be governed by a clear plan, so that there are no longer any characters who drop out of the action altogether or whose parts come to an end prematurely. This striking advance in the handling of the plot and the presentation of incident must be appreciated before we go on to find fault with the dull and uninspired diction. For most of the diction obviously serves a subordinate and utilitarian purpose. Its function is to elucidate the action and comment on it, and to fill out what is happening on the stage; it

[1] Cf. Fischer, op. cit., p. 85.

merely explains the situations arising from the various incidents and the encounters that take place. Even where soliloquies and set speeches of some length occur, they are very largely explanatory of the action, and are more strictly devoted to the events of the story than was the case in the earlier drama. Examples of this are the soliloquy of Cordella which is overheard by the French King (ll. 599–611), that of Perillus, who reappears as Kent in Shakespeare (ll. 743–72), and, at the very beginning, the old King's speech in the council, when, in an episode analogous to the second scene of *Gorboduc*, he asks the advice of his nobles in the matter of his abdication and the division of the realm (ll. 1–31).

In a play consisting predominantly of sober, factual speech of this kind, where a person's inner self is revealed more by what we are given of his intentions and deliberations than by any expression of feeling, there are only a few scenes where states of mind are allowed an extended treatment. And when this happens, the diction becomes more highly coloured,[1] as in the three parallel questions with which the King of France begins his attempt to comfort Cordella:

When will these clouds of sorrow once disperse,
And smiling ioy tryumph vpon thy brow?
When will this Scene of sadnesse haue an end,
And pleasant acts insue, to moue delight?
When will my louely Queene cease to lament,
And take some comfort to her grieued thoughts?
(1230–35)

As the other side to the picture, there is actually one scene with a pronounced emotional content which is carried through with a minimum of rhetorical devices. This is the long scene (ll. 1431–1790) in which Leir passes the night in the open country, where he is discovered by the Murderer and threatened by him, but the Murderer undergoes a change of heart as the result of a speech from

[1] Cf., e.g., 2073 ff. The highly coloured rhetoric of this dialogue is reflected in Leir's answer:

Thou pleasing orator unto me in woe,
Cease to beguile me with thy hopeful speeches.

Perillus. The scene is not without its human appeal – quite apart from Leir's forgiveness of the Murderer there are several other passages of tender feeling in it – but this emotional quality is conveyed as much by the way the situations are presented on the stage as by the language employed. The language reveals no particular artistry, and no sense of poetry; it is, however, closely in touch with what is going on in the way of action. As a result of this 'synchronization' of language and action, of the very close alliance subsisting between them, there is a new kind of directness about the way in which the effects are gained. Though the play is of hardly more than average quality, it does manage to strike this fresh balance between the two sources of interest of pre-Shakespearian drama, and it is from this newly-recovered sense of unity between speech and action that the Shakespearian drama was to evolve.

Woodstock

In view of the faulty transmission of the texts of *The Famous Victories of Henry the Fifth* and *The True Tragedie of Richard the Third*, we must use the greatest restraint and caution in passing judgement on these plays; yet in style and language both of them bear out the supposition that a spontaneity of speech quite foreign to rhetorical tragedy was in the first instance built on the groundwork of an inartistic and in fact downright clumsy diction. Most of the time the style did not get beyond a prosaic matter-of-factness, the language of mere statement. However, once this point was reached, it was possible for an entirely new type of speech to develop, one that was full of vitality, as we shall now see in *Woodstock*. This highly original and surprisingly modern play sets a new standard in the blending of serious and comic material, and in the artistry with which it presents a dramatic situation; but it also displays an unprecedented skill in its subtly ironic characterization.[1] What is more, its diction has a throbbing vitality and richness which

[1] On the place of this play in the history of English drama and for a discussion of its quality, see A. P. Rossiter's excellent Introduction to his edition of *Woodstock*, London, 1946.

are clearly derived from sources very different from the conventions up till this time observed in the rhetorical tragedies, and which at the same time rise far superior to the bareness of language characteristic of earlier chronicle plays.

These qualities are seen at their best in passages in which a conventional situation might have been expected to open the way to a conventional set speech. An excellent example is the official welcome offered to the King and Queen, who enter crowned and 'in great state'. Lancaster embarks upon the speech of welcome, but Woodstock interrupts him with the following words:

> Let me prevent the rest, for mercy's sake!
> If all their welcomes be as long as thine,
> This health will not go round this week, by th' Mass!
> Sweet queen, and cousin – now I'll call you so –
> In plain and honest phrase, welcome to England!
> Think they speak all in me – and you have seen
> All England cry with joy, 'God bless the Queen' –
> And so afore my God I know they wish it.
> Only I fear my duty not misconstr'd –
> Nay, nay, King Richard, fore God I'll speak the truth!
> – Sweet queen, you've found a young and wanton choice,
> A wild-head – yet a kingly gentleman –
> A youth unsettled . . .
>
> (I. iii. 14–26)

This is no longer one of those conventional, stylized speeches of welcome which, as we could see in Peele, represent a kind of word-picture of the formalities taking place on the stage; for here the individuality of Plain Thomas is expressed in the frankness and simplicity of his style of speech, just as in a good many later passages his manner is marked by a similar straightforwardness and familiarity of diction, making a very appropriate and telling use of parentheses. Even where dramatic climaxes are to be given a special impressiveness by means of a more elevated diction, and the familiar types of hyperbole are employed for this purpose, these departures occur only as very occasional high flights from which Woodstock soon returns to his matter-of-fact level of speech. When he is pressed to resign the regency and to deliver up his staff of office, his passionate outburst,

> Then force the sun run backward to the east,
> Lay Atlas' burden on a pygmy's back,
> Appoint the sea his times to ebb and flow;
> And that as easily may be done as this . . .
>
> (II. ii. 149–52)

at once gives place, after the King's rejoinder, to the complete composure that is habitual to him: 'My staff, King Richard? See, coz, here it is.' Such modulations in tone occur fairly frequently in this play, yet there is no question of abrupt transitions or of any changes in style that are inappropriate to the characters concerned. The underlying tone of the whole play is that of normal intercourse, a surprisingly natural, unforced conversational tone,[1] in varying degrees common to all the characters. Even the delightful speech in prose with which Woodstock addresses the 'spruce courtier's' horse is entirely in keeping with his idiom as a whole; he has been taken for a groom by the courtier and treated with some insolence, and his words bring out at the same time his superiority and his amused irony. Even in Greene we seldom come across passages in which the language runs so easily and adapts itself so naturally to transitions in mood, while at the same time remaining eminently good theatre:

> Come on sir, you have sweat hard about this haste, yet I think you know little of the business. Why so I say? You're a very indifferent beast, you'll follow any man that will lead you. Now truly sir, you look but e'en leanly on't: you feed not in Westminster Hall adays, where so many sheep and oxen are devoured. I'm afraid they'll eat you shortly, if you tarry amongst them. You're pricked more with the spur, than the provender – I see that. I think your dwelling be at Hackney when you're home, is't not? . . .
>
> (III. ii. 160–68)

This is not a mere comic interlude in which prose is in place as differentiating low-life material from the tragic main plot. In the

[1] Cf. Rossiter, op. cit., p. 64.

figure of Woodstock pathos and comedy have become fused, and he is equally at home in both.

This is not to say that there are no passages in the play where a rhetorical style of emotional language is employed. In the last two acts especially there are lines which have something of the ring of the typical tragic style.[1] But it is the proportions that are significant, for in the play as a whole it is not the conventional style of tragedy that sets the tone, but this new free and easy manner, giving the impression of spontaneity and capable of infinite modulation. And this is to be noted as an anticipation of the style of Shakespeare.

[1] E.g., the words with which Cheyney announces the Queen's death:

> The lights of heaven are shut in pitchy clouds,
> And flakes of fire run tilting through the sky
> Like dim ostents to some great tragedy.
> (IV. ii. 66–8)

Or the King's lament:

> Then let sad sorrow kill King Richard too,
> For all my earthly joys with her must die,
> And I am killed with cares eternally.
> (IV, iii, 141–3)

PART THREE

14

The Dramatic Lament and Its Forms

In the preceding chapters we have been examining the dramatic set speech in relation to its use and functions in individual plays. From modifications in structure, innovations in style and diction, and the differences to be observed in methods of introducing these speeches and adapting them to their settings, it has been possible to draw significant conclusions about the development of form and style in pre-Shakespearian drama. The interplay between the continued use of long-standing conventions and the originality that was shown in creating new techniques will be seen even more clearly if we abandon the 'horizontal' method of discussing the plays as individual works, and adopt in its place the 'vertical' method; that is, if we select a particular type of set speech that is employed by almost all the playwrights and follow it through its various stages of development.

The Dramatic Lament and the Theme of Complaint in World Literature

The formal lament has been chosen for this purpose, and our object will be to illustrate both the recurrence of the type and the modifications in form that it underwent. Now the lament must be set within the larger context of the Complaint in ancient and modern literature. There are very few literary themes which underwent so many variations and enjoyed so rich a development as that of complaint. In the drama of antiquity we find the *threnos* and the *kommos*, the lyrical and antiphonal laments of the Chorus, and the complainings of those who have been subjected to some incomprehensible fate. In the epic there are the famous laments for the dead and the valedictory and nostalgic laments. In the choral lyric there are traces of threnody, and in the elegy, too, passages of lament are not uncommon. Then we have the Hebrew songs of mourning for the dead, the lamentations of the Old Testament whose phraseology and formulas have to some extent passed into the Church liturgy for the dead by way of the monastic *officium defunctorum*. Furthermore, in the Latin poetry of the middle ages we encounter a wide range of kindred types deriving from ancient models: epitaphs, laments for the dead, and rolls of the departed; and we have as well the *planctus*, the dirge for the Virgin Mary, the *deploratio*, and the *lamentatio*, with their related forms in French, the *complainte* and the *regret*, analogues of which are to be found also in English literature. Nor is the early Teutonic poetry without its lamentations for the dead, and the Middle High German epic is extremely rich in mourning songs and speeches. When we turn to *The Mirror for Magistrates*, one of the most popular and influential works of the English Renaissance, we find that it consists of a series of Complaints in which famous men of the past bewail their sad fates.

Up till now the literary treatment of this theme has been written about only in relation to single *genres* or the literatures of single nations. Most of the studies devoted to it have been restricted to the lament for the dead; one gathers from them, however, that the correspondences and reciprocal influences between these different literary domains are extremely numerous and varied, particularly where the 'topics' of complaint are concerned. An all-embracing study of the complaint-theme in world-literature, one that overstepped the artificial barriers that have been set up between the literatures of the various countries, would be very worthwhile. For our present purposes, however, it will be sufficient to accept the premise that practically all the 'lament-topoi' referred to in the following pages in connexion with the pre-Shakespearian dramatic lament have their roots in the past, whether in medieval Latin poetry, or in patristic literature, or in the medieval vernacular drama and epic, from which their ancestry can in most cases be traced back to ancient times. For already in antiquity a 'Topics' of mourning for the dead had been evolved;[1] this embraced almost everything that the mind of man is able to conceive on the subject of grief and consolation for grief, so that even within the limited field of the Complaint we are given the picture of a long-standing continuity of the kind that Curtius in his comprehensive survey has shown to have existed for a great variety of literary themes.[2]

The Lament in Renaissance Drama

The formal set-speech lament is not peculiar to English drama; it is well-established in the drama of the Renaissance in France and Italy, and there too it is given special prominence as a vehicle for emotional declamation.[3] Indeed it was of the very essence of French and Italian classical drama that inward reactions to an event – the event itself as a rule being only reported – should be represented by means of a long set speech of an emotional or introspective character. Thus a great deal of space is naturally given to formal laments in which the speaker bewails the death of someone dear to him, or the harrowing revelation of some appalling fate in store for himself. Lamentation and anxious or painful reflection came to play so fundamental a part in Garnier's plays that they could reasonably be described as 'dramatic elegies'.[4] In his sonnet of homage to Garnier,

[1] 'In the antique system of rhetoric topics is the stockroom. There are found ideas of the most general sort – such as could be employed in every kind of oratory and writing. Every writer, for example, must try to put the reader in a favorable frame of mind. To this end, until the literary revolution of the eighteenth century, a modest first appearance was recommended. The author had next to lead the reader to the subject. Hence for the introduction (*exordium*) there was a special topics; and likewise for the conclusion. Formulas of modesty, introductory formulas, concluding formulas, then, are required everywhere. Other topoi can be used only for some particular species of oratory – for the judicial oration or the epideictic oration' – E. R. Curtius, *European Literature and the Latin Middle Ages*, transl. from the German by Willard R. Trask, London, 1953, Ch. 5. See this chapter generally. In the present translation the forms 'topics' and 'topos' have been retained.

[2] Curtius, op. cit.

[3] The last two acts of the plays of Cinthio Giraldi and Rucellai, and more particularly of Garnier, almost invariably contain several laments. Sometimes a play will begin with a soliloquy of lament, which serves at the same time as the prologue (e.g., the *Oreste*).

[4] Witherspoon, *The Influence of Robert Garnier on Elizabethan Drama*, p. 46.

Ronsard speaks of Garnier's stage as a place *où les grands lamentent leur fortune*; and this observation might equally well be applied to the classical drama of England. For the subject-matter of his plays Garnier characteristically sought out what was susceptible of a lyrical and elegiac treatment.

Thus the distinctive quality in the drama of this whole period is caught when in his *Poetics* Scaliger lays special stress, among the themes proper to tragedy, on *fletus*, *ululatus*, *conquaestiones*.[1] In the scenario that he sketches out for a tragedy based on the story of Ceyx and Alcyone, he writes: 'The first act is a lament' (*conquaestio*).

The note of lamentation resounds throughout the whole of pre-Shakespearian tragedy. With what frequency are English tragedies described in their titles as 'lamentable' or 'most lamentable'! And pitiable and lamentable indeed is the fall from high estate which, perpetuating the medieval conception of 'tragedye', provides the basic theme of so many of these plays. For the Elizabethan play-wright the formal lament represented a means by which he could combine the expression of painful emotion and suffering with melancholy reflections on life, intellect with feeling, and minute self-analysis with an explosive loss of self-control. We shall continually meet with these characteristic combinations in the examples of lament-speeches that will shortly be considered. Moreover, they are typical also of the formal laments of French tragedy, as represented by Garnier, and of Italian, as represented by Cinthio.

At the same time the dramatic lament is the *locus classicus* for diction heightened by rhetorical adornment; in it the language of passion, 'the melodramatic utterance', is carried to new extremes of artistry. And this results in a curious paradox; for in the very passages where the most profoundly personal emotions or the most unusual states of grief and suffering are crying out for utterance, the playwright gives us only the impersonal formula, the cliché, and the conventional rhetorical pattern. The dramatic lament is often the type of speech that most abounds in commonplace formulas, and is most strictly governed by convention. As we deal with examples individually, one of the questions we must bear in mind is

[1] Cf. *Handbook of French Renaissance Dramatic Theory*, ed. H. W. Lawton, Appendices, p. 133.

whether the smoke-screen of commonplaces and rhetorical devices laid over the expression of grief that would be natural in the circumstances is so thick as entirely to cloak all personal feeling.

The Formal Lament in Ancient Drama

At a time when forms of invocation, prayer, and supplication had not yet hardened into conventional formulas, but still bore some direct relationship to the origin of drama in religious ritual, there was a close association between the expression of personal grief and the form in which it was cast. This association is clear enough in Aeschylus, and also in Sophocles. In Euripides one of the most important basic forms of the lament, the apostrophe, begins to lose its intrinsic meaning and to develop into a formula, the mere husk of what it had earlier stood for.[1] However, even so it cannot be said that in Euripides the grief as such has been entirely drained away, for in his hands the lament took on fresh and original forms of expression that made of it a valid and moving means of self-expression.

Seneca and the Greek Tragedians

Seneca's ways of representing grief are different from those of Sophocles and Euripides, and they foreshadow the developments that were to take place in English drama. In his plays the emotional side of the grief is much more heavily stressed, and correspondingly there is a more deliberate and more obvious use of rhetoric. Seneca's object is to translate the emotional upheavals of his characters into long set speeches charged with emotionalism, and he employs all the resources of language, sharp-edged dialectic as well as the concentrated force of individual phrases; he deliberately heightens, and indeed exaggerates, every utterance of pain or sorrow, and at times even turns the pathetic into the pathological. As a result he has often been reproached for his bombast and his hollow parade of verbiage. In more recent times it has rightly been maintained that judgements of this kind are entirely beside the point.[2] They merely

[1] Cf. Wolfgang Schadewaldt, *Monolog und Selbstgespräch*, Berlin, 1926.

[2] Regenbogen, 'Schmerz und Tod in den Tragödien Senecas'.

prevent us from understanding a type of emotionalism that is essentially different from that of modern times, and it is important that it should be understood, not only as something that made a tremendous impact on the writers of the Renaissance, but also, and equally important, as something stemming from the specific feelings about life and death that were current in the days of the Caesars. Yet even when we have made every allowance for this fact, we can scarcely fail to see in the meticulously ordered rhetoric of Seneca's emotional set-pieces and his pointed and sophisticated dialectic a strongly marked formalism which is bound to lead to some alienation of true feeling – especially in the insistence on pushing the style of utterance to extremes of grandeur and on shrouding it in a closely-woven texture of parallels and correspondences.[1]

Probably the best way to bring out the differences is to examine side by side certain passages in which the Attic playwrights and Seneca have treated the same situations involving the expression of grief and pain. A single example should be enough to illustrate the fundamental differences between the two techniques. In the *Trachiniae* of Sophocles, Heracles, racked by the frightful pangs of his fiery torture, cries out in agony, interrupted by comments and ejaculations from the Old Man, Hyllus and the Chorus. Here are a few passages from his speeches:

O Zeus, where am I? who
These strangers standing by
As tortured here I lie?
Ah me! the foul fiend gnaws anew.
(983–7)

O altar on Cenaean height,
How ill dost thou requite
My sacrifice and offerings!
O Zeus, thy worship ruin brings.
Accursed headland, would that ne'er
My eyes had seen thine altar-stair!
So had I 'scaped this frenzied rage
No incantation can assuage.

[1] Cf. Eduard Norden's study of Seneca in *Antike Kunstprosa*, Berlin, 1923. Vol. I, pp. 306 ff.

Where is the charmer, where the leech,
Whose art a remedy could teach,
Save Zeus alone? If one could tell
Of such a wizard, 'twere a miracle.

O leave me, let me lie
In my last agony.

Ye touch me? have a care!
Would turn me? O forbear!
To agony ye wake
The slumbering ache.
Once more it has me in its grip, the fiend comes on apace. . . .

(993–1010)

. . . Look all of you
On this poor maimed body, and declare
Was ever wretched so piteous as I.
Ah me!
Again the deadly spasm; it shoots and burns
Through all my vitals. Will it never end,
This struggle with the never-dying worm?
Lord of the Dead, receive me!
Smite me, O fire of Zeus!
Hurl, Father, on my head thy crashing bolt!
Again it burgeons, blossoms, blazes forth,
The all-consuming plague.
O hands, my hands,
Arms, breast and shoulders, once all puissant,
Are ye the same . . . ?

(1077–90)

(Translated F. Storr, 1913 – Loeb edition.)

In Seneca's *Hercules Oetaeus*[1] the same agonized cries are required of Hercules, but in accordance with the different technique of Seneca they are presented in the form of four very long, closely-

[1] In recent times Seneca's authorship of *Hercules Oetaeus* has been questioned; cf. W. H. Friedrich, 'Sprache und Stil des *Hercules Oetaeus*', *Hermes*, 82, 1954.

packed set speeches, unaccompanied, however, by any action on the stage. The following passages are taken from the opening lines of the first and third speeches:

Turn back thy panting steeds, thou shining sun,
And bid the night come forth. Blot out the day,
And let the heavens, with pitchy darkness filled,
Conceal my dying pains from Juno's eyes.
Now, father, were it fitting to recall
Dark chaos; now the joinings of the skies
Should be asunder rent, and pole from pole
Be cleft. Why, father, dost thou spare the stars?
Thy Hercules is lost. Now, Jupiter,
Look well to every region of the heavens,
Lest any Gyas hurl again the crags
Of Thessaly, and Othrys be again
An easy missile for Enceladus.
Now, even now will haughty Pluto loose
The gates of Hell, strike off his father's chains,
And give him back to heaven. . . .

(1131–44)

Alas, what Scorpion, what Cancer, torn
From Summer's burning zone, inflames my breast?
My lungs, once filled with pulsing streams of blood,
Are dry and empty now; my liver burns,
Its healthy juices parched and dried away;
And all my blood is by slow creeping fires
Consumed. Destruction on my skin feeds first,
Then deep within my flesh it eats its way,
Devours my sides, my limbs and breast consumes,
Dries up the very marrow of my bones.
There in my empty bones the pest remains;
Nor can my massive frame for long endure,
But even now, with broken, crumbling joints,
Begins to fall away. . . .

(1218–30)

. . . Was't with such arms as these
That I crushed out the Nemean monster's life?
Did this hand stretch that mighty bow of mine
Which brought to earth from out the very stars
The vile Stymphalian birds? These sluggish feet –
Did they outstrip the swiftly fleeing stag,
With golden antlers gleaming on his head?
Did rocky Calpe, shattered by these hands,
Let out the sea? So many monstrous beasts,
So many cruel men, so many kings –
Did these poor hands of mine destroy them all?
Upon these shoulders did the heavens rest?
Is this my mighty frame? Is this my neck?
Are these the hands which once the tottering skies
Upheld? Oh, can it be that ever I
The Stygian watchdog dragged into the light?
Where are those powers, which ere their proper time
Are dead and buried? Why on Jupiter
As father do I call? Why, wretched one,
Do I lay claim to heaven by right of him? . . .

(1235–49)

(Translated by Frank Justus Miller,[1] 1907)[2]

[1] For comparison with later quotations it might have seemed more appropriate to use the Elizabethan versions of Seneca in *Seneca His Tenne Tragedies*, translated by Jasper Heywood, Newton, Studley, etc. (The Tudor Translations, 1927). These translators add much embroidery of their own, however, and a closer modern rendering is a better guide to Seneca's methods. Cf. T. S. Eliot, 'Seneca in Elizabethan Translation', in *Selected Essays*.

[2] Converte, Titan clare, anhelantes equos,
emitte noctem; pereat hic mundo dies
quo morior, atra nube inhorrescat polus;
obsta novercae, nunc, pater, caecum chaos
reddi decebat, hinc et hinc compagibus
ruptis uterque debuit frangi polus.
quid parcis astris? Herculem amittis, pater . . .

(1131 ff.)

Heu qualis intus scorpios, quis fervida
plaga revulsus cancer infixus meas
urit medullas? sanguinis quondam capax
tumidi igne cor pulmonis arentes fibras

Some of the important differences in the language of these passages are due to the different conceptions of pain and suffering held by the two dramatists,[1] but this is not the place to go into these questions. However, there are other dissimilarities for which the different principles of style by which the writers were governed are responsible. In the excerpts from Sophocles every line is closely bound up with the situation that is being enacted, and every line is charged with the physical and spiritual participation of the speaker. In the Seneca, however, the speeches have no integral connexion with the situation; the mighty imprecations and lamentations could have an independent existence, in that they are entirely divorced from the sphere of concrete action and are relegated to an abstract world of mythological parallels and learned allusions. The speech in Sophocles depicts what is actually going on in Heracles' mind; the individual thoughts follow on quite naturally from one another, and from among these thoughts it is the physical pain in each case that finds expression. Thus all the way through a balance is maintained between the spiritual suffering and the physical pain, and finally the two are fused. Seneca, however, in each of his

---

distendit, ardet felle siccato iecur
totumque lentus sanguinem avexit vapor.
primam cutem consumpsit, hinc aditum nefas
in membra fecit, abstulit pestis latus,
exedit artus penitus et costas malum,
hausit medullas . . .

(1218 ff.)

hisne ego lacertis colla Nemeaei mali
elisa pressi? tensus hac arcus manu
astris ab ipsis detulit Stymphalidas?
his ego citatam gressibus vici feram
radiante clarum fronte gestantem caput?
his fracta Calpe manibus emisit fretum?
his tot ferae, tot scelera, tot reges iacent?
his mundus umeris sedit? haec moles mea est,
haecne illa cervix? hasne ego opposui manus
caelo ruenti? . . .

(1235 ff.)

[1] Cf. Wolfgang Schadewaldt, *Sophokles und das Leid*, Potsdam, 1944; Regenbogen, 'Schmerz und Tod in den Tragödien Senecas'. An earlier study is by Karl Kiefer, *Schmerz und Tod auf der attischen Bühne*, Heidelberg, 1910.

speeches takes up a specific motif, isolates it from its dramatic setting, and within a schematized rhetorical framework builds on to it, so to speak, by means of the recurrent formulas of rhetorical question, interjection, and apostrophe. Seneca's Hercules does actually say something at last about his bodily torment (ll. 1218–32); but then it is all the symptoms of physical suffering and decay that he catalogues – indeed it is just as though he were giving a formal medical report. But up to this point he seems to have forgotten that the physical agony caused by the burning robe is every moment bringing him nearer to death. As in the Sophocles (ll. 1090 ff.),[1] the Senecan Hercules, looking down at his arms, recalls the glorious deeds they have done in the past. In Seneca, however, the question,

> Was't with such arms as these
> That I crushed out the Nemean monster's life?

serves as a kind of formula for a whole string of questions relating in turn to the speaker's hand, his feet, his hands, his shoulders, his neck, and once again his hands (ll. 1237–46). From that one question has arisen all this repetition of the formula; each example is improved on by the next, and the whole pattern of parallel utterances has been worked up by a technique of accumulation and crescendo. This method of building out from a single statement by a process of accumulation, employed both as a rhetorical device and for the sake of its rhetorical effect, is continually followed by Seneca, and it is one of the things that early English tragedy was apparently very willing to learn from him.

In the Sophoclean speech Heracles expresses a desire for his own death in the lines,

> Smite me, O fire of Zeus!
> Hurl, Father, on my head thy crashing bolt!

In Seneca this is replaced by a call for the destruction of the whole universe. Heracles' cries of agony in the Sophocles develop in the

[1] And you, my sinewy arms, was it by you
The terrible Nemean lion fell,
The dreadful hydra, and the lawless race
Of Centaurs? . . .
(1090–6)

Seneca into a whole stream of accusations, curses, and frantic exclamations, and everything is cruder, more obvious, more obtrusively ostentatious. Exaggeration of this kind, however, defeats its own ends. The very words are drowned, so to speak, and lose their power to produce the effect of a climax; they have played all their trump cards before the climax is reached.

For moments of the greatest stress both Sophocles and Euripides understood the value of the inarticulate cry, the faltering voice that fumbles for words and cannot find them. This is not Seneca's way of doing things, as we shall see if we compare Heracles' words at lines 988 and 1058 with their Senecan parallels, or those of Oedipus, 'Woe is me! Alas, alas, alas, alas, wretched creature that I am! (*Oed. Tyr.*, 1307) with the corresponding passage in Seneca's *Oedipus* (ll. 998 ff.). Then whereas in the *Hippolytus* of Euripides we have only the cry 'Ah me!' from the lips of Theseus when he has so painfully learnt of his grievous error, and in the following lines only such short ejaculations as 'Curses fall upon me, Goddess!' in Seneca's tragedy of the same title we are treated to a long, admirably constructed set speech in which Theseus calls down upon himself every imaginable kind of horror.[1] Seneca's heroes are never at a loss for words; they never have any feelings of constraint, are never struck dumb, are never so terrified as to lose all power of speech. They always have at their disposal a well-turned set speech and a whole armoury of mythological parallels, of imprecatory phrases, and of the 'topoi' of complaint; and these they bring out one after another without ever putting a foot wrong. However, it was this very 'eloquence' that was bound above all other things to impress Seneca's English readers. It took even Shakespeare some years to outgrow the easy eloquence, the all too rich and ready flow of words, that he always had at his command, and to replace it by those simple words of grief that are so sorely and painfully wrung from his suffering heroes in the moments of their greatest anguish.

Probably, however, the greatest difference between the Greek tragic dramatists and Seneca, as far as the handling of the formal lament is concerned, is the fact that every speech of complaint

[1] Cf. 1201 ff.

and every choral lament in a Greek tragedy is more closely bound up with the development of the play as an organic whole, and with its theme and subject-matter, than is the case with Seneca. Then in Seneca the outbursts of despair or execration given to the sorely tried characters are so like one another that one could quite easily interchange them, or at any rate some parts of them.[1] For example, Alcmena's lengthy song of mourning (*Herc. Oet.*, ll. 1863 ff.), in which she calls in turn on all nations, regions, tribes, and deities to help her bewail her loss, might equally well, with any necessary changes in the names, belong to some other play; and this could also be said of the Chorus's lament in *Thyestes* (ll. 789 ff.). Thus Seneca's laments have developed into mere set declamations which are introduced at appropriate moments in his plots.

Senecan Passions and English Tragedy

A good deal has been written on the ways in which Seneca was adapted to the purposes of English tragedy.[2] However, the unquestionable Senecan influences and parallels that are found in this body of drama have to some extent obscured the dissimilarities and the innovations that closer study reveals, as indeed we have seen in the chapter on *Gorboduc*; developments that took place in the dramatic lament further illustrate this fact.

In English tragedy, as also in French and Italian, the dramatic lament has a much wider range than in Seneca. It is also more intense; indeed it is lament in the true sense of the word. In Seneca lamentation takes the form of outbursts of despair, hatred, and terror rather than of grief and mourning. In the world of 'lamentable tragedy', however, the feeling behind the cry of distress was softened; it was more closely allied to suffering and tears, although a few dramatists were especially strongly impressed by Seneca's vehemence and frenzy, and did their best to emulate these qualities. With Seneca we can only think in terms of *passionate* speeches. A great variety of emotions – those of grief, hatred, self-accusation,

[1] This could be illustrated with *Thyestes*, 1006 ff., or *Hippolytus*, 1201 ff.

[2] See esp. T. S. Eliot, 'Seneca in Elizabethan Translation'. For further reference see the books cited in Chap. 5.

despair, execration, and longing for death, all of them worked up to the highest pitch – combine to form an eddy of violent passions, expressed in the most highly exaggerated diction. However, with his striking powers of psychological insight, Seneca dissects these emotions, and for all their incompatibility with one another, he analyses them in such a way that his passionate effusions become something more than a mere aggregation of strident, irrepressible feelings. It was only very slowly, and after the lapse of much time, that English tragedy learned to appreciate and to adapt to its own ends this balance of psychological tensions, and with it the variety of approach in Seneca's contemplation of what goes on in the minds of his characters. In the earliest English examples of the dramatic lament there are very few signs of real psychological grasp. The different emotions represented are kept more rigidly apart than they are in Seneca. They are treated as separate motifs, even though, as our examples will show, several such motifs may be used in succession within a single speech, the lines of demarcation always, however, being absolutely clear. Furthermore, to a much greater extent in the English plays than in Seneca, the expression of powerful feeling is accompanied by moral reflections and commentary on the lessons to be learnt from the harrowing circumstances in which the speaker is placed; we are never allowed to forget the edifying practical application. The glowing heat of Seneca's passionate outbursts is thus tempered by an element of coolly dispassionate reason and subtle calculation, a weighing up of contrasts in which everything is couched in terms of argument and deliberation. In English tragedy the rationalism which in Seneca is a matter of form rather than of content comes to dominate also the substance and the style of the dramatic lament.

One further point. Seneca's plays have a remarkable uniformity of style, tone, and emotional atmosphere. In the later plays in particular there is no alternation of 'action-scenes' and 'emotion-scenes'; the whole play is a series of static pictures in which a retrospective account of past events is combined with the disclosure of the emotional reactions they produce. The very thin thread of plot on which these 'pictures' are strung has little importance; it merely fulfils the essential requirement of a connecting-link between the scenes, and it could be claimed that these 'pictures', as the means by which events are reported and emotions represented, are ultimately the real plot of the play – they carry on their shoulders what is, from the playwright's point of view, its action. It cannot therefore be said of Seneca's plays (again the later plays in particular) that the long, passionate set-pieces fall outside the main stream of the play, or that they draw exceptional attention to themselves. For though they are put into the form of rhetorical climaxes and are often elaborated for their own sakes, they contain a great deal of the underlying spirit of the play as a whole, and are a part of its very stuff and substance. Moreover, there are so many of them that they can scarcely give the impression of being irrelevant 'insertions', or even of being in any way alien to the action; on the contrary, they must be regarded as the natural points of emphasis, as the passages in which what is especially significant in the work at a particular moment is brought to the fore and given expression.

An attempt has been made in earlier chapters to show that in English tragedy a peculiar relationship between action and the static portrayal of emotion existed from the earliest times. As might be expected from what has already been said in this connexion, formal laments in English drama, especially in its initial stages, do give the impression of being mere 'rhetorical insertions'; they are awkwardly woven into the texture of the plays, and they interrupt and hold up the action. However, we have also seen the developments by which the long set speeches came at last to be centred on the true focal points of the plays and became an essential part of the events being enacted, whether these events were outward, physical actions or inward, spiritual processes.

The 'Topics' of the Dramatic Lament

Thus the emotional set speech, which for our present purposes we are narrowing down to the formal lament, is treated by English playwrights in the first place as something self-contained, something approached very largely from the outside as an exercise in the elaboration of a prescribed theme for which there are patterns and precedents. This can be gathered clearly enough from, among other things, the abundance of recurrent formulas and 'topoi' associated with lament. A review of the 'topoi' of lament that are everlastingly repeated in dramatic laments will very soon show us how extraordinarily often the playwrights have recourse to this stock of firmly established phrases and formulas when they are getting together the material for their speeches. Right up to the time of Shakespeare, it would be difficult to find a dramatic lament that does not contain one or other of these formulas. This does not necessarily imply a want of self-reliance in the playwrights, nor must it be taken to suggest that the dramatic lament remained at a standstill up to the time of Shakespeare. The extensive use of recurrent formulas provides the foundations, however, on which these speeches are built up to their full proportions, and in order to judge them adequately we should know just what these foundations are. Something must therefore be said about the characteristics of the 'topoi' of lament.

The Apostrophe to Fortune and the Invocation to the Gods as 'Topoi' of Lament

The commonest formula of all, one which scarcely ever fails to appear, is the appeal to the powers of destiny, the heavens, or the gods. Out of the prayer with which in ancient drama the man overwhelmed by misfortune turned in the hour of his need to the Powers that were responsible for his suffering, there grew up a regular formula which is no longer either a true invocation, a true question, or a heartfelt supplication, but is an established type of rhetorical adornment which is usually introduced at the beginning of the speech. It is often no more than one of the conventional opening gambits for the formal lament.[1] Thus in the first lament that occurs in *Gorboduc*, Gorboduc begins with the words, 'O cruel fates, O mindful wrath of Goddes' (III. i. 1). In *Gismond of Salerne* Gismond introduces her lament with 'Oh vaine unstedfast

[1] It serves this function already in the Latin drama of the middle ages. Thus in the play on the raising from the dead of Lazarus (Young, *The Drama of the Medieval Church*, Oxford, 1934, Vol. II, p. 211), the lament of the sisters opens with the words, '*O sors tristis! o sors dura!*' In Seneca, cf. *Medea*, 451.

state of mortall thinges!' (I. ii. 1); Renuchio with 'O cruel fate! O dolefull destiny! O heauy hap! O woe can not be told!' (V. i. 1); Tancred with 'O dolorous happe, ruthefull and all of woe!' (V. iv. 1). In many other plays the same, or similar, formulas are employed in the laments;[1] and they are also to be found in French and Italian tragedies of the Renaissance, where they often likewise serve as a kind of formal introduction.[2] English playwrights of the sixteenth century were of course more vividly aware of the idea of 'Fortune' than of 'heavens' or 'gods'. From examples to be cited later, it will be seen that in the lament-speech a reference to Fortune is often made by other means than direct apostrophe of this kind, and that the lament serves the purpose of bringing the unaccountable workings of providence to the attention of the audience by means of examples, as a species of moral *exemplum*.

Although several hundred references are made to Fortune and fate in Shakespeare's plays, and these are phrased in a great many different ways, Shakespeare avoids the isolated apostrophe in which Fortune is merely called upon without anything being required or sought of her, or any other ideas being connected with her. Where on one occasion such an apostrophe is used, that is, in *Romeo and Juliet* ('Unhappy Fortune!' V. ii. 17), it is a sudden cry of terrified foreboding at the very moment when Friar Laurence learns that Romeo has not received the important letter with its explanation of the apparent death of Juliet.

The Preliminary Matter of the Dramatic Lament

It is reasonable therefore to describe the apostrophe to Fortune as a conventional preliminary. However, it is not the only device by which, as part almost of a regular ceremony, a formal preparation for the lament is contrived. This ceremony, especially in the early plays, is hedged about with so many observances that the preparation and the fringe-material almost prevent one from ever

[1] *Wounds*, 2071, 2593; *Soliman and Perseda*, I. iv. 47, 114; *Alphonsus*, V. i. 1559; *Edward I*, I. 58; *Locrine*, 270, 836; *Cambises*, 449.

[2] Cf., e.g., the laments of Hécube in Garnier's *La Troade*, 1729, and of Cléopâtre in *Marc Antoine*, 1792. In the Italian drama cf. the laments in Giraldi's *Orbecche*, V. iii.

getting to the heart of the matter. The grief is swamped by all the ceremonial of indicating grief. In a play it is more difficult indeed to give a convincing impression of grief than it is to deliver a speech of welcome, or one that describes a plan of action or attempts to influence another character. In speeches of these kinds the substance may be presented without any trimmings. In expressing grief, however, the playwright avails himself of all the formulas and conventional phrases that lie ready to hand for such occasions.

Thus, for example, there is a whole battery of questions that belong to the ritual of lament: 'Where shall I find a place wherein I may lament?'[1] 'Whither shall I betake me in my sorrow?'[2] 'Where may I find an echo for my grief?'[3] 'In what words shall I utter my complaint?' Another formula which lays stress on the 'preliminary' nature of these openings is the question, 'With what shall I begin in telling of my grief?' This is a 'topos' which has been taken over bodily into the expression of grief from the technique of narrative and description. It occurs already in Sophocles and in Seneca.[4] But its effect is not always the same. For instance, in the *Trachiniae* of Sophocles the Chorus says:

> Which first of woes, which next,
> Wherewith my soul is vext,
> To wail, I am perplext.
>
> (947–9)

Then in Bajazet's lament in *Selimus*, after various other formulas have been employed in turn, we come upon the somewhat obtrusive lines:

> Ah where shall I begin to make my mone?
> Or what shall I first recken in my plaint . . .
>
> (1760–61)

The first of these utterances springs from genuine need, when in the face of overwhelming sorrow which cries out for lamentation the Chorus is moved to ask itself the question; the second is a mere

[1] Cf. *Locrine*, III. vi. 1; *Span. Trag.*, III. vii. 1.
[2] *Selimus*, 1322; *David and Bethsabe*, 335.
[3] Cf. *David and Bethsabe*, 994; *Locrine*, V. iv. 197.
[4] Cf. *Herc. Oet.*, 180; *Troades*, 1058.

rhetorical flourish which belongs to the repertory of lament-formulas.[1]

The Rhetorical Question as a Convention of Lament

The formulas so far touched on have all taken the form of rhetorical questions. After the apostrophe and the interjection this is the commonest syntactical usage to be found in the dramatic lament.[2] The designation 'rhetorical question' of course tells us little about the nature of this usage. For almost all the choral laments and complaint-speeches in Greek tragedy also provide examples of rhetorical questions, of questions, that is, to which no answers are expected. As Wolfgang Schadewaldt has shown,[3] the question as a means of expressing some affliction of the spirit or as an utterance of helpless sorrow makes its appearance in the lament-passages of tragedy from Aeschylus to Euripides, where it gives the impression, not of a mere rhetorical device, but of an effective form of utterance taking its rise from real suffering. In Seneca, however, these questions have assumed the character of a rhetorical figure; often, indeed, they are nothing more than meaningless formulas. Seneca piles them up on top of one another almost mechanically, and in wearisome profusion, and by means of alliteration, paronomasia, and other rhetorical devices, he forces them to conform to a stiff, symmetrical pattern. In this respect too pre-Shakespearian drama in England had a long way to go before Shakespeare once more, as for example in the great soliloquies of his later tragedies, replaced these empty and ineffectual travesties of emotion by genuine *cris de coeur* wrung from his suffering heroes as they looked about them in helpless perplexity. The plays of the earlier periods are marked by the same devices of accumulation and parallel structure as are found in Seneca, and it is these that determine the shape of the

[1] Cf. also *Gismond*, IV. ii. 33; V. i. 16; *Selimus*, 1287.

[2] This is already the case in Homer. However, there are in Homer examples of laments in which the formula merely leads up to an expression of true grief, bringing the speaker's heavy lot concretely to the fore. Cf. Andromache's lament for the dead Hector in which, in a series of epic pictures, she imagines to herself how the fatherless Astyanax will fare in the future (*Iliad*, XXII. 477–514).

[3] Op. cit., passim.

rhetorical questions. When in *Gorboduc* Marcella is given the task of reporting Porrex's death, it takes some twenty lines of preliminary lament-ritual before we get any idea who it really is whose loss is to be mourned. A series of parallel questions forms the introduction to this lament:

> Oh where is ruth? or where is pitie now?
> Whether is gentle hart and mercy fled?
> Are they exiled out of our stony brestes,
> Neuer to make returne? is all the world
> Drowned in bloud, and soncke in crueltie?
> (IV. ii. 166–70)

One need only put these lines alongside the cry voicing the same feelings which is torn from Juliet, when her angry father has gone out after insisting on her speedy marriage with Paris, to become aware of the difference in technique:

> *Juliet.* Is there no pity sitting in the clouds,
> That sees into the bottom of my grief?
> (*Rom. & Jul.*, III. v. 198–99)

Hecuba, Priam, and Niobe used as Parallels

As we should expect, the dramatic laments, like the other types of set speech, contain plenty of specific parallels between the speaker's own sorrows and those of famous figures of antiquity. These parallels follow on from the question (one of the basic and perpetually recurring formulas of lament), 'Who has suffered sorrows worse than mine?' or 'Can there be a sorrow more hard to bear than mine?'[1] This comparison between the speaker's own suffering and that of others belongs within the broader classification of 'parallels from mythology and ancient story'. It was Hecuba, Priam, and Niobe who constantly provided precedents of suffering, and they were thoroughly familiar figures to the poets of the middle ages and the Renaissance, for whom they stood as the classical types of the mourner. Here again we can trace the processes by which a com-

[1] Cf., e.g., *Herc. Fur.*, 1188; *Phoenissae*, 244.

parison originally full of significance stiffened into a set formula. For in the choral lyrics of Greek tragedy the drawing of parallels between the speaker's own sorrows and examples of sorrow from the higher realm of mythology must be understood as something with a religious meaning. A comparison of this nature provided a background fraught with significance against which the character's own immediate sorrows were endowed with grand, supernatural associations; and an awareness of this connexion could lead to a fuller understanding of the speaker's own sorrows. In Seneca this device is turned into the adduction of mythological parallels for their own sake; it is a rhetorical technique for underlining and exaggerating the suffering in a particular instance. As a further step towards alienation from reality, these parallels from antiquity are in the pre-Shakespearian drama associated with the 'outbidding topos', as it might be called, the device of going one better than anyone else – a usage whose employment in late classical and medieval Latin poetry has been well studied by E. R. Curtius.[1] Thus in *Locrine*, Locrine himself, Guendoline and Camber are one after another moved to protest that neither Priam nor Hecuba nor Niobe suffered or mourned as grievously as they (III. i. 43–57); and in the same play Estrild in a later lament 'proves' that Hecuba had a much easier time of it than she (IV. i. 58 ff.). In *Selimus* Aga's mourning for Bajazet, who has just expired, begins with the words:

> What greater grief had mournful Priamus,
> Then that he liv'd to see his Hector die . . .
> (1862–3)

Naturally this 'outbidding-topos' is found also in the French drama of the Renaissance. At the beginning of Cléopâtre's long speech of mourning towards the end of Garnier's *Marc Antoine* the following lines occur:

> Que je suis misérable! Et jamais femme aucune
> Fut tant que moy confite aux aigreurs de Fortune?
> Larmoyante Niobe, hélas! bien que ton cœur
> Se voist enveloppé d'une juste langueur,

[1] Curtius, op. cit., pp. 169 ff.

Pour tes enfans meurtris, et qu'au haut de Sipyle,
De douleur tu sois faitte une roche immobile,
Qui pleure incessamment, tu n'eus jamais pourtant
Tant de causes d'ennui que j'en vay supportant.
(*Marc Antoine*, 1887–94)

In Shakespeare we no longer find this sophisticated and artificial device of outbidding other people's grief by calling in aid Niobe, Electra or Hecuba.[1] Shakespeare is of course quite familiar with Niobe as the type of the sorrowing, mourning woman, as is evident from Hamlet's short comparison for his mother at his father's burial, 'Like Niobe, all tears' (*Hamlet*, I. ii. 149). When Shakespeare does make use of the outbidding-formula in a lament, he relates it more closely to the characters actually concerned. In the mourning-scene in *Richard III* between the Duchess of York and Queen Elizabeth (II. ii), the personal grief of the speakers is contrasted, not with some historical or mythological parallel, but with the sorrow of the other mourners, and it is only in this way that the two strive to outdo each other. Thus the outbidding formula as a feature of the lament also underwent a certain modification.

The commonest form that the parallel takes is in fact the comparison of present misfortune with past prosperity, according to the formula, 'What has been, and what now is'. As will be further illustrated in a later section, this is constantly linked with some comment on the fickleness and untrustworthiness of Fortune,[2] a favourite theme in pre-Shakespearian drama.

The 'Lugete-Topos'

A very ancient formula associated with mourning, met with already in the Bible and thence taken over into the liturgy for Passion-week, is 'Come ye . . . assist me in my lamentation' – the so-called *lugete* or *plange mecum* 'topos'.[3] The speaker seeks out

[1] Further examples are *Dido*, II. i. 3; Garnier, *Antigone*, 209, 295, 1340, 2304; *Porcie*, 475. Cf. also Seneca, *Octavia*, 57; *Herc. Oet.*, 949.

[2] Cf. Farnham, *The Medieval Heritage of Elizabethan Tragedy*.

[3] Examples of the same 'topos' have been noted in the Middle High German epic, and in the *Deploratio* of the French Renaissance.

those who will ally themselves with him in his grief and help him to mourn. Here a pattern for the playwrights who were especially influenced by Seneca may have been the mourning-song of Alcmena in *Hercules Oetaeus* (ll. 1863 ff.), where a dozen countries, races, localities, and deities are called on in turn to share Alcmena's grief. In *David and Bethsabe* the formula is used to reinforce the Old Testament songs of mourning;[1] and in *Locrine* the deities of nature (Nimphs, Driades, Satiri, Faries), and finally also the 'savadge beares', are successively called upon by Sabren to participate in her grief and mourning for Locrine and Estrild.[2]

The Appeal to the Elements

This formula might then be described as the 'petition for a fellow-mourner'. It is sometimes extended in the form of an appeal to the elements to show their fellow-feeling, to lend an ear to the voice of lamentation, or to look with sympathy on the sufferings of the speaker. Here too a retrospective glance over the early uses of this form of mourning will bring out the contrast between the original and the merely conventional techniques. In Aeschylus's *Prometheus Bound* Prometheus opens his famous first soliloquy as follows:

> Æther divine, and breezes swift of wing,
> Fountains of rivers, myriad-dimpling laugh
> Of billows of the sea, All-mother Earth! –
> Yea, on the sun's all-seeing orb I call: –
> Look on me, what a God endures of Gods!
> Behold, in what torment of outrage, behold,
> I must agonize on through years untold!
> (88–94)
> (Trans. A. S. Way)

For Prometheus the elements are still a reality; they are all around him, and are something very close to him. They are the only friends left to him after he has lost the company of men and been abandoned by the gods. And so he can speak to them as though to sympathetic

[1] *David and Bethsabe*, 994, 999 ff.; cf. 669.
[2] *Locrine*, V. iv. 197; cf. also *Orlando*, 709.

beings which will listen to his voice. The situation of Prometheus in this play, as well as the original link between man and nature of which Aeschylus here makes use, gives to this appeal to the elements a directness and an immediacy which are a very different matter from what we find later. In the *Electra* of Sophocles, again, when Electra calls upon the 'holy light' and the 'air that streams over the face of the earth' as witnesses of her mourning (*Electra*, ll. 86–7), her supplication still holds its original force and reality. When they are taken over by the followers of Seneca, however, these appeals to the elements to participate in the grief and mourning become conventional formulas which no longer bear any essential relationship with what was originally intended by them. This is how some of the formulas run: the heavens are to blush or weep;[1] the sun is to hide its face, the stars to stand still in their courses, and the stream to hold back its waters;[2] the earth is to become parched and fruitless;[3] everlasting darkness is to shroud the world.[4] Several of the passages that come under this heading belong at the same time to the wider group of universal execrations; and from these it is but a short step to the 'topos' of annihilation which has still to be considered as a formula of the lament.

Even within this conventional petition to the elements to share the human grief there is some development. In Guendoline's lament in *Locrine* the theme of 'Blush heauens, blush sunne, and hide thy shining beams' (V. ii. 13) is merely repeated several times with slight variations; in Marlowe's *Tamburlaine*, on the other hand, the same ideas are presented in terms of vast spaces and in a more dynamic form,[5] and thus are assimilated more fully to the

[1] *Locrine*, V. ii. 13; *David and Bethsabe*, 1015; *Tamburlaine*, V. ii. 288; *2 Tamburlaine*, V. iii. 28.

[2] *Wars*, 1643.

[3] *Span. Trag.*, IV. ii. 14.

[4] *Selimus*, 1807; *Jew of Malta*, I. ii. 194; *Orlando*, 1282.

[5] Weep, heavens, and vanish into liquid tears!
Fall, stars, that govern his nativity,
And summon all the shining lamps of heaven
To cast their bootless fires to the earth,
And shed their feeble influence in the air;
Muffle your beauties with eternal clouds . . .
(*2 Tamburlaine*, V. iii. 1 ff.)

spirit of the play. With Marlowe the appeal to the universal powers to give manifestations of grief takes its rise from a deeper impulse than merely the desire of the playwright to introduce a well-tried formula. For the attitude to life of the characters in *Tamburlaine* is as wide and all-embracing as the universe itself, and the frequency with which the elements of heaven and earth, and indeed of the whole universe, are drawn into the speeches, whether for purposes of comparison or in the form of an apostrophe or as imagery, is one of Marlowe's methods of expressing the speaker's proud, dauntless consciousness of being the mid-point of the universe, surrounded by cosmic powers in sympathy with him or subservient to his desires. Even the fantastic visions and wish-fulfilment dreams are an expression of this attitude. Thus, though they move in the realm of cosmic ideas and far-reaching aspirations, the utterances of grief in *Tamburlaine* have the ring of genuineness and sincerity.

In the First Part of *Henry VI* (Shakespeare's authorship of this play is still in dispute) this particular 'topos' of mourning is used at the very beginning in the form of a 'word-accompaniment' appropriate to the action on the stage. In the Folio this action is described as follows: '*Dead March. Enter the Funerall of King Henry the Fift, attended on by . . .*':

Bedford. Hung be the heauens with black, yield day to night;
Comets importing change of Times and States,
Brandish your crystall Tresses in the Skie,
And with them scourge the bad reuolting Stars,
That haue consented vnto *Henries* death.
(*1 Henry VI*, I. i. 1–5)[1]

Earth, cast up fountains from thy entrails,
And wet thy cheeks for their untimely deaths;
Shake with their weight in sign of fear and grief.
Blush, heaven, that gave them honour at their birth . . .
(*1 Tamburlaine*, V. ii. 285 ff.)

Cf. Seneca, *Herc. Oet.*, 970, 1135; *Thyestes*, 1077.

[1] On the question whether Shakespeare wrote these lines, see J. Dover Wilson, *1 Henry VI* (New Shakespeare), p. xxix.

Forms of Self-Apostrophe

In the apostrophes to the elements in *Tamburlaine* there is always a recipient of the appeal, something which is regarded as a sharer, or a counterpart, of the speaker's sorrow. The appeal serves, of course, as the expression and revelation of the speaker's own feelings, so that, in spite of being addressed to a recipient, it remains in the last resort something personal to the speaker himself. The majority of the apostrophes in English tragedy are of this type, and it would be reasonable enough to describe them as a form of 'self-expression', according to Schadewaldt's[1] interpretation of the apostrophes in Euripides. However, when a character addresses, not something external to himself, but his own self, his own eyes and hands, or his own suffering, the I–you relationship and the reciprocal nature of true apostrophe are still further obscured. We must now think in terms of 'self-apostrophe', a device in which the original form of address is employed even though no one outside the speaker himself is concerned. We have seen in earlier chapters how often this practice of addressing oneself is found in passages which, though they are not true soliloquies, since they are spoken in the presence of others, nevertheless assume the form of a monologue. This tendency to drop into monologue is especially pronounced in the dramatic lament. Again and again the lament dissociates itself from the accompanying dialogue, abandons the you-relationship, and becomes a kind of 'pseudo-soliloquy'. For it no longer has the character of a communication addressed to a 'you' and designed to produce a particular effect on another person; it is an expression of the speaker's own sensations of pain, which, however, he is contemplating and describing as though from outside himself. He calls on himself to mourn exactly as if he were some other person.[2] The apostrophe addressed to the speaker's feelings of grief and replacing the straightforward expression of these feelings is yet another figure involving some divorce from reality; it is a

[1] Schadewaldt, op. cit., passim.

[2] This appeal to oneself to mourn is common; cf. *David and Bethsabe*, 577, 'Mourn, Bethsabe, bewail they foolishness', or *Selimus*, 1750, 1788. Cf. also Seneca, *Oct.*, 5.

form of rhetorical colouring, and thus actually leads away from the genuine expression of grief.

Thus in Seneca we find apostrophes addressed to *dolor*, *furor* and *ira*,[1] the apostrophe that the speaker addresses to his own self, or to *anima*, and finally the apostrophe addressed to various parts of the body;[2] Oedipus, for example, appeals to his hand, which is to bring further sorrow upon him,[3] and the Chorus in the *Troades* to the hands with which in their overwhelming grief they beat their breasts.[4] This last form of self-apostrophe is greatly extended in English drama. Not only the heart and the hands, but also, among other things, the eyes[5] and the lips, and tears[6] and sighs,[7] are invoked in the lament. Especially interesting is the apostrophe to *grief*, as also the manner in which the ideas of sorrow, woe and grief are employed within the formal lament. In *The Misfortunes of Arthur* the Griefs are invoked[8] – a reminiscence of Seneca's *Troades*, l. 108 – before Gildas reaches the point of stating the real reason for his sorrow. Here once again we have all the preliminary business of general indications of mourning before we get down to anything concrete. In the long, formalized mourning-scene in *Selimus* in which Bajazet and Aga alternately lament and curse, Bajazet builds up out of his invocation, 'You swelling seas of neuer ceasing care', a long epic simile in which his own existence is likened to a storm-tossed ship carelessly steered by the helmsman Grief.[9] At a later period, it is true, such formal apostrophes to pain and sorrow seldom occur, although representations of grief, sorrow, sadness, woe, sighs, and the like, are plentiful enough in the imagery.[10] In any psychological or naturalistic type of drama, of course, such a presentation of pain and sorrow, as also of other states of mind, would

[1] E.g., *Herc. Oet.*, 308, *Agam.*, 650.

[2] On the earliest examples in Aeschylus, see Schadewaldt, op. cit., p. 43.

[3] *Phoenissae*, 91.

[4] *Troades*, 111.

[5] E.g., *Span. Trag.*, III. ii. 109.

[6] E.g., *Locrine*, V. iv. 3.

[7] E.g., *Span. Trag.*, II. v. 351.

[8] Come cruell griefes, spare not to stretch our strengths,
Whiles bailefull breastes inuite our thumping fists.
(*Misfortunes*, IV. iii. 1–2).

[9] *Selimus*, 1764 ff.

[10] E.g., *David and Bethsabe*, 576, 1432; *Span. Trag.*, III. vii. 486.

be out of the question. It is a convention especially characteristic of Elizabethan drama, and it may be partly explained by the constant endeavour of Elizabethan playwrights to visualize ideas and abstractions as pictures.[1] It also reflects the difference between Elizabethan attitudes towards states of mind and those of today.[2] Shakespeare, with his fine dramatic sense, turned this convention to new uses.[3]

However, the formal apostrophe to grief or woe must also have struck Shakespeare as altogether too rhetorical, and it is rarely found in his plays. In the string of apostrophes uttered by the grief-stricken Nurse at Juliet's death (*Romeo & Juliet*, IV. v. 9 ff.) it is quite obviously employed with the deliberate intention of laying on the colours too thickly:[4]

> O woe! O woeful, woeful, woeful day! . . .

On the other hand, Shakespeare's language is extremely rich in metaphorical representations of grief, sorrow, woe, and kindred feelings, and the ways in which he looked on suffering and sorrow are revealed substantially by means of the numerous indications that he provides in his language.[5]

Desire for Death as a Conventional Formula

A common 'topos' in the pre-Shakespearian dramatic lament, as in world-literature in general, is the question, 'Why did I not die before this moment came, so that I need not have suffered this misfortune?' or 'Why do I yet live?' or 'O that I might now die!' These formulas – 'death-wish formulas' they might be called[6] –

[1] Cf. Bradbrook, *Themes and Conventions*, p. 127.

[2] Cf., e.g., B. Ansell Robin, *The Old Physiology in English Literature*, London, 1911; John W. Draper, *The Humors and Shakespeare's Characters*, Durham, N.C., 1945 (with a bibliography of contemporary literature on the subject, p. 120).

[3] Cf., e.g., Constance on her grief, *King John*, III. i. 68.

[4] An example of the opposite would be, of course, Cassius's words, 'But, O grief, Where hast thou led me?' (*Caesar*, I. iii. 111).

[5] There is as yet no proper study of Shakespeare's handling of pain and sorrow.

[6] The 'topos' *taedium vitae* in ancient literature is treated by Bruno Lier, 'Topica carminum sepulcrarium latinorum', *Philologus* 62/3, 1902–3. Cf. also Statius, *Silvae*, II. i. 25, V. i. 199. Examples are rare in medieval Latin

appear in a great variety of forms. The list may appropriately be headed by an example from Greek tragedy which is both economical of language and poetically effective, even in translation. It occurs there as an utterance of grief, but in comparison with all later examples it has an incomparably less pretentious effect and an altogether more genuine ring; and what is more, it arises directly out of the situation in which it occurs. It is to be found in the *Agamemnon* of Aeschylus, where the Chorus mourns the death of Agamemnon in the following terms:

O earth! that I had lain at rest
And lapped for ever in thy breast,
Ere I had seen my chieftain fall
Within the laver's silver wall,
Low-lying on dishonoured bier!
(*Agam.*, 1538 ff. Trans. E. D. A. Morshead)

In English drama we normally find straightforward questions asking why the speaker should go on living in the face of such misfortune as has befallen him.[1] The formula may also be used as part of the preliminary business of a lament, as for example in *Gorboduc*, in Videna's lament over her murdered son Ferrex:

Why should I lyue, and linger forth my time
In longer life to double my distresse?
(IV. i. 1–2)

A more intense form of the prayer that the speaker himself may die is to be found in the prayers addressed to God,[2] or to the bystanders,[3] or to Death itself,[4] to put an end to his life. In the comparatively unrhetorical atmosphere of the early chronicle play *King Leir*, which with all its artlessness strikes a more human note

literature. It appears in the French *Complaintes*. The following examples of the wish for death as a formula of lament in Garnier's plays may be mentioned: *Cornélie*, 1829; *La Troade*, 1741; *Porcie*, 1675; *Antigone*, 1809. In Seneca cf. *Herc. Fur.*, 1258; *Phoenissae*, 233.

[1] Cf. *Gorb.*, IV. ii. 259; *Gismond*, V. ii. 58; *Leir*, 860; *Locrine*, V. iv. 124; *Tamburlaine.*, V. ii. 185.

[2] E.g., *Gorb.*, V. ii. 106. In a quite different setting, see, e.g., *2 Tamburlaine*, II. iii. 3 ff.

[3] E.g., *Gorb.*, IV. ii. 272.

[4] *Soliman and Perseda*, I. iv. 126.

than we are ever aware of in the rhetorical tragedies, this prayer is uttered with a gentle sincerity which is in marked contrast to the violence and passion usually associated with the formula:

> Ah, gentle Death, if euer any wight
> Did wish thy presence with a perfit zeal:
> Then come, I pray thee, euen with all my heart,
> And end my sorrowes with thy fatall dart.
>
> (862–65)

In Marlowe, too, various characters pray that they may die, and side by side with the execrations that they heap upon themselves, and their appeals for utter destruction, which will be illustrated in a later section, and their parade of exaggerated passions, we find passages that display new levels of lyrical inspiration. An example that comes to mind is Olympia's prayer after her husband's death, when she begins her speech of mourning with the words:

> Death, whither art thou gone, that both we live?
> Come back again, sweet death, and strike us both!
> One minute end our days, and one sepulchre
> Contain our bodies! Death, why com'st thou not?
> Well, this must be the messenger for thee.
> Now, ugly death, stretch out thy sable wings,
> And carry both our souls where his remains.
>
> (*2 Tamb.*, III. iv. 11–17)

Here the formal prayer for death has been turned into an actual colloquy with death. In the heightened lyricism and pathos of this speech, and its turning away from the expected and visible partner in the dialogue (the son who is standing in silence beside the speaker), there are indeed some of the unrealistic and stylized elements that were reckoned appropriate to the formal lament, but at the same time a real relationship with death is developed in place of the mere apostrophe.

Accusation and Malediction in the Lament

These passages and others like them are of course not really typical of the way in which the death-wish formula is handled in pre-Shakespearian drama. With the tragic heroes of the Elizabethan age great suffering is seldom associated with the gentler feelings, sorrow or grief, humility or perplexity; much more often it gives rise to rage, rebellion, and frenzy. Their feelings of grief are readily transformed into the passions of hatred and revenge, into threats and curses. Lament turns into accusation. The dramatic characters of this period cry out in rage and defiance against fate, against the gods and nature; they wish for the destruction of the whole universe, and imperiously demand of the elements or the gods to crush them and to bring about the end of the world. That 'exaggerated dynamic of the will' which Schücking[1] has described as a typical feature in the dramatic art of the whole age is seen here in a characteristic stroke – in the attitude towards suffering and sorrow. And it comes to be associated with a conventional and recurrent phraseology. For the wish for annihilation and the malediction are often found in the mourning-speeches of pre-Shakespearian drama, and the lament is constantly turning into execration.[2] Here too, of course, we are dealing with a 'topos' the seeds of which had been sown by Seneca; but their rapid germination in Renaissance drama could not have come about if the spirit of English tragedy at this time, with its leaning towards the unusual and the extreme, had not found in this Senecan pattern a form of expression particularly well suited to it. On the other hand, this 'annihilation-formula' is also a symbol of that more active emotionalism which determines Seneca's treatment of suffering, and which has been described as a 'fierce energy in doing and suffering'.[3]

The Prayer for Annihilation

Like certain other 'topoi', the prayer for annihilation is usually found in the form of an apostrophe. Already before the time of Seneca, as we have seen, the prayer to the gods had developed into a mere formula which served as a vehicle for the display of emotion and the revelation of the speaker's own feelings. In the formalism of Seneca's style the apostrophe was entirely conventionalized, and

[1] *Shakespeare und der Tragödienstil seiner Zeit*, Chap. IV.

[2] The same is true of Garnier, Giraldi, and others.

[3] Regenbogen, op. cit., p. 183.

the attempt to load it with images of violence and monstrosity, and the frequency with which it is reduplicated, give the impression that Seneca is trying to conceal the lack of reality and sincerity in these forms of invocation with sound and fury, and by the sheer accumulation of striking effects. The prayer for annihilation has already been illustrated in the lament-cum-malediction of Hercules in *Hercules Oetaeus*, which was reproduced on p. 218; but some lines of Deianira's[1] in the same play are worth quoting at this point:

O sire of Hercules,
Destroy me with thy hurtling thunderbolt,
Thy guilty daughter. With no common dart
Arm thine avenging hand; but use that shaft . . .
(847–49)

Conforming remarkably closely to the pattern laid down here, this conventional prayer makes its appearance everywhere in pre-Shakespearian drama, as is exemplified in the quotations below.[2]

[1] perde fulminibus, socer,
nurum scelestam nec levi telo manus
armetur; illud fulmen exiliat pole . . .

Cf. *Medea*, 531; *Herc. Fur.*, 1202; *Thyestes*, 1077.

[2] Send down your wasting flames from wrathful skies,
To reue me and my sonnes the hateful breath.
(*Gorb.*, III. i. 25–6)

O heauens send down the flames of your reuenge.
Destroy I say with flash of wrekefull fier
The traitour sonne, and then the wretched sire.
(*Gorb.*, III. i. 163–5)

Send down, o Lord, from heauen thy whot consuming fire,
to reue this rutheful soule, whome torments to and froe
do tosse in cruel wise with raging waues of woe.
(*Gismond*, IV. ii. 8–10)

But, O Jupiter, of all wrongs the revenger,
Seest thou this injustice, and wilt thou stay any longer
From heaven to send down thy hot consuming fire,
To destroy the workers of wrong, which provoke thy just ire?
(*Damon and Pithias*, 565–8)

And will you not you albeholding heauens,
Dart down on him your piercing lightning brand,
Enrold in sulphur, and consuming flames?
(*Selimus*, 1327–9)

Shakespeare himself follows this tradition, and uses the conventional prayer for annihilation; but as we might expect, he uses it purely as a formula of cursing and imprecation. He so uses it, for example, in the famous wooing-scene in *Richard III*, when the Lady Anne flings out with the words:

> Either, heaven, with lightning strike the murderer dead;
> Or, earth, gape open wide and eat him quick . . .
>
> (*Richard III*, I. ii. 64–5)

and again when Lear hurls his curse at Goneril:

> You nimble lightnings, dart your blinding flames
> Into her scornful eyes.
>
> (*Lear*, II. iv. 167–8)

The Invocation to the Furies

In addition to its use in the prayer to the gods for extermination, the annihilation-formula occurs also in the invocation to the Furies and in the apostrophe to the elements, to the earth, the sun, the ocean, the heavens, and the tempests. They are to be the instruments of destruction, in that the earth is torn asunder and swallows up its unhappy dwellers, the sun is shrouded in darkness, and chaos is spread abroad through the world.

The invocation to the Furies also has its prototype in Seneca,[1] where it is used to intensify the emotional atmosphere. In Elizabethan drama it is nowhere found in so highly exaggerated a form as in Humber's speech of grief and despair in *Locrine*, a speech which, as is so often the case, is a mere succession of the conventional elements of the formal lament:

> Where may I finde some desart wildernesse,
> Where I may breath out curses as I would,
> And scare the earth with my condemning voice;

> Accursed Ioue, King of the cursed gods,
> Cast downe your lightning on poore *Humbers* head . . .
>
> (*Locrine*, IV. iv. 26–7)

[1] Cf. *Medea*, 13; *Herc. Fur.*, 86.

Where euerie ecchoes repercussion
May helpe me to bewaile mine ouerthrow,
And aide me in my sorrowfull laments?
Where may I finde some hollow vncoth rocke,
Where I may damne, condemne, and ban my fill
The heauens, the hell, the earth, the aire, the fire,
And vtter curses to the concaue skie,
Which may infect the aiery regions,
And light vpon the Brittain *Locrins* head?
You vgly sprites that in *Cocitus* mourne,
And gnash your teeth with dolorous laments:
You fearfull dogs that in black *Læthe* howle,
And scare the ghoasts with your wide open throats:
You vgly ghoasts that, flying from these dogs,
Do plunge your selues in *Puriflegiton*:
Come, all of you, and with your shriking notes
Accompanie the Brittaines conquering hoast.
Come, fierce *Erinnis*, horrible with snakes;
Come, vgly Furies, armed with your whippes;
You threefold iudges of black *Tartarus*,
And all the armie of you hellish fiends
With new found torments rack proud *Locrins* bones!

(III. vi. 1–25)

Here, as we see, the speech of mourning, after only six lines, turns into a speech of execration. The 'sorrowfull laments' with which Echo is to help Humber give way to curses. The eightfold invocation to the Furies and their train, interlarded with mythological names and associations, is followed by further imprecations, which are hurled against the gods, the stars and the sea; and eventually Cyclopes and anthropophagi are also called upon to destroy Locrine. Among the speeches discussed in the present context, this absurd sequence is a particularly good example of that exaggerated violence and utter lack of restraint which may be traced right through to the work of Shakespeare's later contemporaries.[1]

Kyd modifies a good many of the conventional devices of the

[1] Schücking, op. cit.

lament, giving them characteristic forms better suited to his special purposes (cf. pp. 272, 275). Instead of an invocation to the Furies in Hieronimo's despairing outburst of grief (III. xiii. 94 ff.), he gives us something that is even more effective in the dramatic sense, that is, Hieronimo's proposal to go down to hell himself and bring back 'a troop of Furies'.[1] He thus turns the purely rhetorical apostrophe into a resolution on Hieronimo's part to act for himself. (Compare with this the way in which the Furies are used in the earlier lament, at III. ii. 16–18.) However, what Hieronimo does here is exceptional; normally the Furies appear in association with invocations or execrations, and this practice is widespread in English tragedy down to the time of Marlowe and Shakespeare.[2] And indeed, even Shakespeare still combines the invocation to the Furies with outbursts of grief and suffering. After Desdemona's death, for instance, as Othello stands at her bedside with Gratiano, he is overcome in turn by thoughts of suicide, feelings of guilt, and grief-stricken love for Desdemona. As he looks down on the lifeless body, his speech shows him torn by these conflicting passions, which are reflected in his words:

> . . . Cold, cold, my girl?
> Even like thy chastity. O cursed, cursed slave!
> Whip me, ye devils,
> From the possession of this heavenly sight.
> Blow me about in winds, roast me in sulphur,
> Wash me in steep-down gulfs of liquid fire.
> O Desdemona! Dead! Desdemona! Dead!
> O! O!
>
> (*Othello*, V. ii. 275 ff.)

The clearly marked full verse-lines in this bold and imaginative apostrophe form a sharp contrast to the broken and faltering

[1] Ile down to hell, and in this passion
Knock at the dismal gates of Plutos court,
Getting by force, as once Alcides did,
A troop of Furies and tormenting hags . . .
(III. xiii. 108–11)

[2] Cf. *Selimus*, 1314; *Misfortunes*, I. ii. 39; *Cornelia*, V. 342; *Tamburlaine*, IV. iv. 17; V. ii. 155.

phrases and agonized groans that precede them, and they are immediately followed by further convulsive cries of grief. It is an outstanding example of the recasting of a traditional usage, and at this point and in this context it comes as a real climax, and has regained all the force of the invocation in its original form. It is true that this particular apostrophe echoes and reechoes, too, with the abounding energy and vehemence of Elizabethan declamation. Yet it is kept in the closest possible relationship with the imaginative world of Othello and with the overwhelming character of his sudden and terrible awareness of his crime. Everything that has occurred earlier leads up to this speech, and the device that had previously worn itself out by its insistence on an unbroken fortissimo is here born afresh with a splendid flourish of trumpets signalizing a great and fateful moment in the play.

Shakespearian Parody of the Invocation to the Furies

That Shakespeare himself was well aware how entirely the conventional invocation to the Furies lost its force when it became a mere rhetorical adornment in association with other formal devices of the dramatic lament is evidenced by his parody of this kind of tragic rhetoric in the Pyramus and Thisbe episode in *A Midsummer Night's Dream.* There we find the whole paraphernalia of the formal apostrophe turned to comic purposes, and in the short Pyramus-Thisbe interlude there are more than two dozen apostrophes. When Pyramus finds Thisbe's bloody mantle he cries:

> Approach, ye Furies fell.
> O Fates! come, come;
> Cut thread and thrum;
> Quail, crush, conclude, and quell.
>
> (*M.N.D.*, V. i. 289–92)

Prayers for Universal Extinction

In addition to the invocation to the gods and the Furies, we find apostrophes to the earth, the sun and the elements used as the vehicle for the prayer for destruction or extinction which, as we have seen, is one of the characteristic 'topoi' of the formal lament. Here once again Seneca is the starting-point, for Seneca quite often uses invocations of this type to express terror and the extremes of suffering.[1] This apostrophe with its demand for extinction sometimes occurs in a condensed form, as in Kyd's *Cornelia*: 'O earth, why op'st thou not?' (V. 39); or it may take the shape of a string of execrations developed in some detail, as in the despairing lament of the Moor in *The Battle of Alcazar*:

> Fight earth-quakes in the intrails of the earth,
> And eastern whirlwinds in the hellish shades!
> Some foul contagion of th' infected heaven . . .
>
> (II. iii. 5 ff.)[2]

Such prayers for extinction must have found themselves peculiarly at home in the spacious and dynamic imaginative world of *Tamburlaine*. It is not surprising that in this play Marlowe makes fairly frequent use of the formula, combining it with utterances of grief,[3] and most effectively decking it out in splendid and highly imaginative imagery. The final lament of the dying Bajazeth reaches its climax in this appeal to the sun:

> O highest lamp of ever-living Jove,
> Accursed day, infected with my griefs,
> Hide now thy stained face in endless night,
> And shut the windows of the lightsome heavens.
> Let ugly darkness with her rusty coach,
> Engirt with tempests wrapt in pitchy clouds,
> Smother the earth with never-fading mists,
> And let her horses from their nostrils breathe
> Rebellious winds and dreadful thunderclaps, . . .
>
> (*1 Tam.*, V. ii. 227 ff.)

[1] E.g., *Herc. Oet.*, 872, 1135; *Thyestes*, 1007. It was from Seneca that Garnier, too, took his prayers for extinction, often combined with an invocation to the Furies. Cf. Hécube's invocation to the Furies in *La Troade*, 2215; Porcie's in *Porcie*, 1639; Thésée's in *Hippolyte*, 2311; Cornélie's in *Cornélie*, 1837.

[2] Further examples in *Orlando*, 1281; *Selimus*, 1807.

[3] *Tamburlaine*, V. ii. 179; V. ii. 285; *2 Tamburlaine*, V. iii. 1; V. iii. 249.

Here the dramatist's sheer delight in his descriptive powers and in the poetic effectiveness of his picture outweighs the force with which the grief is conveyed, so that once more, though this time in a different way, the device has distracted our attention from the reality of the suffering it is intended to express. In *Doctor Faustus*, however, Marlowe succeeds in relating the prayer for extinction more closely to his dramatic situation and in expressing extremes of spiritual anguish by its use.[1] In that famous final soliloquy Faustus essays to bring to a halt the irrevocable fleeting of the hours, and strives for redemption through Christ's grace and for some means of escaping the claims of Lucifer. However, the vision of the redeeming blood of Christ passes from his sight, and in its place he sees the 'ireful brows' of God:

> Where is it now? 'tis gone: and see, where God
> Stretcheth out his arm, and bends his ireful brows!
> Mountains and hills, come, come, and fall on me,
> And hide me from the heavy wrath of God!
> No, no!
> Then will I headlong run into the earth:
> Earth, gape! O no, it will not harbour me!
>
> (V. ii. 154–60)

Here the prayer for extinction reflects an immediate personal experience; the course of the whole agonized spiritual conflict which has been depicted through the entire speech leads up to it with a sense of inevitability. The words 'Earth, gape'[2] are no longer a mere rhetorical formula; they are linked in a close unity of feeling with the preceding line, in which Faustus in his extremity wishes to 'run into the earth'. Moreover, what was observed of Othello's lament (p. 245) holds good here as well: the apostrophe is no longer embedded in a mass of carefully disposed rhetorical figures; it is surrounded by simple expressions which bring out with great directness and intensity all the fluctuating passions of the speaker.

[1] Cf. the formula in an abbreviated form in *Edward II*, IV. vi. 1967 ff.

[2] This formula has its origin in Seneca's '*Dehisce tellus*' (*Oed.*, 868; *Troades*, 519), and is found throughout pre-Shakespearian drama, and right down to Shakespeare's *Richard III* (I. ii. 65). Cf. *David and Bethsabe*, 1497; *Cornelia*, V. 39; *Tamburlaine*, V. ii. 179; *Span. Trag.*, II. v. 330; *Gismond*, IV. ii. 11.

In such a context as this the apostrophe is able quite successfully to carry off its exceptional role. This new use of language, however, is the outcome of a new way of representing feelings. For there is no longer any question here of an emotional motif being detached from the course of action and built up into a static scene with outpourings of lyrical rhetoric, or being used as a 'point of rest'; on the contrary, action is brought about as a part of the speech itself, an 'inward' action which is conceived as something running concurrently with the speech, and not merely reviewed subsequently.

However, the prayer for extinction may be introduced in other ways, not only in inward action as we have seen it employed by Marlowe. In Kyd's *Spanish Tragedy* there is an example which illustrates how the demand to be destroyed may be linked with external events taking place on the stage. This occurs in the scene (IV. ii) in which Isabella mourns Horatio's death in a soliloquy, at the end of which she kills herself. In this soliloquy there is something that goes beyond mere formal lament, declaimed without any accompanying action, for with a sword Isabella sets about laying waste the garden in which her son was murdered and his body hanged, slashing down trees and branches and hacking up the ground, and crying out, 'I will reuenge my selfe vpon this place . . .' And out of these actions, which are implied by the internal stage-directions in the speech itself, there emerges quite naturally the withering curse:

> Fruitlesse for euer may this garden be,
> Barren the earth, and bliselesse whosoeuer
> Immagines not to keepe it unmanurde.
> An Easterne winde, commixt with noisome aires,
> Shall blast the plants and the yong saplings; . . .
>
> (IV. ii. 14–18)

In Shakespeare too the merely formal and rhetorical use of the apostrophe calling for extinction is replaced by something which is fully fused with the dramatic content. In *Richard III* the Lady Anne's lament for her husband characteristically enough develops into execration – execration of his murderer, of course, not the indiscriminate calling down of judgement on all and sundry; and at the beginning of the First Part of *Henry VI*, as we have seen, the lament for the dead King Henry V is introduced by a formula allied to the prayer for general annihilation. In the Second Part of *Henry VI*, however, there is an example of the device not employed in a merely formal manner. Young Clifford comes upon his father's body lying on the battlefield, and cries out:

> O, let the vile world end,
> And the premised flames of the last day
> Knit earth and heaven together!
>
> (2 *Henry VI*, V. ii. 40–2)

These lines express a real and powerful emotion, and they occur at a moment of crisis which has been prepared for by what has been happening on the stage. Although in a different way from the passage in *Tamburlaine*, the exaggerated diction of the lines represents a momentary blaze of passion translated into violent phraseology, for nothing else in the context is expressed in such violent and forceful terms.

In *Antony and Cleopatra* there is an even bolder and more impressive example of the figure, illustrating its use in a moment of anguish at the climax of a most movingly dramatic expression of grief; in keeping with the imaginative world of the whole play, it provides in a few words an image that lights up the farthest spaces of the world:[1]

> O sun,
> Burn the great sphere thou movest in! darkling stand
> The varying shore o' the world! O Antony . . .
>
> (*Ant.*, IV. xv. 9 ff.)

So cries Cleopatra when she has word of Antony's approaching death. Instead of the traditional lament, with its string of rhetorical apostrophes, Cleopatra's grief has been concentrated into a single cry of anguish. Looking back at the lines in *Tamburlaine* in which exactly the same motif was handled (p. 247), or at Seneca's use of

[1] Cf. Clemen, *The Development of Shakespeare's Imagery*, pp. 159 ff. For similar types of imagery, ibid., p. 93.

this 'topos',[1] it is not difficult to see the continuity; but at the same time there is a considerable difference between the poetic reshaping of the formula and its use as a mere rhetorical figure.

The process that can be traced in Shakespeare may be seen, in its earliest stages, at work already in his predecessors; the lament as a set speech in the full sense of the term is in some of them being replaced by short speeches and by spontaneous remarks and ejaculations that form an integral part of the dialogue. Even in these condensed laments and ejaculations of grief, however, it is easy enough to see, on the basis of the short survey we have been making, the survival of the established formulas. Two examples will suffice here. In Greene's *James IV*, Sir Bartram tells poor, deceived Queen Dorothea about her husband's plot to murder her, and this is her answer:

> What should I do? ah, poore vnhappy Queen,
> Borne to indure what fortune can containe!
> Ah lasse, the deed is too apparent now!
> But, oh mine eyes, were you as bent to hide . . .
>
> (III. iii. 1385 ff.)

In his later plays Marlowe, like Shakespeare, often associates the lament with dialogue or compresses the conventional formulas for expressing grief. When Edward II has taken leave of his loyal followers and is being led away, Young Spencer cries:

> O, is he gone? is noble Edward gone?
> Parted from hence? never to see us more?
> Rent, sphere of heaven, and, fire, forsake thy orb,
> Earth, melt to air! gone is my sovereign,
> Gone, gone, alas, never to make return.
>
> (IV. vi. 99–103)

Here the lament-'topos' which had in earlier times provided material for a set speech entirely composed of rhetorical figures has been

[1] Converte, Titan clare, anhelantes equos,
emitte noctem; pereat hic mundo dies . . .
(*Herc. Oet.*, 1131 ff.)

Cf. *Thyestes*, 1092.

converted into genuinely dramatic language, and in this context and at this point of the plot it gains new force and conviction.

These last few examples illustrate very clearly the point we have been trying to make, that is, that the dramatic lament, and in Shakespeare the shorter outbursts of grief as well, take their direction from firmly established formulas laid down in the distant past. Sometimes these formulas are taken over mechanically and imposed on the speech as mere rhetorical adornments; sometimes they are dovetailed into the structure of the play and adapted to its intention and its atmosphere. They may serve as climaxes developing naturally out of the context, or they may fail of their effect because they are sandwiched in among other formulas of a similar type. The great poet can give them back their original imaginative character and force of expression; as Shakespeare sometimes does with his apostrophes, he can embody in them what is essentially a new experience, and thus endow them with new life. Furthermore, he may entirely discard certain devices because they seem to him to be too superficial, or too exaggerated, or too artificial. However, the dramatic lament, even when it is concentrated into a few lines, always proceeds on traditional lines, usually following traditions that go a long way back into the past. Indeed tradition plays as important a part in the types of passage we are concerned with here as the individuality of the poet. To appreciate these passages fully, we must be conscious of what lies behind them; we must be able to see through to the basic pattern.

15

The Pre-Shakespearian Dramatic Lament

Though certain basic forms of expression persisted in the dramatic lament, they were continually being modified, and by varying the structure and organization of their laments playwrights could show the various devices they had inherited in very different lights. Now the time has come to illustrate these developments by analysis of some complete laments, and this will serve as a complement to our examination of the individual motifs that traditionally belonged to this type of speech.

Gorboduc

As our first specimen we shall take the King's lament at the beginning of Act III in *Gorboduc.*

Gorboduc. Eubulus. Arostus.

Gor. O cruel fates, O mindful wrath of Goddes,
Whose vengeance neither *Simois* stayned streames
Flowing with bloud of *Troian* princes slaine,
Nor *Phrygian* fields made ranck with corpses dead
Of *Asian* kynges and lordes, can yet appease,
Ne slaughter of vnhappie *Pryams* race,
Nor *Ilions* fall made leuell with the soile
Can yet suffice: but still continued rage
Pursues our lyues, and from the farthest seas
Doth chase the issue of destroyed *Troye.*
"Oh no man happie, till his ende be seene."
If any flowing wealth and seemyng ioye
In present yeres might make a happy wight,

Happie was *Hecuba* the wofullest wretch
That euer lyued to make a myrrour of,
And happie *Pryam* with his noble sonnes.
And happie I, till nowe alas I see
And feele my most vnhappye wretchednesse.
Beholde my lords, read ye this letter here.
Loe it conteins the ruine of our realme,
If timelie speede prouide not hastie helpe.
Yet (O ye Goddes) if euer wofull kyng
Might moue ye, kings of kinges, wreke it on me
And on my sonnes, not on this giltlesse realme.
Send down your wasting flames frõ wrathful skies,
To reue me and my sonnes the hatefull breath.
Read, read my lordes; this is the matter why
I called ye nowe to haue your good aduyse.

(III. i. 1–28)

This speech opens a meeting of the Privy Council. Accompanied by two counsellors, the King enters and at once embarks on his complaint. But the actual cause of his grief is not suggested until the end of the speech, when he produces the letter, and is only made clear by the subsequent reading of the letter. We know of course from the last two scenes, and also from the dumb show which precedes the third act, that some mischief is brewing against the state and the King.[1] However, the true nature of the evil, and with it the full and real cause for Gorboduc's lamentation, that is, Porrex's murder of his brother Ferrex, is only revealed to us by a messenger in the middle of the scene. Gorboduc's lament as yet shows no awareness of this fact. It merely prepares us in general terms for a disastrous situation, the concrete realization of which comes later and on the whole bears no very close relationship to the lament itself. The description of the events and the representation of the emotional and mental reactions to them are not yet dovetailed in any way, as we saw in our discussion of the whole play

[1] Ferrex's purpose to take the field against his brother arose from the previous two scenes. The danger of internal dissension to the state, a theme already several times touched on, was the basis of the final song of the Chorus.

in Chapter IV; they are allowed to stand side by side, and there is not the slightest attempt made to amalgamate them. It was evidently taken for granted by the author that this scene, in which through the fratricide the first great catastrophe bursts upon the realm and its king, should be introduced by appropriately mournful reflections on the part of the King himself, in precisely the same way as the other council-scenes are opened by the King.

The first two-thirds of Gorboduc's lament, therefore, are a reflective commentary on the generally threatening and calamitous state of affairs which has been led up to in the preceding scenes and the dumb show. Thus the preparatory 'lament-ritual' is longer than the more concretely presented lament proper; and it is couched in such general terms that it might equally well have stood in another context. If we glance at the other two comparatively long laments in *Gorboduc*, Videna's speech of mourning for Ferrex (IV. i. 1 ff.) and Marcella's woeful report of Porrex's death (IV. ii. 166 ff.), we find a very similar type of structure. In them too there is a fairly long introduction of an essentially 'interchangeable' character (in Videna's speech 22 lines, in Marcella's 14), made up of the conventional formulas and only later giving place to concrete grounds for lament. The real subject-matter of the mourning and the 'lament-ritual' are not brought into any kind of unity; they fall apart into two clearly distinguishable halves. For the transition from the one to the other is so abrupt, that one can speak only of a line of division, not of a transition. Seneca's emotional set speeches had a much stronger internal coherence than we find here. This parallelism in the structure of the dramatic lament, its tendency to fall apart into distinct and separate compartments, is a further step towards its loss of personal application.

The lament-'topoi' figuring in Gorboduc's speech are already familiar to us. Needless to say, there is the opening apostrophe to the Fates; there are Hecuba and Priam used for purposes of comparison; there are the desire for death and the prayer for extinction. To begin with the first of these 'topoi', the apostrophe to the Fates and the gods: this two-fold apostrophe loses all its exclamatory character in that it is qualified by a long compound relative clause, with a complex array of added negative clauses introducing a whole host of subjects and objects, all of them dependent on the apostrophized 'wrath of Goddes'. And after all this we are given no predicate to the apostrophe, as is surely necessary from the grammatical point of view. Broken up into separate compartments, and falling apart into a series of antithetical clauses balanced one against the other, this complicated sentence finally remains incomplete. It is an example of an author's indulging his fondness for artistic expansion by means of noun-phrases carefully weighed against one another and set down in well-matched pairs (*neither–nor*, *ne–nor*), and the result is that what is said is neither easy to follow nor properly rounded off. The reduplications and other inflationary devices are obviously intended to intensify the force of the utterance, but what actually happens is that it loses both in force and in clarity. The rhetorical garnish in fact has a watering-down effect. The loose sentence-structure is padded out with a great deal of redundant matter, an example of that principle of 'copiousness' of style which was inculcated by all Renaissance teachers of rhetoric.[1]

The maxim dragged in at line 11 in the manner of the Senecan *dicta*, 'Oh no man happie, till his ende be seene', serves as a kind of headline to the comparison with Priam and Hecuba which follows. This enlarges upon the maxim, and the fourfold repetition of *happie*, employing anaphora in lines 16 and 17, is by yet another rhetorical figure negatived by the concluding *vnhappye*, and provides a connecting-link for the different parts of the sentence. The prayer for extinction exemplifies the same type of inflation by means of carefully contrived reduplications and involutions. The actual prayer, 'Send down your wasting flames' (l. 25), is preceded by a doubly limiting conditional clause ('Yet . . . if'), in which the second of the apostrophes, 'kings of kinges', quite unnecessarily introduced, picks up the word *king* from the preceding line, where it appears as the subject, and by the device known as 'paronomasia' now uses it as part of the object. A good many other rhetorical figures might be mentioned in connexion with this speech, including the continual use of alliteration. They are not employed here, as in Seneca, in order to impart more weight and pregnancy to particular phrases; their effect is rather to overlay the whole speech with a complicated

[1] Cf. Chap. 45, p. 67. Cf. also Doran, *Endeavors*, p. 46 ff.

pattern of correspondences for the most part only slenderly connected with the main theme.

The tendency towards conditional, hypothetical and otherwise limiting forms of utterance is even more pronounced in Videna's long speech of mourning for Ferrex (IV. i. 1 ff.).[1] Though her other son Porrex is not present, Videna calls down the wrath of the gods upon him (ll. 32–5); then she addresses three questions to him, parallel in structure, and in substance merely variations on the same theme. But these are purely hypothetical questions, and each begins with an if-clause. Thus in this play even a lament for a murdered son is spun out with casuistry, and the sophisticated method of argument characteristic of deliberative or dissuasive speeches finds its way even into a speech which is essentially emotional in character (cf. Chapters 4 and 5). It is quite obvious that this involved style, with its wealth of conditional clauses and its decided predilection for hypothetical and other restrictive forms of expression, reflects the legalistic Inns of Court outlook of the authors, and their academic pedantry is only very thinly disguised by the *gravitas* of the diction. In the development of the English dramatic lament it is certainly not without significance that its starting-point was a type of language which, in its involved and clumsy sentence-structure, is almost the exact opposite of what we should consider appropriate in speeches intended to convey powerful emotion.

In the course of the years this pedantically legal style was replaced by other techniques in the emotional set speech. The fact remains, however, that for a very long time to come speeches of this nature continued to be composed according to a preconceived, carefully disposed pattern; the speaker contemplates his feelings from a distance, as it were, weighs them quite objectively, and arranges them in a rational order. In other words, the emotional speech remains a derivative product, a linguistic structure organized by the intellect, and not a spontaneous expression of the feelings. The advice which the eighteenth-century writer Gottsched gave to the poet in his *Critische Dichtkunst*[2] would be equally appropriate here: 'The emotion must be allowed to subside somewhat if you are to take up your pen and represent your griefs in an orderly sequence.'

[1] Cf. IV. i. 5, 7, 11, 36, 45, 53. [2] P. 121.

Locrine

Locrine contains more laments than any of the other rhetorical tragedies, and an example chosen from this play will illustrate further developments in the style of the English dramatic lament:

Enter the souldiers leading in Estrild

Estrild. What prince so ere, adornd with golden crowne,
Doth sway the regall scepter in his hand,
And thinks no chance can euer throw him downe,
Or that his state shall euerlasting stand:
Let him behold poore *Estrild* in this plight,
The perfect platforme of a troubled wight.
Once was I guarded with mauortiall bands,
Compast with princes of the noble blood;
Now am I fallen into my foemens hands,
And with my death must pacifie their mood.
O life, the harbour of calamities!
O death, the hauen of all miseries!
I could compare my sorrowes to thy woe,
Thou wretched queen of wretched *Pergamus*,
But that thou viewdst thy enemies ouerthrow.
Nigh to the rocke of high *Caphareus*,
Thou sawst their death, and then departedst thence;
I must abide the victors insolence.
The gods that pittied thy continuall griefe
Transformd thy corps, and with thy corps thy care;
Poore *Estrild* liues dispairing of reliefe,
For friends in trouble are but fewe and rare.
What, said I fewe? I! fewe or none at all,
For cruell death made hauock of them all.
Thrice happie they whose fortune was so good,
To end their liues, and with their liues their woes!
Thrice haplesse I, whome fortune so withstood,
That cruelly she gaue me to my foes!
Oh, souldiers, is there any miserie,
To be comparde to fortunes trecherie.
(IV. i. 46–75)

These are the words with which the captive Estrild bewails her fortune as she is being led over the stage by soldiers after her husband Humber has been killed by Locrine. The fact that she speaks more about herself in this lament than, for example, Gorboduc had done does not mean that the speech has any closer personal application than Gorboduc's. For the object of Estrild's speech is not that she should express her own personal grief in it; she is much more concerned with holding up her fate as an *exemplum*. She approaches her miserable situation from the outside, turns it over in her mind, and compares it with that of other unfortunates; and she makes of it a cautionary tale the rhetorical effect of which is increased by the use of the 'outbidding-topos'. Or to state it in clearer terms, it is not Estrild who is speaking about herself here, but the author speaking about her. In order to clarify the situation of the Scythian queen who has fallen into captivity and wretchedness, and whose misery is being enacted before our eyes, he accompanies the stage-picture with these lines in much the same way as a painting is sometimes explained by a 'legend' attached to it. This is especially obvious in the first six lines, which are so worded as to suggest the author standing there with outstretched forefinger and explaining to the audience the meaning of the picture displayed on the stage. When the nature of the set speech in the classical drama was being discussed (Chapters 5 and 6), we saw that this is not in any way exceptional, but that for much of the time we must be thinking in terms of a 'depersonalized' mode of speech. The set speech was a form of authorial commentary on the tableau shown on the stage; it was not thought of as an expression of personality or even of character.

The lines that come after these first six, those in which Estrild changes over from speaking in the third person to the first, are merely a variant of what she had just said, and the contrast of *Once* and *Now*, one of the regular 'topoi' of the dramatic lament, provides the formal basis of this part of the speech. The apostrophes which follow, antithetically balanced against each other, syntactically parallel, and bound together by the alliterated synonyms *harbour* and *hauen*, are brought in so abruptly, and with so little relevance to their context, that their absence would not be noticed if they were removed bodily. Now comes a comparison with Hecuba, though she is not actually mentioned by name. This, coupled with the academic touch in the opening words ('I could compare . . .') and the allusion to 'the rocke of high *Caphareus*', intensifies the learned flavour of the passage; and the next two lines, in which Estrild goes back to speaking of herself in the third person, follow on somewhat awkwardly. When after this she drags in the proverbial comment, 'For friends in trouble are but fewe and rare' – very much in the manner of a Senecan *dictum*, though here it is masked as a subordinate clause – and goes on to correct it, as it were interrupting herself to do so, this too must be taken merely as an artificial contrivance intended to suggest a personal manner of speaking. For the 'fewe' is seized upon as a patent excuse for its confutation with the opposite idea contained in the words 'none at all'. The antithesis employing the 'outbidding-topos', 'Thrice happie they . . . Thrice haplesse I', brings to a close this typical lament, which reads like an academic exercise in poetic rhetoric exemplifying the lament as a *genre*; quite apart from the rhyme, a great variety of rhetorical figures is called in aid to embellish the composition. In the last two lines an attempt is made to relate the speech to the other people present, for it has developed into a regular monologue; but this is even more weakly and awkwardly managed than the corresponding attempt in *Gorboduc* to bring about a transition to dialogue by the production of the letter.

As we saw in the chapter on *Locrine*, its author was clearly intent on making as many opportunities as possible for the introduction of set speeches of an emotional character, and for the most part they are laments of one kind or another. He obviously manipulated his plot to this end. In the present context it is interesting to note that immediately after this speech of Estrild's, Locrine, the enemy of the Scythians and slayer of their king, sets eyes on Estrild for the first time and at once falls passionately in love with her. This sudden love of Locrine's finds expression, only five lines after Estrild has finished her lament, in a speech which also takes the form of a lament, and which, in the manner of an operatic duet, is delivered from the other side of the stage as a kind of antiphon to Estrild's grief:

If she haue cause to weepe for *Humbers* death,
And shead sault teares for her ouerthrow,
Locrine may well bewaile his proper griefe,
Locrine may moue his owne peculiar woe. . . .
(IV. i. 81 ff.)

The occasion for this 'lament' is far-fetched. The author's determination to bring in laments at all costs and as often as possible leads him at this point to introduce one in which it is not despair at the speaker's own misfortunes or grief at the death of someone dear to him that furnishes the pretext, but merely a love that is unhappily timed.

It is likely that the author of *Locrine*, though he obviously delighted in this ability to drag in the greatest possible number of laments, was also inclined to laugh at himself for doing so. For in this play there are not only a great many highly sophisticated formal laments, crammed with rhetorical tricks of every kind, but also, somewhat surprisingly, there is a parody of this style of lament. Side by side with the serious plot in the vein of high tragedy there runs a sub-plot figuring a set of clowns (cf. Chapter 6). Immediately after Albanact's pathetic suicide on the battlefield comes the comic interlude in which Trumpart finds Strumbo lying stretched on the ground. In order to escape a hero's death, Strumbo is cunningly shamming dead, and in answer to Trumpart's questions he persistently declares, 'I will not speake, for I am dead, I tel thee.' Whereupon Trumpart cries:

And is my master dead?
O sticks and stones, brickbats and bones,
  and is my master dead?
O you cockatrices and you bablatrices,
  that in the woods dwell:
You briers and brambles, you cookes shoppes and shambles,
  come howle and yell.
With howling & screeking, with wailing and weeping,
  come you to lament,
O Colliers of *Croyden*, and rusticks of *Royden*,
  and fishers of *Kent* . . .
(II. v. 98 ff.)

This is a parody of the high pathos of the lament proper, complete with all its usual paraphernalia, the apostrophes, the rhetorical questions and the '*lugete*-topos', and once such a bold and witty parody of a highly cultivated style becomes possible, its days are numbered (cf. Chapter 11, p. 177).

Peele, 'David and Bethsabe'

As examples from *Gorboduc* show, the dramatic lament often takes the form of a single isolated speech, when, conforming to the pattern of the Senecan *domina-nutrix* scene, it is occasionally followed by a speech of consolation, as can also be illustrated from *Gorboduc*, in Arostus's speech at III. i. 42 ff. Or alternatively it is made part of a full-scale scene of mourning in which the lament of the principal character, presented in a set speech of some length, is elaborated by a group of sympathisers. In this way choric scenes are built up, scenes in which the antiphonal mourning of ancient drama is to some degree extended; with this difference, however, that it is not the Chorus and the leader of the Chorus, or the Chorus and a single actor, who face each other and exchange their lamentations, but a number of characters take part in the exchange. The following passage, taken from Peele's *David and Bethsabe*, will illustrate this extension of the lament uttered by a single person into one in which a number of people take part:[1]

Enter David, Ithay, Sadoc, Ahimaas, Jonathan, *with others;*
David *barefoot, with some loose covering over his head;*
and all mourning.

Dav. Proud lust, the bloodiest traitor to our souls,
Whose greedy throat nor earth, air, sea, or heaven,
Can glut or satisfy with any store,
Thou art the cause these torments suck my blood,
Piercing with venom of thy poisoned eyes
The strength and marrow of my tainted bones.
To punish Pharaoh and his cursed host,
The waters shrunk at great Adonai's voice,

[1] Cf. also Chap. 5, p. 89.

And sandy bottom of the sea appeared,
Offering his service at his servant's feet;
And, to inflict a plague on David's sin,
He makes his bowels traitors to his breast,
Winding about his heart with mortal gripes.
Ah, Absalon, the wrath of heaven inflames
Thy scorched bosom with ambitious heat,
And Satan sets thee on a lofty tower,
Showing thy thoughts the pride of Israel,
Of choice to cast thee on her ruthless stones! –
Weep with me, then, ye sons of Israel;
Lie down with David, and with David mourn
Before the Holy One that sees our hearts;
(*Lies down, and all the rest after him.*)
Season this heavy soil with showers of tears,
And fill the face of every flower with dew;
Weep, Israel, for David's soul dissolves,
Lading the fountains of his drowned eyes,
And pours her substance on the senseless earth.
Sa. Weep, Israel; O, weep for David's soul,
Strewing the ground with hair and garments torn,
For tragic witness of your hearty woes!
Ahi. O, would our eyes were conduits to our hearts,
And that our hearts were seas of liquid blood,
To pour in streams upon this holy mount,
For witness we would die for David's woes!
Jonath. Then should this Mount of Olives seem a plain
Drowned with a sea, that with our sighs should roar,
And, in the murmur of his mounting waves,
Report our bleeding sorrows to the heavens,
For witness we would die for David's woes.
Ith. Earth cannot weep enough for David's woes:
Then weep, you heavens, and, all you clouds, dissolve,
That piteous stars may see our miseries,
And drop their golden tears upon the ground,
For witness how they weep for David's woes.
(VIII. 1–43)

The only function of the first part of the scene, as it is reproduced here, is to establish an emotional atmosphere; the plot, such as it is, is entirely forgotten, and the action comes to a standstill; moreover, the language touches on nothing that has the remotest bearing on future events. It is in fact a set tableau, the import of which has already been indicated in the grief-stricken behaviour and mourning-garments of the characters when they come trooping on to the stage in a body, as the opening stage-direction describes them. The lamentations of this party of mourners are merely the caption printed beneath the tableau. As has already been shown in previous chapters,[1] this is a type of dramatic representation which often occurs in Renaissance and baroque plays.

David opens his lament with an apostrophe to 'Proud lust', which he pillories as the real cause of his present sorrow. In comparison with the arid and extremely abstract language of the laments in *Gorboduc* and *Locrine*, these first six lines have a pronouncedly pictorial and sensuous quality. That was Peele's special strength as a dramatist; in the diction he used he painted with a richer palette than most of his contemporaries. Thus here and in the subsequent lines we have a more vivid impression of physical reality than is to be found in other works of these years. The anguish of the mourners is conveyed to us in physical terms; and the apostrophe to Absalon displays a similar forcefulness in its pain-imagery, appealing strongly as it does to the senses, as for example in the words, 'the wrath of heaven inflames Thy scorched bosom with ambitious heat'. On closer examination, however, we find even here a greater concern with the art of elaborating details and using colourful single touches than with the need to give the impression of a coherent picture; the lines suggest a brightly coloured tapestry in which the gay threads have been chosen entirely for the sake of the single colours. Much of the passage is nothing more than padding. Thus the familiar principle of amplification is seen at work in this play too, except that this time the amplification is achieved by different means from those generally used. Although the customary devices of accumulation and reduplication are employed to add to the emotional intenstity, their excessive use neutralizes much of the

[1] Cf. p. 129.

emotion and blurs the focus; examples from the first six lines alone are 'nor earth, air, sea, or heaven', 'glut or satisfy', and 'strength and marrow'.

Like other early examples, this lament also falls apart into several clear-cut sections, for each of which a single motif or a single 'topos' provides the material. In the first section 'Proud lust' is apostrophized as the abstract cause and origin of the present sorrows; in the third (ll. 14–18) Absalon is addressed as the personal originator of the calamity. In the intervening lines, which are not linked either syntactically or by sequence of thought with what precedes and follows them, there is a description of the punishment that the sea is capable of inflicting; and this is like the *exempla* drawn from classical mythology, though of course it is derived from a Biblical example, the story of Pharaoh. Here again, therefore, use is made of the well-worn contrast between *once* and *now*, and this is emphasized by the parallelism between 'To punish Pharaoh' and 'to inflict a plague on David's sin'. In the fourth section the '*lugete*-topos', the appeal for fellow-mourners, is introduced, and in the following lines this is repeated several times with variations.

No sustained line of thought gives coherence to this particular lament; even more than those of *Gorboduc* and *Locrine*, it is chiefly noteworthy for its completely static character. The whole speech 'marks time'. There is no development, no progression towards any clearly-defined end; the various motifs follow one another like so many logs of wood laid in a row. Thus the very structure of the speech reflects the static nature of the tableau on the stage. And the transition from this leading speech to the antiphonal laments of David's companions certainly cannot be called a transition to dialogue; nor does it bring about any increase in movement. The individual speakers are not answering one another; none of them even says anything fresh. All they are doing is to split up a long lament and share it out among a variety of mourners. If the names of the speakers were struck out, we should no longer be aware that these lines were supposed to be spoken by different persons.

The four speakers who follow David do no more, in fact, than produce a set of variations on a single theme, the theme that he has inaugurated at the end of his speech, that is, weeping and tears. This is given poetic expression and embroidered with a great deal of hyperbole, as was the practice in the Elizabethan lyric. The choric lament of David and his attendant priests is, indeed, nothing more than a sequence of pictures described in lyrical terms. The poet in Peele has got the upper hand of the playwright; as so often happened, he seems almost to have forgotten that it was a play he was writing.

We must remember, of course, that in *David and Bethsabe* Peele's method of composition, even down to particular points of style, was determined and directed by his two narrative 'sources', the Old Testament and the *Seconde Semaine* of Du Bartas.[1] In certain matters of detail it could be shown, too, that Peele stopped half-way in his dramatization of narrative material, a process that should involve not only the recasting of subject-matter and plot, but also some modification of the diction.[2]

And yet, in the lyrical expression of feeling in this choric lament there resides a quality which was to show itself peculiarly susceptible of development, and was to enrich in special ways the multiple orchestration of Elizabethan drama. Peele's handling of his effects in this scene is restricted and somewhat schematic; but his method was taken over by Marlowe, who made by his use of it a telling and thoroughly dramatic element of tragedy; and Shakespeare was supremely successful in fusing this technique of Peele's with the other formative influences on his dramatic art. As a vehicle for the expression of deep feeling, the rhetorical set speech, in *Gorboduc* and the later classical plays still concerned entirely with deliberation, generalizations, arguments and dreary moralizing, is here well on the way to shaking off didactic abstractions, employing in place of them a type of imagery which is capable of expressing emotion. The images may still be very largely conventional, may be devised for their own sake out of a sheer, self-sufficing delight in picturesque diction, may belong essentially to the domain of lyrical narrative

[1] A discussion of the Biblical passages will be found in Bruno Neitzel, *George Peeles David and Bethsabe*, Halle, 1904. P. H. Cheffaud, *Peele*, Paris, 1914, draws comparisons with Du Bartas (pp. 136 ff., pp. 176 ff.).

[2] Cheffaud gives immoderate praise to Peele's dramatic ability.

rather than of drama; but at least the first steps have been taken away from a style consisting substantially of abstract ideas worked up and disposed in accordance with rhetorical theory, and in the direction of an expressive poetic diction in which the eyes play a part as well as the mind. For in the other laments in *David and Bethsabe* it is just as obvious as it is here that the inward eye of the poet has cooperated with the other faculties – that in each of these situations involving the expression of grief he has visualized in pictorial terms something of the real situation of the persons concerned. Thus when Tamar is thrust out of doors, she imagines in her lament (III. 76 ff.) how she will fly 'to desert woods, and hills with lightning scorched', and there with her 'windy sighs' will lure 'night-ravens and owls to rend [her] bloody side'. Thus too for the mourning Bethsabe, in her lament at the beginning of Scene IV, her miserable situation is made concrete by her rejection of the otherwise comfort-affording musical instruments, the 'tinkling cymbal', the 'ivory lute' and 'David's kingly harp', and before her eyes she sees Jerusalem filled with lamentation and grief sitting in its streets:

> Jerusalem is filled with thy complaints
> And in the streets of Sion sits thy grief . . .

And thus too in his last lament, at the end of the play (XV. 165 ff.), David sees himself sitting in his grief 'in some cedar's shade', his ivory lute broken 'in thousand shivers', while in the woods the sighing winds and threatening tempest mingle with his lamentations. These are all of them merely tentative beginnings, but beginnings fraught with significance and opening up new forms of expression for the emotional set speech.

Kyd, 'The Spanish Tragedy'

In these developments Kyd is once again the man in whom we may see most sharply defined the conflict between the various stylistic tendencies in the dramatic lament with which we are now familiar and the new methods that were growing up of adding dramatic qualities to the emotional set speech.

First to be considered is the Viceroy's lament in Act I, Scene iii, of *The Spanish Tragedy*:

Then rest we heere a while in our vnrest,
And feed our sorrowes with some inward sighes,
For deepest cares break neuer into teares.
But wherefore sit I in a Regall throne?
This better fits a wretches endles moane:
Yet this is higher then my fortunes reach,
And therefore better than my state deserues.
(*Falles to the ground.*)

I, I, this earth, Image of mellancholly,
Seeks him whome fates adiuge to miserie:
Heere let me lye; now am I at the lowest.
Qui iacet in terra non habet vnde cadat.
In me consumpsit vires fortuna nocendo,
Nil superest ut iam possit obesse magis.
Yes, Fortune may bereaue me of my Crown:
Heere, take it now; let Fortune doe her worst,
She will not rob me of this sable weed.
O no, she enuies none but pleasant things.
Such is the folly of dispightfull chance.
Fortune is blinde, and sees not my deserts;
So is she deafe, and heares not my laments;
And could she heare, yet is she wilfull mad,
And therefore will not pittie my distresse.
Suppose that she could pittie me, what then?
What helpe can be expected at her hands,
Whose foote is standing on a rowling stone,
And minde more mutable than fickle windes?
Why waile I then, wheres hope of no redresse?
O yes, complaining makes my greefe seem lesse.
My late ambition hath distaind my faith;
My breach of faith occasiond bloudie warres;
Those bloudie warres haue spent my treasure;
And with my treasure my peoples blood;
And with their blood, my ioy and best beloued,

My best beloued, my sweete and onely Sonne.
O wherefore went I not to warre my selfe?
The cause was mine; I might haue died for both:
My yeeres were mellow, his but young and greene,
My death were naturall, but his was forced.

(I. iii. 5–42)

Unlike the speeches so far dealt with in this chapter, this lament is not introduced without any preparation; it is preceded by a short four-line passage of dialogue, in which, moreover, we have the Viceroy's first words, addressed to his companions. However, the antithesis between *rest* and *vnrest* in the first line of the long speech clearly warns us to expect the rhetorical language of the usual type of lament. But the announcement of the first three lines, amounting to 'Now let us mourn', is immediately followed by the question, 'But wherefore sit I in a Regall throne?' And with the answer, which he himself supplies, the Viceroy comes down from the throne and throws himself to the ground. In this way his lamentation is reinforced, and also brought into sharper focus, by means of some appropriate stage-business. And this time the earth is not merely apostrophized by way of a rhetorical gesture; it is thought of as something quite concrete, and becomes in a sense a stage-property in that the Viceroy actually 'falles to the ground'. Thus the words spoken and the visible stage-business are closely bound up with one another, even if it is done here in an obvious and undeveloped fashion and with the sole intention of making the situation clearer by combining a visual effect with the rhetorical effect. That Kyd could not be satisfied with this, but felt that he must also introduce an erudite effect by the use of a Latin *dictum* is indicated by the Latin quotation that follows – actually a pseudo-quotation, as the dog-Latin shows – which, however, does not embody any general moral truth, but provides in allegorical terms a further interpretation of the lying on the ground.

The 'interpretative' stage-business is continued as the speech proceeds. The Viceroy's thoughts turn to his crown, of which Fortune may yet bereave him, and with his own hand he puts it from him. He looks down at his mourning attire, his 'sable weed', but 'O no, she envies none but pleasant things.' A new style of soliloquy seems here to be in the course of development. In place of the long periods, hypotactic in their structure and clearly subdivided, following one another without any mutual interdependence, the characteristic style of *Gorboduc* and similar plays, this speech progresses with the ebb and flow of dialectic, involving a process on the speaker's part of agitated 'reasoning with himself' in which he interrupts himself and in the tone of conversation asks questions and answers them (l. 23, 'Suppose . . . what then?'; l. 28, 'O yes . . .'; l. 35, 'O wherefore . . .?'). At the same time a preference is shown for short sentences and clauses, following one another in rapid sequence, and linked to one another by word-chains of the kind illustrated in lines 29–34 (*faith/faith; bloudie warres/bloudie warres; treasure/treasure;* etc.). The tempo of the whole speech is more rapid than that of any of the others so far treated. The Viceroy's sharp, biting self-reproach finds its outlet in stroke after stroke of inexorable logic, and his questions and answers, his affirmations and denials, emphasize his 'vnrest'; it is evident that his creator wanted to give the fullest force to his self-tormenting sorrow. As in other laments of the period, the 'topos' of the incalculable, blind and fickle Fortune is dragged into the Viceroy's reasonings with himself, but no longer in the manner of earlier playwrights, as a mere statement or as a conventional ejaculation of grief. Of course, if we examine it more closely, even this self-communing of the Viceroy's, spontaneous as it sometimes appears, is seen to be no more than a conscious and ingenious building-up of dramatic effects. Like our other examples, this is a thoroughly sophisticated speech, its train of thought being directed by its attitude of rational, hair-splitting argumentation; indeed it is much the same as what we found in the speeches of *Gorboduc*, except that the rhetorical artifices are now pressed into the service of a new speech-style in which a more conscious attempt is made to reproduce the situation represented by the soliloquy than has hitherto been the case, and the various individual motifs are brought into a new relationship with the speaker's feelings.

As a speech illustrating in an extreme form the art of rhetorical organization and the conscious use of linguistic devices, Hieronimo's famous lament, probably the best known of all emotional set speeches in pre-Shakespearian drama, must now be considered:

O eies, no eies, but fountains fraught with teares;
O life, no life, but liuely fourme of death;
O world, no world, but masse of publique wrongs,
Confusde and filde with murder and misdeeds.
O sacred heauens, if this vnhallowed deed,
If this inhumane and barberous attempt,
If this incomparable murder thus
Of mine, but now no more my sonne,
Shall vnreveald and vnrevenged passe,
How should we tearme your dealings to be iust,
If you vniustly deale with those, that in your iustice trust?
The night, sad secretary to my mones,
With direfull visions wake my vexed soule,
And with the wounds of my distresfull sonne
Solicite me for notice of his death.
The ougly feends do sally forthe of hell,
And frame my steps to vnfrequented paths,
And feare my hart with fierce inflamed thoughts.
The cloudie day my discontents records,
Early begins to regester my dreames,
And driue me forthe to seeke the murtherer.
Eies, life, world, heauens, hel, night and day,
See, search, shew, send some man, some meane, that may –
(*A Letter falleth.*)
Whats heere? a letter?. . .
(III. ii. 1–24)

Here our first feeling is that formal rhetorical patterns have never, surely, been so consciously and deliberately employed as in these lines. The speech is a masterpiece of rhetorical art. Its structure and proportions are worked out with an almost mathematical exactness, and a variety of stylistic figures are harmoniously dovetailed in order to make a powerful emotional impact. The speech falls into two halves of almost equal length, the conclusion of each half being marked by a pair of rhymes, *iust/trust* and *day/may*. It opens with three apostrophes, all three identical in syntax and structure and all three at once turned into negatives, the whole sequence broadening out from what is of close personal concern to the speaker ('eies', 'life') to the more comprehensive conception of the 'world'; thence the speech proceeds to a further apostrophe, 'O sacred heauens', an invocation to the highest of all abstractions which is differentiated from the preceding apostrophes by the epithet ('sacred') appended to it. This leads up to three if-clauses, each one twice the length of the one before, and each in turn an amplification of the same idea, until at last we come to the predicate of this multiple conditional clause. This predicate, 'pass', is given a special emphasis by the two corresponding participles, 'vnreveald' and 'vnrevenged'. The whole sentence, gathering weight as it proceeds, is brought to an end with the great question concerning justice, which closes with yet another conditional clause introduced by 'if'; and this – surely, like line 23, quite deliberately – is given a line which is extra long, linked with the preceding line both by the rhyme and by the twofold repetition of words.

The second half of the speech has the same tripartite organization, and again there is a carefully controlled parallelism in the syntactic structure of the sentences. One after another the three powers whose function it is to remind Hieronimo of his loss and incite him to revenge are introduced ('the night', 'the ougly feends', 'the cloudie day'); and as we should expect, the Furies are among them. The penultimate line once again names the four faculties or powers apostrophized in the first half of the speech and the three described in the second half, and all these are made the object of the alliteratively linked imperative verbs of the next line. By this ingenious touch, by including all the leading ideas of the speech in a single line, Kyd has contrived to draw together all of its individual sections and to round them off most satisfactorily. If we also take into account the way in which he has used the various rhetorical figures (*correctio*, *paronomasia*, *progressio*, *polyptoton*,[1] *anaphora*, antithesis, parallelism, etc.), the impression is strengthened of a confident and calculating expertise capable of handling rhetorical

[1] The repetition, with different forms, of the same word.

and stylistic artifices as they had not been handled by any earlier playwright.[1]

However, one has only to read this speech aloud and fall under the spell of its word-music to see that the accomplished academic exercise in rhetoric, as it is exemplified here, is only the one side of the picture. Kyd has been much more successful than the authors of all the other laments so far considered in subordinating the arts of rhetoric to the requirements of the spoken word, and in this way he has brought them back closer to their original functions. In his hands the rhetorical set speech became a theatrical medium of outstanding effectiveness; he realized to the full the value of rhetoric on the Elizabethan stage, while his predecessors had for the most part been governed by their feeling for the power of the written word alone.

Kyd's handling of the arts of rhetoric in this passage may add considerably to the effectiveness with which Hieronimo voices his feelings, provided that we are willing to be guided by the standards of late sixteenth-century taste, and not by present-day tastes and standards. With regard to these effects of *spoken* rhetoric, attention must be drawn to the way in which, in the first half of Hieronimo's speech, both the inner stress of the speaker and the tone of his language show a progressive increase in intensity until we come to the last line with its extra length; the way, too, in which the hammer-blows of the single-line apostrophes, each one with its associated negative producing the effect of an echo, lead up to longer sentences communicating a more powerful feeling of suspense. We can hear how the desperate father has to make three fresh starts in his attempt to find more telling ways of describing the 'vnhallowed deed'. And finally we observe that, after the abrupt, incomplete sentences so far used, the great question in which the justice of the heavens is arraigned takes the form of two self-contained clauses (and verse-lines) profound with meaning, which by reason of their high proportion of monosyllabic words have to be spoken very slowly, the metre ensuring that the most significant words are given the greatest emphasis. Thus even the structure of the speech contributes to its

[1] On the use of rhetoric in this speech see Kenneth Muir, 'Shakespeare and Rhetoric', *Shakespeare-Jahrbuch*, 90, 1954, p. 52.

auditory effect. If, lastly, we examine the imagery, we find that, although the motifs of the three images developed in the second half are conventional, they are well attuned to the sombre spirit of the play as a whole; moreover, they are closely related to the speaker, in that they represent the three forces that are driving Hieronimo on to his deed of vengeance.

This analysis of its stylistic features should not be taken as an aesthetic evaluation of Hieronimo's speech. For nowadays we are apt to regard the extravagance and artificiality, the affectation and sophistication of this style as something absurd, indeed as mere turgid bombast. As is shown by the parodies of this very speech that had begun to appear in English drama before the turn of the century, a reaction was already by then setting in against the excesses and rhetorical extravagances of so melodramatic a style.[1] Nevertheless, at that time, and indeed for many years to come, as the extraordinary success of *The Spanish Tragedy* on the stage shows, it was accepted as a very great achievement. It is our duty today, therefore, to examine all the resources of this art, so that we may be able to do it full justice within the context of its period.

We have described this speech as a fully-rounded and self-contained entity. But in fact the completeness and roundness break down at the very end, when Kyd ingeniously introduces the device by which he is to effect a convincing transition to action. After the string of verbs almost tumbling over one another and the rush of the words 'some man, some meane, that may – ', Hieronimo stops short in the middle of the sentence, for a letter drops at his feet. And this is the means by which the transition to a continuation of the visible action is brought about. However, there is also an inner, psychological transition, for in that last line the talk was of a means of revenge, and the audience automatically connects the appearance of the letter with this – a supposition that is justified, as is shown within a few moments. We see therefore that with his sure dramatic instinct Kyd has been using the lament as a preparation for the dropping of the letter. The scene could hardly have begun with this

[1] Cf. Schücking, *Die Zusätze zur Spanish Tragedy*, Sächs. Akad. der Wissenschaften zu Leipzig, 1938; Harry Levin, 'An Echo from *The Spanish Tragedy*', *MLN*, LXIV, 1949.

incident; Hieronimo had to be on the stage beforehand, doing or saying something. Thus Kyd, accomplished man of the theatre as he was, has shown considerable dramatic skill in getting over the awkwardness of opening the scene with a speech of lament.

However, Kyd had at his command further stylistic resources with which to express grief and other strong emotions. Even within this limited field he shows himself a real master, capable of ringing all the changes. This is well exemplified in the soliloquy at the beginning of Act III, Scene vii, where Hieronimo again mourns the loss of his son. In the first part of the speech Kyd plays his own variations on the two well-worn themes of 'Where shall I go to voice my grief?' and 'Nature grieves with me'; then he embarks on a finely expressive image of a helpless suffering that is thrown back on itself, a suffering whose impassioned pleas cannot force their way through to heaven.[1]

Here for the first time in pre-Shakespearian drama, it would seem, we have sorrow conceived of in terms of a coherent picture of movement, for it is not merely a state of mind that is described, but activity; and, moreover, all the conventional formulas are abandoned. Kyd was not only a craftsman and a man of the theatre; at times he could also be a poet.[2]

However, self-contained laments of the type illustrated by the last two examples are by no means fully representative of the kinds of speech to be found in *The Spanish Tragedy*. As was pointed out in Chapter 7, Kyd in several passages shows his ability to synchronize action and emotion within the same speech, and to fuse the different types of speech that are necessary to this end; and he

[1] Yet still tormented is my tortured soule
With broken sighes and restles passions,
That winged mount, and, houering in the aire,
Beate at the windows of the brightest heauens,
Solliciting for iustice and reuenge:
But they are plac't in those empyreal heights,
Where, countermurde with walles of diamond,
I finde the place impregnable; and they
Resist my woes, and giue my words no way.
(III. vii. 10–18)

[2] As is shown, among other things, by the cumulative imagery in the visionary speeches in some later scenes (e.g., III. xii. 1 ff.; III. xi. 56 ff.).

manages to make the resulting product fully dramatic. Thus every now and then, where in the normal course there would have been a speech of unbroken lamentation, we come across a speech which succeeds in conveying simultaneously inward and outward action, and is thus at the same time a manifestation of feeling and a contribution to the plot (cf. pp. 109–10).

There is of course no consistency of execution in Kyd's efforts in this mode. He still owes a great deal to the hackneyed style of the conventional expression of high emotion, and the departures from this style in the direction of a speech-technique regulated by the actions and mental processes of the speaker remain for the present nothing more than tentative experiments. It is only in the later so-called additions to the play that these experiments are carried a stage further.[1] A good example is the fifth scene of Act II, which has already been discussed in an earlier chapter (see p. 109). In this scene there is an 'action-speech' which deliberately blends visible actions on Hieronimo's part with the expression in words of his inward agitation. However, it develops later into a conventional lament in which four parallel apostrophes embodying commonplace 'topoi' of this type of speech are set down in a row;[2] and Isabella adds to the list a few lines lower down with two equally conventional appeals to tears and sighs.

In this connexion reference must be made to Schücking's claim that the 'additions' to *The Spanish Tragedy* are not in fact additions, but substituted episodes taking the place of scenes, speeches or passages which were conspicuously outdated and bombastic in their style, and hence no longer acceptable to the changed taste of a later period. If, as Schücking suggests, we run the first, longer 'addition' straight on from the first part of the speech we have just been discussing, that is, from II. v. 15, the lines that would drop out would be those which retain the commonplaces of the classical

[1] Cf. Schücking, op. cit.

[2] O heauens, why made you night to couer sinne?
By day this deede of darkenes had not beene.
O earth, why didst thou not in time deuoure
The vilde prophaner of this sacred bower? . . .
(II. v. 24 ff.)

lament. The new version would also convey Hieronimo's grief and despair more realistically, and in a manner that would give greater force and dramatic tension to his discovery of his son's body; and at the same time the partial replacement of the long unbroken speech by dialogue would be entirely in keeping with the developments that we have in earlier chapters tried to show taking place. It is true that even in this scene we still find in Hieronimo's final speech the conventional prayer for extinction[1] and the conventional desire for death. But at any rate there are no longer the four apostrophes, so stiffly wooden in their identical structure; the style is altogether more spontaneous and dynamic, and the formal symmetry is done away with, even though the sentiments expressed are the same as those of the earlier lines.

The other so-called additions are similarly revealing, for they too use new means, means perhaps later developed, of communicating sorrow and spiritual stress. What is more, in addition to the deeper psychological understanding and the move in the direction of more dialogue and greater concreteness, there is now a completely new element that we have not so far met with, and that is a cynical realism which points the way to the spirit of a later period.

Marlowe

Marlowe was a greater poet than Kyd. The calculated sophistication of the rhetorical patterns still employed by Kyd in the emotional set speech must have seemed to him altogether too limited and inflexible for his purposes. The careful interlocking of rhetorical figures is rare in his work, and there is little 'patterned speech'. In its place he gives us the new language of his mighty, full-flowing blank verse and his bold, aspiring imagery. It was his special gift to be able to translate feelings into the language of melody, of rhythm, and of images. He opens up rich and hitherto undreamt of resources of language for the emotional set speech. In his hands it

[1] Confusion, mischiefe, torment, death and hell,
Drop all your stinges at once in my cold bosome,
That now is stiffe with horror; kill me quickly: . . .
(II. v. 89 ff.)

breaks away from the methods of argument and rationalization which even Kyd did not relinquish. With the disappearance of the devices of formal rhetoric it takes on a new and astonishing force and expressiveness. In Marlowe, at any rate in some passages, we can speak of the dramatic lament as a true expression of personality.

Most of Marlowe's formal laments occur in *Tamburlaine*. They range from the more conventional use of the *genre* in choric scenes of mourning to prose speeches in which the grief and despair are much too powerful to be contained within the rigid structure of verse – as in Zabina's speech at V. ii. 243 ff. First a few words about the choric use of the lament.

Just before the dying Tamburlaine comes driving in, drawn by the captive kings in his royal carriage, three of his faithful viceroys, Theridamas, Techelles and Usumcasane, give voice to their grief for their afflicted master and their forebodings of his death. Theridamas begins:

> Weep, heavens, and vanish into liquid tears!
> Fall, stars that govern his nativity,
> And summon all the shining lamps of heaven
> To cast their bootless fires to the earth,
> And shed their feeble influence in the air;
> Muffle your beauties with eternal clouds,
> For hell and darkness pitch their pitchy tents,
> And Death, with armies of Cimmerian spirits,
> Gives battle 'gainst the heart of Tamburlaine.
> Now, in defiance of that wonted love
> Your sacred virtues pour'd upon his throne,
> And made his state an honour to the heavens,
> These cowards invisibly assail his soul,
> And threaten conquest on our sovereign;
> But if he die, your glories are disgrac'd,
> Earth droops and says that hell in heaven is placed.
> (*2 Tamb.*, V. iii. 1–16)

This is the first of the three laments whose choric character is emphasized by the fact that the rhyming couplet at the end is repeated as a kind of refrain at the end of the third speech while the second speech is also rounded off with a rhyming couplet. The three laments form a ceremonial introduction to the deathbed scene that follows. In this scene we observe once more that in this style of dramatic representation certain significant events being enacted on the stage are accompanied by speeches of some length, so that we are confronted, not by either a fast-moving, complex stage-action or a merely static tableau, but by the gradual unfolding of highly important events which are for the most part to be interpreted symbolically (cf. the section on *Tamburlaine* in Chapter 8). For here the presence of the three mourning viceroys as a group is soon seen to be only the first of a series of tableaux which ends with the bringing in of the hearse (l. 223). The words 'Weep, heavens' introduce the familiar 'topos' in which the elements are called upon to share in the speaker's grief. However, this appeal to the elements is used with greater justification than is usual and arises quite naturally from the central imagery and the imaginative world of the play as a whole. In almost every one of his speeches Tamburlaine had appealed to the powers of the universe; he had held converse with them, threatened them, dictated to them. We have seen that this 'reaching for the stars' means on his lips more than a mere artistic delight in hyperbole for its own sake, and we have tried to understand why his imagination and will continually express themselves in cosmic images. Not the least important reason for the metaphorical force and the bold spaciousness that are so appropriate to all the vast, universal execrations in *Tamburlaine* is the fact that, while Marlowe was writing this play, his own imagination must all the time have been possessed by the elemental powers and the vast expanses of heaven. And so, when here at the end of the play the cosmic powers are arrogantly set at defiance by Tamburlaine's followers, and assailed with reproaches, commands and threats so that they shall not suffer Tamburlaine to die, such ideas are fundamental to the theme of the play and express its very life; this is not just a conventional 'topos', taken up for the moment and then replaced by other well-worn formulas. The same ideas form the basis of both the other speeches, though now it is 'the powers that sway eternal seats' that are called upon. This is a quite normal choric extension of a theme by variations, and yet it is more than this; for it prepares us to accept the death of the 'scourge and wrath of God' as an event of universal significance, and it is not by accident therefore that the whole play ends with a prayer for the annihilation of the universe:

> Meet heaven and earth, and here let all things end . . .
> (*2 Tamb.*, V. iii. 249 ff.)

The laments uttered by Tamburlaine himself at Zenocrate's death-bed, just before and after she dies (2 Tamb., II. iv), are more individual in expression than those of the present ritual mourning-scene, with their stylized choric presentation. In them too, it is true, there is a fundamental connexion between the partly lyrical and partly rhetorical style of the more important speeches and the stylized grouping of the characters, the solemn set tableau in which only a few slight changes of position take place (cf. Chapter 8). However, Tamburlaine's lament for his dying consort takes the form chiefly of a paean of praise. It begins indeed with the conventional lament-'topos', 'Black is the beauty of the brightest day', but then it proceeds to the hymn-like vision of the angels waiting on the walls of heaven to receive Zenocrate (cf. p. 122). The second speech of Tamburlaine which may reasonably be described as a lament, that during which music is sent for at Zenocrate's bidding (*2 Tamb.*, II. iv. 78 ff), is entirely taken up by the image of the beloved one whom he is mourning. No strange and remote ideas and figures are needed now to convey Tamburlaine's grief; he makes no use of rhetorical questions that fall ineffectually upon the empty air, or of apostrophes to far-distant powers. His grief expresses itself as something present and immediate; his thoughts about the dying Zenocrate call up visions of her present and her future existence, and shed a poetic radiance about her. For even the 'outbidding-topos' which belongs so inevitably to formal panegyric contributes towards this transfiguration – if Zenocrate had lived in ancient days, not Helen nor Lesbia nor Corinna would have been sung by the poets, but Zenocrate.

While music sounds during a pause, Zenocrate dies, and then Tamburlaine breaks out into a further speech of lament; and now, with a true Elizabethan reversal of feeling, he is shown as 'raving, impatient, desperate, and mad'. And once again a conventional 'topos' of lament, the prayer for extinction, is given a new lease of life as Marlowe uses it, in that it is converted into an impulse to be doing something, into a call for some realistic action:

> What, is she dead? Techelles, draw thy sword,
> And wound the earth, that it may cleave in twain,
> And we descend into th' infernal vaults,
> To hale the fatal Sisters by the hair, . . .
>
> (*2 Tamb.*, II. iv. 96 ff.)

True poet as he was, Marlowe was able, with his vivid pictorial imagination, to visualize all these traditional usages of the formal lament in terms of actuality; by extending them and filling them out, he moulded them into new creations. In this instance Tamburlaine sees in the cloven earth the path leading down to hell, just as in Part 1 the same formula, 'Gape, earth', brought to the mind of the mourning Zabina a vision of hell:

> Gape, earth, and let the fiends infernal view
> A hell as hopeless and as full of fear
> As are the blasted banks of Erebus,
> Where shaking ghosts with ever-howling groans
> Hover about the ugly ferryman,
> To get a passage to Elysian.
>
> (*1 Tamb.*, V. ii. 179–84)

Thus in Marlowe grief and despair were expressed in a fresh and forcefully dynamic way by means of these images of the universe and the underworld; and this is true also of his practice with regard to the other formulas of lament.[1]

The speech of Zabina just instanced belongs to a sequence of laments and utterances of despair exchanged between her and Bajazeth, and leading up to the suicide of Bajazeth. A few moments earlier Zabina has gone out and left Bajazeth alone. When she comes

[1] Compare Bajazeth's apostrophes to life and to his eyes (V. ii. 192, 196), and Zenocrate's to her eyes (V. ii. 278), with the parallel passages in *Span. Trag.* (III. ii. 1 ff.). Cf. Zabina's despairing question, 'Then is there left no Mahomet, no God, / No Fiend, no Fortune, nor no hope of end . . .? (V. ii. 176 ff.), and her question on the meaning of life (V. ii. 185 ff.).

in again and sees what has happened, she begins another lament which from the point of view of style is probably the most remarkable in the whole play:

> What do mine eyes behold? my husband dead!
> His skull all riven in twain! his brains dash'd out,
> The brains of Bajazeth, my lord and sovereign!
> O Bajazeth, my husband and my lord!
> O Bajazeth! O Turk! O emperor!

> Give him his liquor? not I. Bring milk and fire, and my blood I bring him again. Tear me in pieces, give me the sword with a ball of wild-fire upon it. Down with him, down with him. Go to my child; away, away, away! ah, save that infant! save him, save him! I, even I, speak to her. The sun was down, streamers white, red, black. Here, here, here! Fling the meat in his face. Tamburlaine, Tamburlaine! Let the soldiers be buried. Hell, death, Tamburlaine, hell! Make ready my coach, my chair, my jewels. I come, I come, I come!
>
> (*She runs against the cage, and brains herself.*)
>
> (*1 Tamb.*, V. ii. 242–56)

Zabina is beside herself with despair, and her passion cannot contain itself within the regular blank verse with which the speech opens; syntax and coherence of thought go by the board as well, and a new prose of high emotion is born, a prose that may almost be described as realistic,[1] a faltering speech that struggles to find words, that breaks off abruptly, and just as abruptly begins to tumble out incoherent thoughts and delusions. The passage is a significant early example of the language of madness on the Elizabethan stage,[2] for which in time prose came to be accepted as the normal medium. The random succession of confused thoughts and impressions that rush through Zabina's mind with her approaching death; the way in which her thoughts turn again to the red and white flags, and her recollection of the child drives away the fierce lust for revenge; the grand, monumental quality of the command with which the out-

[1] Cf. Levin, *The Overreacher*, p. 47.

[2] Cf. R. R. Reed, *Bedlam on the Jacobean Stage*, Harvard U.P., 1952; Milton Crane, *Shakespeare's Prose*, Chicago U.P., 1951, p. 17.

burst ends, 'Make ready my coach . . .': all this has a striking dramatic immediacy of a kind that had not been achieved before. It has already been shown in the section on *Tamburlaine* in Chapter 8 that these dying words of Zabina, a companion-piece to the final speech – and suicide – of Bajazeth which precedes it, provide a most effective focal point in the scene as a whole.

The two speeches by Zenocrate that follow (ll. 257 ff., 285 ff.) take us back from the disorderliness of this speech to the regularity of blank verse. They too are laments, but laments in which the well-tried formulas – 'O wretched me, that I should live to see this' (ll. 257 ff.), and the appeal to earth and heaven to weep and to blush (ll. 285 ff.) – are merely introductory to other methods of expressing the speaker's grief. These take the form, first of a horror-stricken account of the outrages she has witnessed, and then of an appeal to the absent Tamburlaine, the author of all this woe, an appeal that wavers between love, reproach, and condonation.

The concreteness given to the lament in these passages is characteristic of its further development in Marlowe's plays. More and more it discards the established formulas, becoming ever more closely bound up with what is actually going on, and with the perceptions and experiences and immediate concerns of the speaker. As was shown in the chapter on Marlowe, more frequent use is made now of the 'condensed' lament which expresses the grief in two or three lines, or translates it into a deep sigh or a passionate desire.[1] At the same time the lamentation begins to be mixed with other kinds of utterance, with entreaties, with the imparting of information, or with anything else, indeed, that comes up in the natural flow of dramatic dialogue at this point.

In other words, the formal lament as such has ceased to exist; in its place there are only utterances in the form of dialogue or of set speeches in which, among other things, grief and mourning are expressed. It is interesting to consider from this point of view the complaints of King Edward II about his miserable existence in the dungeons of Kenilworth Castle (*Edward II*, V. iii. 3 ff.; 16 ff.; 34 ff.; V. v. 51 ff.; 58 ff.). Here the element of complaint comes out

[1] *Jew of Malta*, I. ii. 194 ff., 259 ff.; V. vi. 87 ff.; *Mass. at Paris*, XVIII. 81 ff., 161–2; *Edward II*, III. i. 4–5; V. i. 110–111.

in the powerfully graphic representation of this degrading incarceration in a noisome sewer and in the delineation of the spiritual and bodily suffering that this causes the King. It is true that on one occasion, in his humiliation at being washed with 'puddle water', there is the traditional cry for help from the 'Immortal powers, that knows the painful cares . . .' (V. iii. 37); but an apostrophe of this kind is exceptional. Where the established formulas of lament do find admittance, they are now so closely integrated with the visible action taking place that in their new guise we scarcely recognize them as formulas. An example is the conventional petition for death in the following passage, in which Edward is once again describing his wretched condition:

> They give me bread and water, being a king;
> So that, for want of sleep and sustenance,
> My mind's distempered, and my body's numb'd,
> And whether I have limbs or no, I know not.
> O would my blood dropp'd out from every vein,
> As doth this water from my tattered robes . . .
> (*Edward II*, V. v. 61 ff.)

With these few observations on Marlowe's plays we may take our leave of the task we set ourselves in this chapter, that is, to trace the techniques of the formal lament; for we have now travelled some way along the path of development that is to govern the expression of grief in Shakespeare's plays. It is only the early plays, and in particular *Titus Andronicus*[1] (Shakespeare's authorship of which is in any case still disputed) and *Richard III*, that contain types of speech which might have found a place in this analysis of the sustained formal lament. In his later work he devised entirely different methods and developed new potentialities for the expression of grief and suffering; but the study of these methods must remain a subject for future research.[2]

[1] Cf. *Tit. And.*, III. i.

[2] A useful start, limited to *King Lear*, has been made by Wolfgang Schadewaldt, 'Lear und Oedipus', *Das Neue Forum*, 1951.

The Chronicle Plays ('Leir' and 'Woodstock')

However, before leaving the subject, we must consider whether anything like formal lament is to be found in the pure chronicle plays which were written either a short time before Shakespeare's history plays or contemporaneously with them. In plays of this type we find that what would earlier have appeared as unadulterated lament takes the form of a 'review of the situation', whether its function be explanation, comment, or retrospect; and such speeches contain only a few lines of complaint which play a modest part beside the other topics handled. Two soliloquies from *King Leir and His Three Daughters* may suffice to illustrate this. At the beginning of the third act Perillus, the prototype of Shakespeare's Kent, comes in to tell us of the misfortune that has befallen his master. In the classical tragedy this would have been the occasion for a full-scale lament. In this play, however, it merely provides an opportunity for the delivery of an informative and comprehensive consideration of the present state of affairs, and only two exclamatory lines are reminiscent of the normal style of the lament:

> Oh yron age! O times! O monstrous, vilde,
> When parents are contemned of the child!
> (ll. 761–2)

In the same way the soliloquy of Leir when he has just been repulsed by Gonorill (ll. 854–65) is a piece of sober analysis which only towards the end introduces the conventional petition for death, used here, however, without any of the usual rhetorical formulas (cf. pp. 239–40).

A more characteristic procedure, however, is to relegate the lament to the interval between the acts, so that it is mentioned only in retrospect. Thus the proportions have been reversed: whereas in earlier times the lament had held first place, and on its account the action of the play had been neglected and consigned to the interval between the acts, now it is obviously felt as a type of speech that holds up the continuity of the action, and therefore as something which preferably should be avoided. Again this can be illustrated by an example from *King Leir*. The fourth scene of Act IV opens with some questions that the French King puts to Cordella:

> When will these clouds of sorrow once disperse,
> And smiling ioy tryumph vpon thy brow?
> When will this Scene of sadnesse haue an end,
> And pleasant acts insue, to moue delight?
> When will my louely Queene cease to lament,
> And take some comfort to her grieued thoughts?
> (ll. 1230–5)

This is not followed, however, by any actual exhibition of grief on Cordella's part, but merely by her explanation that she is 'bound by nature to lament' (l. 1240).

Woodstock offers a further example of the same thing:

> *Enter the King and Scroope.*
>
> *Scroo.* My dearest lord! Forsake these sad laments.
> No sorrows can suffice to make her live.
> *King.* Then let sad sorrow kill King Richard too,
> For all my earthly joys with her must die
> And I am killed with cares eternally.
> For Anne a Beame is dead, for ever gone!
> (IV. iii. 139–44)

Here too the actual 'lament' has taken place earlier, off stage. Only an echo of it remains in a few lines of grief whose simplicity of diction is particularly effective in a passage the main purpose of which is to provide information. The end of the scene, too, with the King's words,

> Come, come let's go:
> My wounds are inward. Inward burns my woe,
> (IV. iii. 181–2)

illustrates a new terseness and lack of emotionalism in the language of grief. In these plays it is made abundantly clear that new potentialities in the expression of grief were being exploited in chronicle plays which were not influenced by the techniques of rhetorical tragedy, and it was these that Shakespeare was to apprehend and develop.

16

Conclusion

This brings us to the end of the task we undertook at the beginning of this book, that is, the development of a new approach to the history of serious drama before Shakespeare. The change-over from a drama of set speech and declamation to a drama rich in action may now be seen as a slow process of evolution, embracing many stages, and many movements and influences continually merging with one another; when it is examined more closely, what at first sight, and seen from a distance, appeared likely to show as a single, straightforward line of development has turned into something very much more complex. But that is what happens in all researches whose object is the close study of a period in which a revolution in style has taken place; one's hopes of discovering some unifying principle or some comprehensive formula survive only so long as one fails to recognize the many different factors that operate from time to time within the period and that govern and define the changes that occur. So too in the present instance we cannot escape the conclusion that the developments in form and style in pre-Shakespearian drama had more aspects and more causes than is generally realized. Not the least important reason for this was that the conventions underlying the composition of the set speech were interpreted very differently by different playwrights, and modified accordingly; at times, moreover, there was some conflict between individual styles of expression and the traditional forms that adhered to established conventions. However, as far as the function and techniques of the set speech in early Elizabethan drama are concerned, all qualifications notwithstanding, one continuous line of development stands out very clearly. We can follow it through from the stage where the set speeches are merely juxtaposed without any kind of relationship between them to that in which they are clearly interrelated and closely associated with character, situation and underlying theme. We can watch the set speech gradually assuming individuality and becoming more and more dramatic, and all the time its potentialities for expressiveness are being enriched.

In retrospect therefore we may see the history of pre-Shakespearian drama as a gradual fusing of all the basic components of drama. In the earlier period they are found side by side in little watertight compartments, and some of them appear only in rudimentary stages of development. An essential attribute of all great drama is that it represents the integration and mutual harmony of all the constituents of dramatic art, a rich multiplicity of dramatic effects welded into unity by the creative vision of the dramatist. It is not until Shakespeare that our drama reaches this supreme level of achievement. None of his predecessors manages anything of this order, though here and there we can see some of them struggling towards it. We must remember, of course, that with many playwrights current views on the nature of drama stood in the way of any development towards organic unity. Some of the plays of Peele and Greene even suggest that many playwrights thought it quite natural to use as many unrelated elements as possible in their work. These methods of his predecessors did not come amiss to Shakespeare; but even while he was exploiting all the potentialities to be found in diversity, as in *A Midsummer Night's Dream*, he wove all the heterogeneous elements of his work into a fresh unity, establishing many correspondences and interrelationships between the different worlds represented in the play. The study of the dramatic set speech contributes to our understanding of these developments.

It will perhaps be helpful to recapitulate some of the points that have been made in this study, for the failure to take them into account is a frequent source of error in the appreciation of Elizabethan drama. We have seen how misleading it can be in this particular period to start out from some preconceived ideal of drama and use it as our yardstick in assessing what we find in the plays. In the span of time covered by our survey the conception of what drama is and ought to be was continually changing. The history of drama in the sixteenth century goes back to origins and prototypes that are essentially different in character and background; they include the Miracle Play, the Morality, the Interlude, the Masque, and Senecan tragedy. No single, fixed conception of drama, therefore, such as was possible a hundred years or so later with the classical drama of France, could be evolved by taking these prototypes as a starting-point and working over the various ways in which their methods were developed. Thus to do reasonable justice to any particular play, it is important to discover what particular conception of drama underlay its composition. For we are continually finding ourselves confronted by 'special' forms of drama.

It is evident that we must not regard the history of pre-Shakespearian drama as a continuous process of growth towards realism, towards greater truth to life. This is another of the criteria which are often, though perhaps as a rule unconsciously, applied to the age that preceded Shakespeare. However, our study of the set speeches in the drama of this period has perhaps helped us to a better understanding of certain aspects of the plays, and intentions on the part of their authors, that have nothing whatever to do with realism.

Considerations of form and style and details of dramatic technique have been our main concern in this study. Even in the pre-Shakespearian drama, however, we have found that these aspects of plays can have different kinds of significance according to the contexts in which they are used and the ways in which they are related to meaning. The set speeches have forced us to consider what attitudes of mind lay behind the particular form and style employed. Here again our findings have varied. Whereas in some plays there has been a correspondence between form and content, the one being apprehended as the expression of the other, in many cases there has been an appreciable lack of harmony between the subject-matter and the form. With these plays the assumption that there is a concord of style and content is bound to lead us astray. Our analyses of styles of expression, which played an especially important part in the chapters on the lament, were designed both as a corrective and as a complement to the one-sided conclusions that are drawn in many stylistic studies of pre-Shakespearian plays.

As has already been suggested, this survey of Elizabethan drama also looks forward, for any study of the foundations on which Shakespeare built must increase our understanding of his development. In such an approach there is of course the danger that we may judge everything in the pre-Shakespearian drama in the light of Shakespeare's later achievement. However, we ought certainly to be clear about what Shakespeare, when he began writing his plays, had at his disposal in the way of structural potentialities, forms of expression, and dramatic conventions. But here we are confronted by something of a paradox. At every turn in Shakespeare's early and middle plays we encounter conventional usages, forms of style, literary artifices, and dramatic features which have their origins, and many parallels, in the pre-Shakespearian drama. In this respect Shakespeare might well be regarded as a figure of the Elizabethan theatre who was thoroughly at home in the techniques and methods of representation that had been tried and approved by his predecessors.[1] Nevertheless, his work as a dramatist is not to be understood merely as a logical continuation or a further development of the dramatic art that we meet with before his time. For already in his early plays, from *Richard III* onwards, we constantly feel ourselves in the presence of something entirely new and unexpected, something that belongs to him alone, even though he may have borrowed so much of his material, his themes and situations from pre-Shakespearian drama. For what is so often used there as a single detail, a mere matter of technique, a superficial trick of style, turns up again in Shakespeare in a new context; but in him it is organically related to the meaning of the play as a whole, and often too it reappears in an entirely different garb and with a different function to fulfil.

One of the distinctive features of Shakespeare's development is his constant modification of the existing dramatic kinds, and of the conventions and styles of expression that lay ready to his hand. More than any of his contemporaries he delighted in experiment; he enjoyed developing, recasting and mixing the kinds.[2] But it must not be forgotten how very far in advance of his contemporaries Shakespeare was in these matters, and how much more of an innova-

[1] Cf. Fluchère, *Shakespeare and the Elizabethans*.

[2] Cf. Clemen, 'Tradition and Originality in Shakespeare's *Richard III*', *Shak. Quart.*, V, 3, 1954.

tor he was than they. The arguments put forward in recent years for dating many of his plays earlier than has hitherto been accepted[1] further strengthen this impression of his originality, and suggest that much in his early plays, his mastery of 'the well-built chronicle play', for example, was a contribution of his own to dramatic literature.[2]

However, in spite of our claim that Shakespeare is no mere offshoot of earlier movements, a more exact acquaintance with the art of his predecessors cannot fail to help anyone who is studying his work. For the very way in which Shakespeare adapts what has seized his fancy, modifies it, develops it, and echoes its tones – in short, his whole method of setting about his material – gives evidence of his quite extraordinary expertise and his conscious artistry. For a long time, indeed right up to the Romantic period, critics were unwilling to credit Shakespeare with this highly finished and conscious artistry, and his finest strokes were put down to 'nature', and not to 'art';[3] but his supreme artistry will be clear and obvious if his work is approached along the lines we have just indicated. Although historical and comparative methods of scholarship have fallen into some disrepute, and with them 'background studies' of all kinds, on the grounds that they pay far too little attention to the appreciation of the plays as works of art in their own right, we cannot do without them. They must be regarded as a complement to interpretative methods, not only furnishing criteria relevant to Shakespeare's time and its usages, but also deepening our insight into his creative processes and providing evidence from other directions that he was a highly skilled and conscious craftsman. One of the objects of this study has been to prepare material for such an approach.

Finally, we are faced with the question how far the method of inquiry followed in this work, that is, using the dramatic set speech as our basis in tracing the history of form and style in the plays

[1] Cf. Peter Alexander, Introduction to *William Shakespeare: The Complete Works*, London, 1951.

[2] Cf. Wilson, *Marlowe and the Early Shakespeare*; A. P. Rossiter, Preface to *Woodstock*.

[3] Cf. Peter Alexander, *Shakespeare's Life and Art*, London, 1939, pp. 6 ff.

under discussion, is applicable to the plays of Shakespeare. Some light may be thrown on the growth of Shakespeare's dramatic art by various characteristics of style and problems of form that are revealed by a study of the dramatic set speech in the history plays. At the same time, however, it becomes increasingly difficult to mark the frontiers between the set speech and dialogue, for with Shakespeare the lines of demarcation become ever fainter and fainter. The forms of speech and of dialogue that he uses are so many and various as to preclude isolation and classification, and hence also any specialized treatment of a particular form. In the pre-Shakespearian drama the lines of demarcation were much clearer, and, as we have seen, it was not until the end of the period that they came to be overstepped to any considerable degree. However, particular types of set speech ceased in time to be identified with their original functions; the dramatic set speech came increasingly to represent a complex of functions, losing its close association with any single one of the types that had previously been so clearly defined; and for this reason it is difficult to group Shakespeare's speeches into specific classes or to treat them under comprehensive headings. Nor does it help to single out only the 'orations', the set speeches and harangues that are delivered on public occasions, and to subject them to methodical study,[1] for this leads to considerable difficulties of other kinds, difficulties both of classification and of analysis, as has been suggested in an earlier chapter (p. 50).

However, the difficulties that stand in the way of any specialized study of this kind are an indication of the many levels at which Shakespeare is working, and of the richness of his dramatic art. In Shakespeare the various dramatic elements and forms constantly overlap; they are so delicately adjusted to one another, and so carefully interlaced, that only a method of inquiry that embraces his art as a whole could really do justice to it, only a type of interpretation that treats the various individual properties of this art according to the bearing they have on other properties. And this is an undertaking that must be left to the future.

[1] Kennedy, *The Oration in Shakespeare*.

Select Bibliography

Plays cited

Gorboduc, Gismond of Salerne, The Misfortunes of Arthur: *Early English Classical Tragedies*, ed. J. W. Cunliffe, Oxford, 1912.

Locrine: *The Shakespeare Apocrypha*, ed. C. F. Tucker Brooke, Oxford, 1908.

The Spanish Tragedy: *The Works of Thomas Kyd*, ed. Frederick S. Boas, Oxford, 1901.

Peele: *The Works of George Peele*, ed. A. H. Bullen, 2 vols., London, 1888.

Greene: *The Plays and Poems of Robert Greene*, ed. J. Churton Collins, 2 vols., Oxford, 1905.

Marlowe: *The Works and Life*, ed. R. H. Case, 6 vols., London, 1930 ff.

Selimus, The Wounds of Civil War, The True Tragedie of Richard the Third, King Leir and His Three Daughters: The Malone Society Reprints (General Editor, W. W. Greg).

Woodstock: ed. A. P. Rossiter, London, 1946.

Cambises: *Specimens of the Pre-Shakespearian Drama*, ed. J. M. Manly, Boston, 1897.

The Troublesome Reign of King John: ed. F. J. Furnivall and J. Munro (The Shakespeare Library), London, 1913.

The Famous Victories of Henry the Fifth: *Chief Pre-Shakespearian Dramas*, ed. Joseph Quincy Adams, New York, 1924.

Seneca: *Seneca's Tragedies*, ed. F. J. Miller (The Loeb Classical Library), London, 1929.

Garnier: *Œvres Complètes de Robert Garnier*, avec notice et notes par Lucien Pinvert, Paris, 1923.

Works most frequently cited

J. W. H. Atkins, *English Literary Criticism: The Renascence*, London, 1947.

Howard Baker, *Induction to Tragedy*, Louisiana State U.P., 1939.

M. C. Bradbrook, *Themes and Conventions of Elizabethan Tragedy*, Cambridge, 1935.

E. K. Chambers, *The Elizabethan Stage*, Oxford, 1923.

W. Creizenach, *The English Drama in the Age of Shakespeare*, London, 1916.

E. R. Curtius, *European Literature and the Latin Middle Ages*, trans. from the German by Willard R. Trask, London, 1953.

Madeleine Doran, *Endeavors of Art: A Study of Form in Elizabethan Drama*, Madison, 1954.

Una Ellis-Fermor, *Christopher Marlowe*, London, 1927.

Willard Farnham, *The Medieval Heritage of Elizabethan Tragedy*, Berkeley, 1936.

Rudolf Fischer, *Zur Kunstentwicklung der englischen Tragödie von den ersten Anfängen bis zu Shakespeare*, Strassburg, 1893.

Sister Miriam Joseph, C.S.C., *Shakespeare's Use of the Arts of Language*, New York, 1947.

Harry Levin, *The Overreacher: A Study of Christopher Marlowe*, Harvard U.P., 1952.

Thomas Parrott and **R. H. Ball,** *A Short View of Elizabethan Drama*, New York, 1943.

Levin L. Schücking, *Shakespeare und der Tragödienstil seiner Zeit*, Berne, 1947.

Levin L. Schücking, *Character Problems in Shakespeare's Plays*, London, 1922.

C. F. Tucker Brooke, *The Tudor Drama: A History of English National Drama to the Retirement of Shakespeare*, London, 1912.

F. P. Wilson, *Marlowe and the Early Shakespeare*, Oxford, 1953.

INDEX OF AUTHORS AND SUBJECTS

INDEX OF PLAYS